THE AMERICAN GARDEN
GUIDES

annual
gardening

Consultants
Donald Buma, Botanica, the Wichita Gardens
Galen Gates, Chicago Botanic Garden
Mary Irish, Desert Botanical Gardens, Phoenix, Arizona
Kim Johnson, Old Westbury Gardens, Old Westbury, New York
Lucinda Mays, Callaway Gardens, Pine Mountain, Georgia
Julie Morris and Gail Reade, Blithewold Mansion and Gardens
Susan E. Nolde, Brookside Gardens, Wheaton, Maryland
Michael Ruggiero, The New York Botanical Garden

Enabling Garden Consultant: Eugene Rothert, Chicago Botanic Garden

Botany Consultant: Dr. Lucile McCook

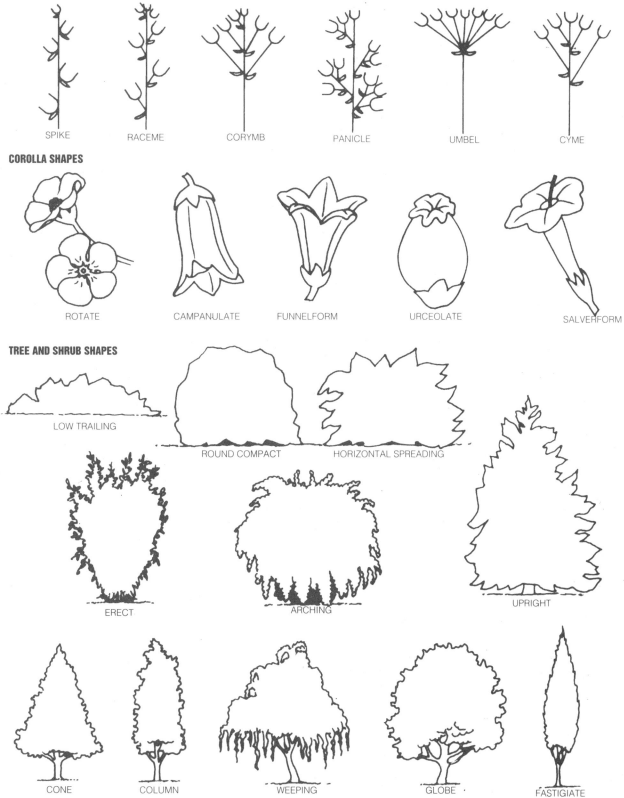

FLOWER TYPES

SPIKE

RACEME

CORYMB

PANICLE

UMBEL

CYME

COROLLA SHAPES

ROTATE

CAMPANULATE

FUNNELFORM

URCEOLATE

SALVERFORM

TREE AND SHRUB SHAPES

LOW TRAILING

ROUND COMPACT

HORIZONTAL SPREADING

ERECT

ARCHING

UPRIGHT

CONE

COLUMN

WEEPING

GLOBE

FASTIGIATE

annual gardening

Missouri Botanical Garden

By June Hutson
CURATOR, TEMPERATE HOUSE, ROCK GARDENS, DWARF CONIFER COLLECTION

assisted by
Brian Ward
FORMERLY, CURATOR, ANNUAL BEDS

with Ruth Rogers Clausen

Preface by Dr. Peter H. Raven
Series Editor: Elvin McDonald
Principal Photography by James Cuidon

Pantheon Books, Knopf Publishing Group
New York
1995

Acknowledgments
This book was created with the help, expertise, and encouragement of a great many people. We would like to thank all the consultants who contributed so much to it, and Dr. Shannon Smith, Dr. Peter Raven, Janine Adams and the entire staff of Missouri Botanical Garden. We also appreciate the efforts of Brenda Ward, Jack Jenson, Sari Amen, Kathy Grasso, Susan Ralston, Amanda Gordon, Altie Karper, Alan Kellock, David Pryor, Susan Kilpatrick, Marlin Hardeo, Doug Jensen, Jaime Gutierrez, Sadie and Fred Sammis, Peg Streep, Patrick Markham, Ian Adams, Jay Hyams, Susan Lurie, Kate Learson, Penny Byham, Shirley Stein, Sarah and Rachel Stein, Chani Yammer, Etti Yammer, Michelle Stein, and Deena Stein.

Project Director: Lori Stein
Book Design Consultant: Albert Squillace
Editorial Director: Jay Hyams
Associate Art Director: Chani Yammer

Library of Congress Cataloging-in-Publication Data
Clausen, Ruth Rogers.
Annual gardening / Missouri Botanical Garden ; Ruth Clausen, writer
p.   cm. –(The American garden guides)
Includes index.
ISBN 0-679-75831-3
        1. Annuals (Plants) 2. Flower gardening.   3. Annuals
(Plants)–United States. 4. Annuals (Plants)–Canada. 5. Flower gardening--United States. 6. Flower gardening--Canada. I. Missouri Botanical Garden.   II. Title III. Series.
SB422.C58 1995   94-32984
635.9'312–dc20   CIP

Manufactured in Singapore

First Edition

9 8 7 6 5 4 3 2 1

Opposite: The tiled Moorish garden in the Missouri Botanical Garden's Shoenberg Temperate House illustrates the use of annuals in formal garden designs.

contents

Zinnias and heliotrope.

Petunia x *hybrida* 'Polo Red'

3. Garden Design

4. Techniques 180

5. Special Conditions 202

Petunias and nicotiana.

the american garden guides

The network of botanical gardens and arboreta in the United States and Canada constitutes a great treasure chest of knowledge about plants and what they need. Some of the most talented, experienced, and dedicated plantspeople in the world work full-time at these institutions; they are the people who actually grow plants, make gardens, and teach others about the process. They are the gardeners who are responsible for the gardens in which millions of visitors exclaim, "Why won't that plant grow that way for me?"

Over thirty of the most respected and beautiful gardens on the continent are participating in the creation of The American Garden Guides. The books in the series originate with manuscripts generated by gardeners in one or several of the gardens. Drawing on their decades of experience, these originating gardeners write down the techniques they use in their own gardens, recommend and describe the plants that grow best for them, and discuss their successes and failures. The manuscripts are then passed to several other participating gardens; in each, the specialist in that area adds recommended plants and other suggestions based on regional differences and different opinions.

The series has three major philosophical points carried throughout:

1) Successful gardens are by nature user-friendly toward the gardener and the environment. We advocate water conservation through the precepts of Xeriscaping and garden health care through Integrated Pest Management (IPM). Simply put, one does not set into motion any garden that is going to require undue irrigation during normal levels of rainfall, nor apply any pesticide or other treatment without first assessing its impact on all other life—plant, animal, and soil.

2) Gardening is an inexact science, learned by observation and by doing. Even the most experienced gardeners often develop markedly dissimilar ways of doing the same thing, or have completely divergent views of what any plant requires in order to thrive. Gardeners are an opinionated lot, and we have encouraged all participants to air and share their differences–and so, to make it clear that everyone who gardens will find his or her own way of dealing with plants. Although it is important to know the rules and the most accepted practices, it is also important to recognize that whatever works in the long run for you is the right way.

3) Part of the fun of gardening lies in finding new plants, not necessarily using over and over the same ones in the same old color schemes. In this book and others in the series, we have purposely included some lesser-known or underused plants, many of them native to our vast and wonderful continent. Wherever we can, we call attention to endangered species and suggest ways to nurture them back to their natural state of plenty.

This volume was originated by June Hutson of Missouri Botanical Garden; she worked closely with Brian Ward, who managed the annual plantings at Missouri Botanical Garden for over thirty years. The manuscript was written by Ruth Rogers Clausen, and reviewed by eight gardens in different regions of the country.

Elvin McDonald
Houston, Texas

Director's preface

The horticultural showcase that is the Missouri Botanical Garden is the result of the hard work of expert horticulturists. Through the use of an abundant variety of plant material, including extensive use of annuals, the Garden is able to enjoy a long, colorful growing season.

The home gardener can also have a showpiece of a garden by using the information and techniques presented in this book. June Hutson, the author of *Annual Gardening,* is one of our many valued horticulturists. June's expertise in growing and designing with annuals is one of the reasons that 700,000 visitors flock to the Missouri Botanical Garden annually.

Annuals provide our landscapes with the seasonal colors so popular with home gardeners and visitors to display gardens. While trees, shrubs, groundcovers, and perennials all may be used to add interesting textures, forms, fragrance, and color to our gardens, annuals, seasonally planted, provide a flexibility that longer-lasting plants do not possess. There is a nearly endless array of colors, sizes, shapes, seasons of bloom, and uses for annuals. They are readily available, inexpensive to replace, and most are easy to grow.

The uses for annuals are many. Historically, they are famous for colorful borders, edging, as fillers between other plants and for summer bedding and carpet bedding so popular in the great Victorian gardens. These uses continue today, but we also see annuals used in containers, hanging baskets, flowerboxes, for fragrance, cut flowers, and groundcover, and in naturalistic and even xeriscape gardens. They can also be used in mass plantings to add great swaths of color to our streets, parks, commercial landscapes, and botanical gardens. Take a look at any of the seed catalogs and the uses and array of these popular plants will be obvious. Some annuals even reseed themselves, and thus appear year after year.

The Missouri Botanical Garden uses many different kinds of annuals. Visitors to the Garden's seventy-nine acres enjoy a range of garden experiences from a Japanese garden to an English woodland to a tropical rainforest. In 1996, home-gardeners will have the opportunity to learn even more about the craft of gardening when twenty-four residential-scale demonstration gardens open.

I hope this book will give you a better understanding of the joys of using annuals in your own garden. It is a great pleasure for the staff of the Missouri Botanical Garden to share its expertise with gardeners everywhere.

Peter H. Raven, Ph.D
Director, Missouri Botanical Garden

INTRODUCTION

Above: Planting annuals around garden ornaments, like the "Zerogee" sculpture by Paul Granlund at the Missouri Botanical Garden, allows the gardener the flexibility to experiment with different color and texture accents each year. *Oppositeand previous pages:* At the Missouri Botanical Garden, the Heckman Rock Garden contains a full array of plants. In addition to the traditional woodies and perennials, annuals are used for color and to camouflage bulbs.

Vigorous, dependable, free-flowering, and versatile, annuals are the stalwarts of the flower garden. When the perennial border is gasping in the August sun, and the blossoms of flowering shrubs and trees are little more than fading memories, most annuals are still pushing out bloom with an enthusiasm that borders on the reckless. And while many perennials take two or more seasons to flower, annuals offer close to instant gratification. But reliability and vigor are only a small part of their appeal: For sheer take-your-breath-away impact, annuals are far and away the horticultural champions, from the massive nodding heads of helianthus to the intense, almost neon-blue flowers of the diminutive lobelia. And lest you think that the realm of annuals is limited to the impatiens, begonias, salvias, and geraniums of your local garden center, consider that thousands of plants are classified as annuals, making them arguably the *most* varied of all garden plants. From the stately cleome, with its delicate, spidery racemes, to the cottage-garden tangle of jewel-toned nasturtium, annuals offer a staggering variety of color, form, habit, and size.

DEFINITION Strictly speaking, an annual is a plant that lives out its life cycle in a single year, from germination through flowering and setting of seed to the death of the plant itself. For the purposes of this book, however–and for most gardeners as well–the definition is expanded to include the so-called tender perennials–plants that are hardy in warmer climates but can't survive the cold winters that predominate in much of the continental United States. These plants, which include coleus and heliotrope, don't die after setting seed as true annuals do, but are withered easily by frost and lack the hardy root systems of true perennials.

USING ANNUALS Though annuals have been cultivated for centuries, they saw their great heyday in the late 1800s, when their exoticism and brilliant coloration made them indispensable in the fashionable Victorian garden. With the ascendancy of the herbaceous perennial border as championed by Vita Sackville-West and others, however, annuals came to be disparaged for exactly those qualities that had endeared them to the Victorian sensibility. To the haute horticulturists of Sackville-West's day, they were unrestrained, over-bright, and vulgar. This low opinion persisted for decades, although ordinary gardeners, of course, continued to cultivate annuals, blithely unaware of their tarnished reputation. And why not? Annuals weren't just dependable, they were enormously versatile. The very characteristic that shortened their lives–the lack of a complex root system–made them, as a rule, eminently portable. If you needed to fill a bare spot in the garden, you could simply dig up a clump of petunias and plunk them down again, with the near certainty that they would continue to thrive. And if the grand schemes of May proved less than grand in July, there was always the consolation that next spring you could start again from scratch.

It was inevitable that the horticultural pendulum would swing back, ushering in a new era of popularity for annuals. After all, what other group of flowering plants can fulfill so many needs and fit so many niches? Annuals can be used in beds and borders, either by themselves or alongside perennials and shrubs. (Indeed, in newly planted perennial borders they are almost a necessity, filling in the blanks, as it were, until the perennials attain their long-awaited maturity.) Because their roots aren't likely to demand too much in the way of water and nutrients, they can be interplanted with even the fussiest roses. Smaller annuals like sweet alyssum and portulaca are naturals in alpine rock gardens, prodigiously spilling over crags and crevices and even, at times, acting remarkably like perennials by self-seeding with abandon. And the larger annuals, including the startlingly hued Mexican sunflower and the above-mentioned cleome, rival even larger flowering shrubs as showy garden specimens.

From a purely practical standpoint, annuals like morning glory and moonflower provide quick cover for stumps, drainpipes, and other eyesores, while a hedge of giant sunflowers can pinch-hit for shrubs when instant privacy is required. Interplanted with vegetables, annuals attract bees and other necessary pollinators (though the idea that marigolds actually repel such pests as nematodes and potato beetles is no longer widely believed). Because their mission in life is to produce seed, annuals are the mainstay of the cutting garden, becoming ever more prolific as their bounty is plundered.

And finally, what is more emblematic of summer than a hanging basket filled to the brim and over with gaily colored annuals? In fact, their short roots and long-flowering habit make them ideal for containers of every sort, from windowboxes and terracotta pots to recycled wine casks and old watering cans.

HISTORICAL NOTES

Humanity's first attempts at gardening were more practical than ornamental. For just about every primitive culture there is evidence that humans began to experiment with growing their own food at about the same time they began to set up the homes. These experiments involved enclosing plots, irrigation, making tools, and figuring out how to plant seeds so that a supply of food would be readily available when foraging and hunting were unsuccessful.

But it did not take long for art and beauty to become involved in the practice of horticulture. Even the earliest gardens of Egypt and Assyria were planted in patterns and decorated with statues. Estates usually included flower gardens with beds of poppies, cornflowers, and papyrus. Famous for their sense of style, early Egyptians usually planted in blocks of color, which might be the origin of the still-popular "carpet bedding" style. Flowers were often grown in pots or wooden boxes placed along pathways. Cut flowers—ivy, poppy, mignonette, cornflowers, and lilies—were used indoors and as perfumes. The Assyrians of Mesopotamia also were great gardeners, and probably introduced the practice of hanging vines, an art perfected in the famous hanging gardens of Babylonia. a multileveled landscape of terraces with shrubs, vines, and flowers. In ancient India and China, too, flowers were grown and used abundantly.

Ornamental horticulture took hold in Europe during the reign of the Roman Empire. Even the homes of ordinary citizens included garden plots where flowers for religious ceremonies—violets, hyacinths, narcissi—were grown. In many homes, carefully laid out beds of lilies, roses, violets, pansies, poppies, and iris were planted. Country homes boasted even more elaborate gardens.

Sophisticated techniques of topiary, edging, and irrigation were developed for these gardens, and avid gardeners collected exotic specimens from abroad.

With the fall of the Roman empire, many ornamental horticultural practices were lost. But as the Renaissance dawned, horticulture reemerged as an art form and interest in exotic plants resurfaced. This was a time of world exploration, and explorers returned to Europe with not only spices and textiles, but also with exotic plants. Throughout the sixteenth century, the French and English aristocracy favored flowering exotics, probably to brighten the dreary winters of northern Europe. As Renaissance gardens grew in size and complexity, the privileged Europeans copied Italian gardens.

Technologic advances during this time resulted in movement of people from rural areas into cities and gave them an unknown possession–leisure time. Women of the upper middle classes had technology to help with the household chores, leaving them time to cultivate themselves and beautiful growing things.

Flowers became a focal point of society as they were given special sentiments involving all aspects of life. Plant collecting expeditions fanned out across Africa, Asia, New Zealand, Australia, and South America, and British gardens such as Kew became renowned for their exotic collections.

When colonists arrived in the South America, they found elaborate gardens that rivaled the best that Europe had to offer. Ornamental gardening by colonists in the New World began slowly; colonists had little time for pleasurable hobbies. However, they did bring seed from many of the plants they loved back home, and often incorporated hollyhock, canterbury bells, calendula,

and primroses into utilitarian vegetable and herb gardens. Though formal gardens were a rarity, they did exist; a notable example was the governor's mansion in Williamsburg, Virginia. Acclaimed plantsman John Bartram of Philadelphia (1699-1777) collected specimens of the many new plants he found here and sent them back to England, among them shooting stars, wild asters, gentians, honeysuckles, and dogtoothed violets. He also imported many plants such as snapdragons, poppies, and carnations for distribution here, and created new hybrids. George Washington and Thomas Jefferson were avid gardeners as well.

Horticulture was promoted by the publication of books, the foundation of garden clubs, and by many flower shows. Plant crazes periodically swept the country: chrysanthemums in 1890, asters in 1900-1910, sweet peas in 1912.

Until recently, Americans have been influenced by England in their choice of garden design. Until the end of the nineteenth century, that meant following the stylized, enclosed gardens of Capability Brown and Humphrey Repten. In the twentieth century, William Robinson and Gertrude Jekyll broke this tradition, placing an emphasis on a more natural look. Jekyll, a British garden designer, is considered by many to be the most influential voice in garden design, particularly with perennials. She placed importance on juxtaposition of plants, studying each one for shape, texture, and color, and popularizing many new plants. Today, the "new American garden" style accepts many of Jekyll's ideas and extends them, incorporating the native plants that were found on this continent by the original settlers into gardens that echo the country's natural landscape.

BASIC NEEDS Annuals are among the most adaptable of garden plants, demanding little more than good light, sufficient water, and reasonably fertile soil. Even if your conditions fall short of this rather general ideal, you're likely to find annuals that will work for you. In fact, some of the most striking annual gardens can be found in what would appear to be the most inhospitable sites—on rocky, sunbaked slopes; in sandy seashore soil; under the enveloping shade of mature trees.

Soil The majority of annuals prefer full sun and well-drained, slightly acid soil with a moderate humus content; but most grow quite well in alkaline soil as well. If your soil is clayey, you can amend it with compost or well-rotted

The brilliant colors of annuals are rarely seen in other plant groups. They add seasonal color to the dwarf conifers, as shown above in the Kassabaum Dwarf Conifer Garden at the Missouri Botanical Garden.

A BRIEF LESSON IN BOTANY

Plants are living things and share many traits with animals. Plants are composed of millions of individual cells that are organized into complex organ systems. Plants breathe (take in and expel gases) and extract energy from food; to do this they require water, nutrients, and atmospheric gases. Like animals, plants reproduce sexually, and their offspring inherit characteristics through a genetic code passed along as DNA and, unlike animals, some plants reproduce asexually.

Plants, however, can do one thing that no animal can do. Through a process called photosynthesis, plants can capture energy from the sun and convert that energy into compounds such as proteins, fats, and carbohydrates. These energy-rich compounds are the source of the energy for all animal life, including humans.

THE IMPORTANCE OF PLANTS

Because no living animals can produce the energy they need to live, all their energy comes from plants. Like other animals, we eat green plants directly, in the form of fruits, vegetables, and grains (breads and cereals), or we eat animals and animal products that were fed green plants.

The oxygen we need to live on Earth is constantly pumped out of green plants as a byproduct of photosynthesis. Plants prevent the erosion of our precious soils and hinder water loss to the atmosphere.

Plants are also an important source of drugs. Fully one-quarter of all prescriptions contain at least one plant-derived product. Aspirin, one of the most commonly used drugs, was originally isolated from the bark of the willow tree. Today, scientists are screening plants from all over the world in search of new compounds to cure cancer, AIDS, and other diseases.

THE WHOLE PLANT

Basically, a plant is made up of leaves, stems, and roots; all these parts are connected by a vascular system, much like our circulatory system. The vascular system can be seen in the veins of a leaf, or in the rings in a tree.

LEAVES

Leaves are generally flattened and expanded tissues that are green due to the presence of chlorophyll, the pigment that is necessary for photosynthesis. Most leaves are connected to the stem by a stalk, or petiole, which allows

the leaves to alter their position in relation to the sun and capture as much energy as possible. Plants that have leaves year-round are often called "evergreen," while plants that lose all their leaves at one time each year are termed "deciduous."

Leaves come in an astounding variety of shapes, textures, and sizes. Some leaves are composed of a single structure, or blade, and are termed simple. Other leaves are made up of many units, or leaflets, and are called compound (see endpapers).

STEMS

Technically, a stem is the tissue that supports leaves and that connects the leaves with the roots via a vascular system. Stems also bear the flowers on a plant. Therefore, a stem can be identified by the presence of buds, which are the unexpanded leaves, stems, or flowers that will develop at a later time.

Plants that send up leaves in a rosette or clump may have stems so short that they are difficult to distinguish. Other plants, like the iris, have a stem, called a rhizome, that travels horizontally underground. Many plants of arid regions have very reduced leaves or have lost their leaves altogether in order to avoid loss of water to the atmosphere. The barrel cactus is an example of a plant that is almost entirely stem.

ROOTS

Although out of sight, roots are extremely important to the life of the plant. Roots anchor a plant in the soil, absorb water and nutrients, and store excess food, such as starches, for the plants' future use. Basically, there are two types of roots: taproots and fibrous roots. Taproots are thickened, unbranched roots that grow straight down, taking advantage of moisture and nutrients far below the soil surface. Taproots, such as carrots, store carbohydrates. Fibrous roots are fine, branching,

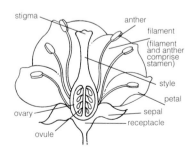

and generally more shallow. They often form dense mats of roots, making them excellent agents of soil stabilization. Fibrous roots absorb moisture and nutrients from a shallow zone of soil and may be more susceptible to drought.

Roots obviously need to come into contact with water, but they also need air in order to work properly. Except for those adapted to aquatic environments, most plants require well-drained soils that provide them air as well as water.

VASCULAR SYSTEMS

Plants have a well-developed vascular system that extends throughout the plant body and that allows movement of water and compounds from one part of a plant to another. Once the roots absorb water and minerals, the vascular system funnels them to the leaves, where they are used in photosynthesis. Likewise, energy-rich compounds that are produced in the leaves must travel to the stems and roots to provide nutrition for further growth. The vascular system also strengthens plant tissues. Although much of the vascular system is part of the internal anatomy of a plant, some parts can be seen.

PHOTOSYNTHESIS

A green plant is like a factory that takes raw materials available in the environment and converts them into other forms of energy. In a complex series of energy transfer and chemical conversion events called photosynthesis, plants take energy from the sun, minerals and water from the soil, and gases from the atmosphere; these raw materials are converted into chemical forms of energy that are used for plant growth. These same energy-rich compounds (proteins, sugars and starches, fats and oils) can be utilized by animals as a source of food and nutrition. All this is possible because of a green pigment, chlorophyll.

Photosynthesis is an extremely complex series of reactions that takes place in the cells of leaves, the byproducts of which are connected to other reactions throughout the cell. The most basic reactions of photosynthesis occurs like this. Energy from the sun strikes the leaf surface, and electrons in the chlorophyll molecule become "excited" and are boosted to a higher energy level. Excited electrons are routed through a chain of reactions that extracts and stores energy in the form of sugars. As a byproduct of electron loss, water molecules (H_2O) are split; hydrogen moves in to replenish the electrons lost from chlorophyll, and Oxygen is released, finding its way into our atmosphere. In another photosynthetic reaction, carbon dioxide from the atmosphere is "fixed," or converted into organic compounds within the plant cell. These first chemical compounds are the building blocks for more complex reactions and are the precursors for the formation of many elaborate chemical compounds.

PLANT NUTRITION

Plants require mineral nutrients from the soil, water, and the atmosphere in order to maintain healthy growth and reproduction. Macronutrients, those nutrients needed in large amounts, include hydrogen, oxygen, and carbon so essential for photosynthesis. Other macronutrients are nitrogen, phosphorus, potassium, sulfur, and calcium. Nitrogen is an important component of chlorophyll and of proteins, which are used to construct DNA, cell membranes, and other vital compounds in the cell. Phosphorus is also used in building DNA and is important in cell development. Potassium is important in the development of tubers, roots, and other storage organs. If macronutrients are in limited supply, growth and development in the plant will be strongly curtailed. Micronutrients, such as iron, copper and magnesium, are required in smaller amounts and are of variable importance to different kinds of plants.

LIFE CYCLE

Higher plants (except for ferns) begin life as a seed. Given the right set of conditions (temperature, moisture, light), a seed will germinate and develop its first roots and leaves using food stored in the seed (humans and other animals take advantage of the high-quality food in seeds when we eat wheat, rice, and corn, just to name a few). Because of the presence of chlorophyll in the leaves, the small plant is soon able to produce its own food, which is used immediately for further growth and development. As the seedling grows in size, it also grows in complexity. The first, simple root gives way to a complex root system that may include underground storage organs. The stem is transformed into an intricate system of vascular tissue that moves water from the ground upward into the leafy part of the plant, while other tissues transport energy-rich compounds manufactured in the leaves downward to be stored in stem and root systems.

Once the plant reaches maturity, flower initiation begins. Flowers hold the sexual apparatus for the plant; their brilliant colors and glorious odors are advertisements to attract pollinators such as insects or birds. In a basic, complete flower, there are four different parts, given below. However, many plants have incomplete flowers with one or more of these parts missing, or the parts may be highly modified.

1. Sepals. The outermost part of the flower, the sepals cover the young floral buds. Although they are often green, they may be variously colored.

2. Petals. The next layer of parts in the flower, petals are often colorful and play an important role in attracting pollinators.

3. Stamens. Stamens are located next to the petals, or may even be basally fused to the petals. The stamens are the "male" reproductive parts of the flower; they produce the pollen. Pollen grains are fine, dustlike particles that pollinate the female portion of the flower. The tissue at the end of the stamen that holds pollen is called the anther.

4. Pistil. The innermost part of the flower holds the female reproductive apparatus for the plant. The stigma, located at the tip of the pistil, is often covered with a sticky substance and is the site where pollen is deposited. The stigma is held by a floral tube, called the style. At the base of the style, the ovary holds one to many ovules, which contain eggs that represent undeveloped seeds.

Pollination is the transfer of pollen from an anther to a stigma and is the first step in the production of seeds. Pollen can be transferred by an insect visiting the flower, by the wind, or even by the splashing of raindrops. After being deposited on a compatible stigma, the pollen grains grow into tubes that travel from the stigma down the floral tube into the ovary, depositing sperm cells to the ovules. If all goes well, sperm cells unite with the eggs inside the ovules, and fertilization takes place.

After fertilization, the entire floral structure is transformed into a fruit. Fruit can be fleshy, like an apple, or dry like a pea pod. Within each fruit, fertilized eggs develop into seeds, complete with a cache of storage tissue and a seed coat.

BINOMIAL NOMENCLATURE

Scientific nomenclature of plants can be confusing and intimidating. However, once you are comfortable with the naming system, you'll appreciate its logic and simplicity, particularly in identifying plants correctly. Common names are often used to refer to plants. Unfortunately, several plants can have the same common name, adding to the confusion. To be absolutely certain of a plant's identity, use its scientific name. Every plant in the world has only one correct scientific name (usually in Latin or Greek) that is recognized throughout the world.

Binomial nomenclature means that each name has two parts. Almost all plants have at least a genus and species name. The genus name designates a group of plants that have more in common with each other than any other group. Examples of genus are *Dianthus*, *Pelargonium* and *Tagetes*. The specific epithet is the second word in the name and is usually descriptive of the individual plant. For example, *Portulaca grandiflora* is in the genus *Portulaca*. Its specific epithet, *grandiflora*, is the Latin word for large-flowered. The species name, consisting of the genus and specific epithet, for moss rose is *Portulaca grandiflora*.

Plants that are developed and cloned by humans are generally designated with a cultivar name (cultivar comes from "cultivated variety"), for example, *Ricinus communis* 'Carmencita' or *Rudbeckia hirta* 'Double Gold'. If a plant is a hybrid, either occurring in nature or man-induced, the plant will usually have two names connected by an "x", indicating a hybrid. For example, *Coleus* x *hybridus* indicates that these coleus are hybrids.

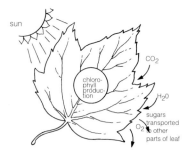

sun

chloro-phyll production

CO_2

H_2O

O_2

sugars transported to other parts of leaf

An annual garden is a perfect venue for experimentation. Whether you plant a few old favorites in a new combination (such as the marigolds, sages, and zinnias above), a plant that is new for you (such as jewels of opar, shown with celosia on the opposite page) or a mix of every plant you like (such as the garden on the far right), you never know exactly how it is going to look.

manure; after the first year, you should need only a light reapplication in spring, along with an application of start-up fertilizer. Be aware, however, that some annuals, including cosmos, gazania, and nasturtium, require little in the way of fertilizer and, in fact, do better in relatively infertile soil. Portulaca, for example, is at its best where the soil is poorest, which is why its multicolored roselike blossoms brighten so many seaside gardens; try to grow it in the nice fertile soil of a typical perennial bed, however, and you're likely to reap only frustration. The same holds true for poppies, whose gorgeous blooms are at their best in the dry, fast-draining soil of stony banks and alpine rock gardens.

pH If your soil pH falls within the 6.0-7.4 range, you should be able to grow most annuals; if tests reveal your soil to be too acid or alkaline, it can be altered with amendments, such as lime for acid soil and aluminum sulfate for alkaline. Of course, some soils, specifically those found in the desert Southwest, are extremely alkaline and can't be modified sufficiently to suit the vast majority of annuals. This doesn't mean that Southwesterners are consigned to cultivating cactus gardens (striking as they may be); annuals like dianthus and strawflower, for example, do quite nicely in alkaline soils, as does the notoriously hard-to-please sweetpea.

Water As a rule, annuals require about an inch of water a week; if nature fails to provide, you'll have to do it yourself, either with overhead sprinklers, soaker or other hoses, or an old-fashioned watering can. If you live in a very dry climate—or if you're concerned about conserving water—you can choose among a fair number of annuals whose requirements for water are minimal, among them cleome, dusty miller, globe amaranth, and even those old standbys petunia and zinnia. If summer rainfall in your area is actually above average, or if your garden is in wet or boggy soil, you'll find a host of annuals who like to get their feet wet, including browallia, fuchsia, nicotiana, and pansy.

Sun Most annual gardens are sited where they can receive at least six to eight hours of full sun a day, because that's what the majority of annuals prefer. But as America's suburbs mature, and the trees planted in those suburban back-

Containerized annuals provide seasonal color for formal displays, as shown here in the Shoenberg Temperate House at the Missouri Botanical Garden. The walls of a garden can be softened by the addition of cascading annuals in containers.

yards expand their canopies, sun becomes an increasingly scarce commodity. If you're intent on growing annuals in a tree-shaded yard, you have two basic alternatives: You can prune or cut the trees to admit more sunlight, or you can choose plants that are shade tolerant. This doesn't mean that you can start an annual garden on a forest floor; few, if any, annuals can grow in complete shade. But a surprising number do very nicely, and even prefer, the kind of partial shade you're likely to find in most home landscapes, including ageratum, browallia, coleus, dianthus, fuschia, impatiens, lobelia, pansy, salvia, vinca, and wishbone flower.

CHOOSING ANNUALS For many gardeners, selecting plants is the most enjoyable aspect of annual gardening; it can also be the most perplexing. Once you've narrowed the list to those annuals that suit your specific growing conditions, you'll still have to choose among a vast number of plants, especially if you start your annuals from seed. (Seed catalogs and exchanges offer an abundance of annual plants unlikely to be found at local nurseries or garden centers.)

Since half the beauty of an annual garden derives from the felicitious combination of flowers planted in it, it's wise not just to think of a plant's individual attributes but to consider how all the plants in the garden will work together. Do the colors complement or contrast with one another, or are they a motley assortment of clashing hues? Do the shapes, sizes, and textures present a pleasing variety, or do they look unrelentingly the same, like edgy soldiers awaiting inspection?

Don't forget to consider foliage as well as bloom: Though most people choose annuals for their flowers, many of these plants are valuable for their foliage alone, from the exotic multihued leaves of the common coleus to the silvery plumage of dusty miller to the subtly colored whorls of ornamental cabbage. And others, while grown primarily for their flowers, offer foliage that packs its own aesthetic punch. Think of the feathery, bright-green foliage of cosmos, or the lovely fingerlike leaves of cleome. Because both of these flowers tend to tower over the rest of the garden, their foliage is very much a part of its overall design. Annual vines like morning glory, hyacinth bean, and cardinal vine also offer showy foliage that stands out in the landscape. Among the many other plants with interesting foliage are plumed thistle, echium, annual poinsettia, and ivy geranium.

Season, too, is an important, and often overlooked, consideration. Most gardeners think of annuals as strictly long-season plants, flowering abundantly from June through September. In reality, many—like pansies and linaria—flower primarily in spring, and others—including flowering kale—are at their best at the end of the season.

Finally, don't hesitate to try the unusual and the unexpected. Though gardeners are often advised to look to their neighbors for inspiration (on the generally wise premise that what grows well next door will grow equally well in your own dooryard), this tends to promote an unrelenting sameness in the landscape. With so many exotic and heirloom seeds now available to the general gardening public, it would be a shame to hew strictly to the familiar. This isn't to suggest that you throw out your packets of zinnia and cosmos, but to coax you into expanding your horticultural repertoire. Why not, for instance, plant a few bells-of-Ireland with their white-veined bell-like green calyxes? (Who ever thought that green flowers could be such stand-outs in the garden?) Or consider diascia, a modestly sized plant that simply covers itself in small deep-pink snapdragonlike flowers. For foliage, tuck in a few polka-dot plants, whose pretty dark green leaves are improbably dotted with the brightest pink, as if some careless painter had been walking about the garden with a still-dripping brush. Or plant one or more of the scented geraniums, whose flowers are insignificant but whose appealingly cut leaves give off the intriguing fragrance of lemon, or chocolate, or rose. Consider, too, some variations on the ordinary: Instead of the ubiquitous red salvia, choose St. John's fire 'Firecracker', with its smashing peach-colored flower tiers. And though it's hard to imagine anyone tiring of the glorious *Helianthus annuus*, an intriguing alternative is the Mexican sunflower, whose orange-red blossoms fairly blaze above the dark green foliage. One of the objectives of America's great botanical gardens is to encourage diversity, and nowhere is that diversity more apparent than in the glorious grouping of plants known as annuals. We urge you to experiment, not just for the sake of the landscape, but for your own enrichment as well.

June Hutson has gardened since she was ten years old. Although she began her career in a different field, she volunteered at the Missouri Botanical Garden and returned to college for a degree in horticulture. She was soon hired by the Garden and she has been there for the past eighteen years, working in the perennial, vegetable, annual, rose, and herb gardens, as well assisting in the Climatron and Mediterranean House and at seasonal flower shows. June is currently curator of the Temperate House, the Rock Garden and the Dwarf Conifer Collection. She teaches in the Adult Education Master Gardening Program and lectures to gardening clubs on annuals, perennials, rock gardens, ornamental grasses, herbs, bulbs, and dried flowers.

PLANT SELECTOR 2

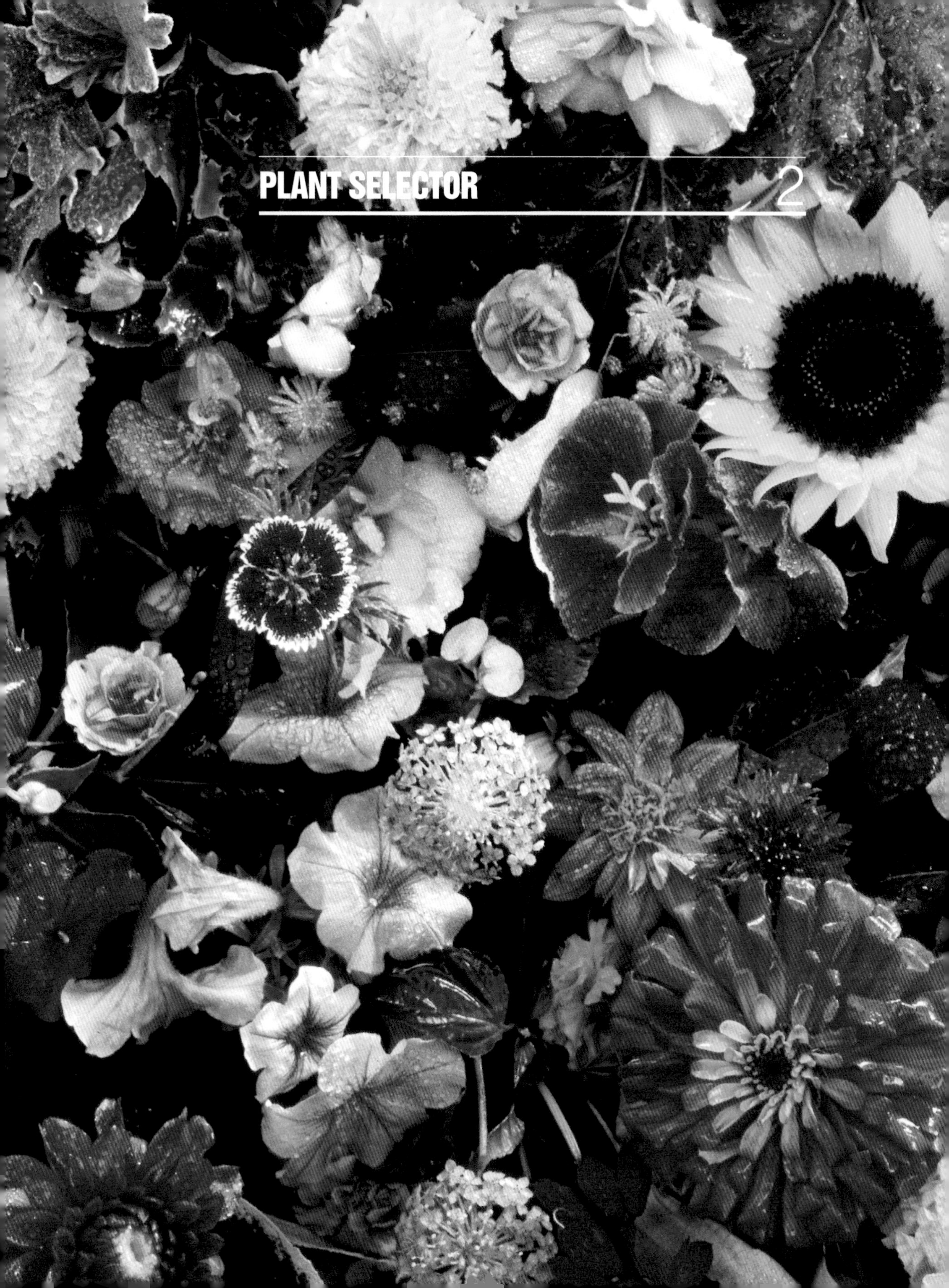

Plants in this volume are arranged according to their Latin or scientific names. Here are the Latin names of some common herbs; see the index of table of contents for complete listings:

Basil: *Ocimum*
Black-eyed Susan: *Rudbeckia*
Cabbage: *Brassica*
California poppy: *Eschscholzia*
Cockscomb: *Celosia*
Dusty miller: *Senecio*
Four o'clock: *Mirabilis*
Geranium: *Pelargonium*
Hollyhock: *Alcea*
Larkspur: *Consolida*
Marigold: *Tagetes*
Moonflower: *Ipomoea*
Morning glory: *Ipomoea*
Nasturtium: *Tropaeolum*
Pansy: *Viola*
Pepper: *Capsicum*
Periwinkle: *Catharanthus*
Pink: *Dianthus*
Poppy: *Papaver*
Sage: *Salvia*
Sea Lavender: *Limonium*
Snapdragon: *Antirrhinum*
Statice: *Limonium*
Stock: *Matthiola*
Sunflower: *Helianthus*
Sweet alyssum: *Lobularia*
Sweet pea: *Lathyrus*
Tobacco flower: *Nicotiana*
Vinca: *Catharanthus*

CHOOSING ANNUALS

Gardeners don't always enjoy every part of the gardening process–but finding a great new plant is pure pleasure for just about everyone. Since thousands of different varieties and cultivars are currently being sold, and nurseries, botanists, and private gardeners all over the world are busy finding and creating more, there will never be a shortage of new plants to discover. Moreover, new methods of transportation and communication are making it easier for us to find and use annuals that are common in other parts of the world. The key is finding out which ones are right for you.

This plant selector chapter is designed to give you basic information about annuals to grow in your own garden. For information on how to design a garden, see Chapter 3. For information on techniques like how to plant or how to start seeds indoors, see Chapter 4; in this chapter, you will find portraits of individual annuals. Our gardening experts have selected about two hundred varieties that work well for them; they mixed some common, easy-to-find selections with others that you might not know about, but should. Gardeners from other botanic gardens around the country added varieties that do well in their regions.

When deciding which annuals to grow, ask yourself:

1. Do I want to specialize in a particular type of plant, such as dahlias or pansies? Do I want annuals to use for cutting in fresh or dried arrangements? There is, of course, no reason not to mix types.

2. Do I live in the right geographical region for this plant? If you live in a warm region, you may be able to overwinter some plants like lantana or hollyhock, but nasturtiums, which require a cooler climate, won't grow for you. If you are not sure about your climate zone, talk to your county extension service, local nursery, or botanic garden. But don't forget that your site is unique; it has its own "microclimate," and conditions may be different from those two blocks away let alone at the nursery ten miles down the road. Even within your own yard, the climate in a sheltered spot near the house might be different from the site on the other side of a hill. (See page 182 for information on choosing a site, and Chapter 5 for information on growing herbs in difficult climates.)

3. How much care will this plant need? And how much time do I wish to spend caring for it? Is it susceptible to a disease that is rampant in my area? Will it need staking? Pruning? Extra watering? How much care is it worth? You can grow almost anything if you are willing to take the time to pamper it.

4. Can I find the plants and seeds I want in regional catalogs and local nurseries? Regionally grown plants are already acclimated to your climate and will be easier to care for.

Answer these questions honestly. It's easy to fudge–but the plant will know. Much heartache and wasted effort can be saved by putting the right plants in the right place right from the start.

When choosing plants, you will find dozens or even hundreds of varieties available for each annual. Every gardener has his or her personal favorites; one gardener's heaviest yielder is another's certain failure. A species that yields beautiful blooms for dried arrangements may not provide the long blooming period desired by a gardener who wants it to look great outdoors.

Some terms you will find throughout this chapter need to be defined. Annuals are often referred to as hardy, half-hardy, and tender, but these terms don't imply hardiness as we usually think of it, as plants that will last through winter. Hardy annuals are those that can be sown directly in the ground whenever the soil can be worked (fall in mild climates, early spring in cooler regions). Tender annuals need to be sown in completely warmed soil, after all danger of frost is passed. Half-hardy annuals fall somewhere in between; they will survive a very light frost. Another term frequently used in relation to annuals is F_1 (or F_2) hybrid. These refer to first (or second) generation hybrids, usually produced from two uniform inbred parents by hand pollination and often among the best selections available.

We have listed varieties that have worked for our gardeners; the only way to find the ones that will work for you is to try them yourself. If you find a plant you love that seems only marginally suited to your climate, plant it–and see if it grows.

The U.S. Department of Agriculture has prepared this map, which separates the country into climate zones; many seed companies use these zone numbers to indicate where a particular variety will survive the winter. In annual gardening, this is not a very important factor, since you don't expect your plants to overwinter. The climate zone map will help you choose shrubs and perennials used in your garden. Find out what zone you're in, and pay attention to the growers' recommendations–but remember that climate zone is only one part of the picture.

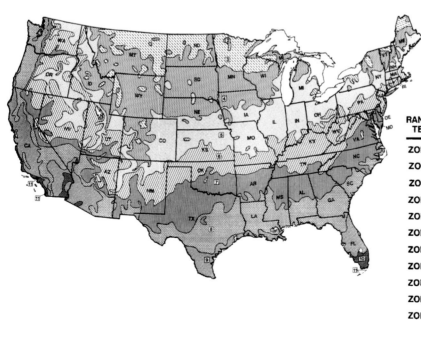

RANGE OF AVERAGE ANNUAL MINIMUM TEMPERATURES FOR EACH ZONE	
ZONE 1	BELOW –50° F
ZONE 2	–50° TO –40°
ZONE 3	–40° TO –30°
ZONE 4	–30° TO –20°
ZONE 5	–20° TO –10°
ZONE 6	–10° TO 0°
ZONE 7	0° TO 10°
ZONE 8	10° TO 20°
ZONE 9	20° TO 30°
ZONE 10	30° TO 40°
ZONE 11	ABOVE 40°

BLUE/PURPLE FLOWERS
ageratum, 28
arctotis, 35 (blue eye)
begonia, 36
brachycome, 41
brassica, 41
browallia, 42
callistephus, 46
centaurea, 53
collinsia, 60
consolida, 61
cynglossus, 66
datura, 70
dianthus, 70
dolichos, 74
eustoma, 76
evolvulus, 78
gilia, 80
gomphrena, 81
helichrysum, 86
heliotrope, 84
limonium, 98
lobelia, 100
lobularia, 102
morning glory, 93
nemophila, 108
nigella, 110
oxypetalum, 115
petunia, 120
petunia, 120
phlox, 125
portulaca, 127
rhodochiton, 129
salpiglossus, 131
salvia, 132
scabiosa, 137
*scaveola, 138
strobilanthus, 143
torenia, 151
trachymene, 151
verbena, 153
viola, 155

WHITE FLOWERS
abelmoschus, 28
acidenthera, 28
alcea, 31
ammi majus, 33
ammobium, 33
antirrhinum, 36
arctotis, 36
begonia, 36
bellis, 46
brachycome, 41
callistephus, 46
canna, 47
catharanthus, 49
chrysanthemum, 55
clarkia, 56
cobaea, 58
dahlia, 66
datura, 70
dianthus, 70
eschscholzia, 75
eustoma, 76
gladiolus, 81
gomphrena, 81
helianthus, 83
helichrysum, 86
heliotrope, 86
impatiens, 88
lantana, 95
lobelia, 100
lobularia, 102
moonflower, 91
nicotiana sylvestris, 111
nierembergia
petunia, 120
phlox, 125
cosmos, 63
*polianthes, 127
portulaca, 127
solanum, 142
viola, 142
zinnia, 156

YELLOW FLOWERS
abelmoschus, 29
alcea, 31
antirrhinum, 36
calendula, 45
canna, 47
celosia, 50
chrysanthemum, 53
coreopsis, 63
cosmos, 63
dahlia, 66
dyssodia, 74
eschscholzia, 75
gaillardia, 78
gazania, 80
gladiolus, 81
helianthus, 83
helichrysum, 86
lantana, 95
melampodium, 106
*petunia, 120
portulaca, 127
rudbeckia, 131
salpiglossus, 132
sanvitalia, 137
tagetes, 144
thunbergia, 149
tithonia, 149
tropaeoleum, 152
verbena, 153
zinnia, 156

GREEN FLOWERS
Amaranthus caudatus 'Viridis' 32
brassica, 41
molucella, 108
nicotiana alata, 109
Nicotiana langsdorfii, 111

RED/ORANGE FLOWERS
alcea, 31
amaranthus, 32
antirrhinum, 36
begonia, 36
bellis, 40
calendula, 45
callistephus, 46
canna, 47
celosia, 50
chrysanthemum, 53
cosmos, 63
cuphea ignea, 66
*dahlia, 66
dianthus, 70
gazania, 80
gladiolus, 80
gomphrena, 81
helichrysum, 86
hibiscus, 87
impatiens, 88
impatiens balsamina, 88
lantana, 95
matthiola, 108
mirabilis, 106
papaver, 115
pelargonium, 117
pentas, 120
petunia, 120
portulaca, 127
salpiglosssus, 132
sanvitalia, 137
silene, 143
tagetes, 144
tropaeolum, 132
verbena, 153

PINK FLOWERS
alcea, 31
antirrhinum, 31
*begonia, 36
bellis, 40
brassica, 41
callistephus, 46
canna, 47
catharanthus, 49
celosia, 50
chrysanthemum, 53
clarkia, 56
consolida, 61
convolvulus, 61
cosmos, 63
dahlia, 66
dianthus, 70
eustoma, 76
gladiolus, 81
gomphrena, 81
helichrysum, 86
hibiscus, 87
impatiens, 88
lantana, 95
lavatera, 98
lobularia, 102
mandevilla, 102
matthiola, 105
pelargonium, 117
petunia, 120
phlox, 125
portulaca, 127
silene, 143
zinnia, 156

FOLIAGE PLANTS
*alternanthera, 32
Amaranthus tricolor, 33
caladium, 45
coleus, 58
euphorbia, 76
hypoestes, 88
kochia, 88
ocimum, 113
oxalis, 115
perilla, 120
talinum, 147
phormium, 126
ricinus, 129
senecio, 141
strobilanthes, 143
setcreasea, 142

GRASSES
Agrostis nebulosa, 31
Briza maxima, 42
hordeum, 878
pennisetum, 119

Ageratum with dahlias, cleome, and alternanthera.

ABELMOSCHUS MOSCHATUS MUSK MALLOW *Malvaceae (Mallow family)*

Closely related to hibiscus, cotton, and okra, musk mallow is a tender annual seldom seen in American gardens. Each two- to three-inch flower lasts only a single day, but blooms continue to open until the frost. Native to southeastern Asia, musk mallow thrives in sunny places in hot humid climates and adds an exotic tropical note to the garden scene. In the North it is seldom worth seeding too early in the spring as growth is frustratingly slow, until the soil has really warmed up. Seed directly out of doors for best results or sow individually in peat pots or containers and transplant eighteen to twenty-four inches apart in early summer; avoid disturbing the roots. Cherry red 'Mischief' and 'Pink Mischief' are on the market, both about eighteen inches tall. In regions with cool summers, musk mallows make excellent container plants for conservatories or sunrooms. *A. manihot* is a stately plant six feet or more tall, bearing foot-long leaves, lobed or cleft three to seven times and elegantly borne on extended petioles. The five- to six-inch pale yellow or cream flowers, eyed in maroon, are carried on the upper part of the plant. Ideal to add an exotic note to the back of a late summer border. Its relative okra, *A. esculentus,* which bears beautiful flowers as well as edible fruits, is also sometimes used as an ornamental plant.

ACIDANTHERA BICOLOR PEACOCK ORCHID *Iridacea (Iris family)*

Now considered part of the *Gladiolus* genus, the peacock orchid is native to South Africa. The two-foot graceful plants with gladioluslike foliage and orchidlike white fragrant flowers with maroon centers bloom in late summer to fall. The peacock orchid needs to be surrounded by lower-growing plants; its stem is not very attractive. Purple foliage plants like alternanthera or coleus are good companions. It likes full sun (it tolerates some shade in Missouri) and ample moisture in a well-drained soil. It is stunning when massed or as an exotic accent to a border. It grows from a corm and is easily propagated by dividing cormels produced at its base, or by seed. It can be dug up in the fall and stored in a cool (but not freezing) dry place.

AGERATUM HOUSTONIANUM FLOSS FLOWER *Asteraceae (Daisy family)*

Floss flower is found in the wild in Mexico and parts of tropical and subtropical America. In cooler regions it is treated as a tender annual; its clusters of long-lasting, fluffy rayless flowers are a familiar sight in countless parks and gardens. Typically edging a path or flower border, they are also excellent in containers and may be used as winter pot plants given long day treatment indoors. Best from seed, ageratum is most satisfactory sown indoors in a temperature of 60-70° F. and will germinate in about ten days. Then lower the temperature to 0° or so at night to avoid soft spindly growth. Set the young plants out of doors only when all danger of frost has passed, since they are very sensitive. Alternatively seed may be sown outside at this time, but the minute seeds are difficult to handle. Plant the dwarf forms about six inches apart, the tall ones about a foot apart. Ageratum thrives in full sun, although

ABELMOSCHUS MOSCHATUS 'PACIFIC PINK LIGHT' (MUSK MALLOW) Hibiscuslike leaves and two- to three-inch flowers on a twelve- to fifteen-inch-tall plant. Needs full sun and rich, organic soil.

ACIDANTHERA BICOLOR (PEACOCK ORCHID) Two-foot graceful plants with gladioluslike foliage. Orchidlike clear white fragrant flowers with maroon centers. Blooms late summer to fall. Provide full sun and ample moisture in a well-drained soil.

AGERATUM HOUSTONIANUM 'BLUE HORIZON' (FLOSS FLOWER) Up to thirty inches tall, usually about twelve inches tall, with crinkled dark green leaves. Flowers in puffy blue clusters that bloom May through October. Plant in full sun or partial shade and well-drained soil with plenty of moisture.

AGERATUM HOUSTONIANUM 'CAPRI' (FLOSS FLOWER) Eight-inch rounded mound with crinkled dark green leaves. Flowers in puffy deep blue and white clusters that bloom May through October. Plant in full sun or partial shade and well-drained soil with plenty of moisture.

AGROSTIS NEBULOSA (CLOUD GRASS) Twelve- to fifteen-inch-high mound with short, narrow leaves. Cloudlike tan flower panicles. Blooms mid to late summer. Plant in full sun or partial shade in well-drained soil.

ALCEA ROSEA 'SUMMER CARNIVAL' (HOLLYHOCK) Five- to six-foot erect plants with large light green leaves. Large double flowers with papery petals in many colors, arranged along stalks. Treated as an annual since it flowers early in season. Plant in full sun and well-drained soil.

ALTERNANTHERA DENTATA 'RUBIGINOSA' (INDOOR CLOVER) One- to two-foot erect, bushy plant that is grown for its red-purple leaves. White to greenish-white, fairly insignificant flowers. Plant in full sun in well-drained, somewhat poor soil.

AMARANTHUS CAUDATUS 'HOPI RED DYE' (LOVE-LIES-BLEEDING) Three- to five-foot-tall, upright plant with stout branches and red to purplish large leaves. Drooping chenillelike deep red flowers that often touch ground. Plant in full sun and well-drained soil.

light shade is preferable where the sun is intense. Average well-drained soil is acceptable, but rapid wilting will occur if it dries out. Of the dwarf cultivars 'Midget Blue' grows about four to five inches tall, but 'Blue Mink' will reach nine to twelve inches. 'Blue Hawaii', white 'Summer Snow', and the only pink one, 'Pinkie', are about six to eight inches. 'Blue Horizon', a fine tall cultivar perhaps reaching thirty inches, is seen at its best toward the middle of the border. Deadheading is seldom necessary, except for 'Pinkie', whose browned, spent flowers are very noticeable. White fly and aphids are frequent pests and mildew may be a problem, particularly if the plants are allowed to dry out, or if air movement is poor. In areas with hot humid summers ageratum may not last the whole season, but in cooler climates, such as that of Rhode Island's Blithewold Mansion and Gardens, they will bloom until frost if deadheaded. Ageratum makes a lovely and long-lasting dried flower, especially 'Blue Horizon'. It combines well with 'Lady Bird' cosmos or 'Cherry Rocket' snapdragon, and looks great with celosia.

AGROSTIS NEBULOSA CLOUD GRASS *Poaceae (Grass family)*

Cloud or cloud bent grass is a delicate ornamental grass, grown to provide an airy effect in the flower border or as a cut flower both fresh and dried. In the dried state it is very long-lasting, but is rapidly destroyed by cats, which seem to love it! A lovely companion for Johnny-jump-ups. The graceful flower clusters are carried above six- to twelve-inch plants. Although a native of Spain, it can be treated as a hardy annual and seeded directly in the garden in spring. It is one of the fastest annuals to grow, going from seed to full flower in about six weeks. Position cloud grass where it will get full sun or very light shade; average, well-drained soil is fine. For drying the stems can be cut green or wait until the plant turns tan color and just remove the roots. The seeds remain viable for years, but are difficult to obtain on the market.

ALCEA ROSEA [ALTHAEA ROSEA] HOLLYHOCK *Malvaceae (Mallow)*

In many people's minds, no cottage garden scene is complete without a group of stately hollyhocks. Generally considered to be herbaceous perennials, they are often grown as biennials and discarded after flowering to avoid infection of rust, an unsightly fungal disease. Early flowering strains such as 'Majorette' and 'Summer Carnival' are treated as annuals. They may be seeded indoors six to eight weeks before the last frost or may be direct sown as soon as the soil is workable. Indoors, a night temperature of 50-55° F. is ideal. Plant out into average soil in a sunny spot, about one to two feet apart depending on their ultimate height. Avoid too rich a soil, which promotes soft, disease-prone growth, which may need staking. This is one of the few plants which looks best growing in a stand of mixed colors, preferably of course with a thatched cottage as a background! Flower colors include white, yellow, pinks, reds and crimson, with both single and double strains, ranging from two-and-one-half to six or seven feet in

Hollyhock fits perfectly in a cottage garden, or can lend a cottage garden feeling wherever it is planted.

Joseph's coat is a marvelous foliage plant that blends well in most annual and perennial beds. Although it suffered from overuse in the past, new and more interesting forms are making it popular once again. *Above:* Alternanthera with canna foliage, dahlias, and fountain grass.

height. Popular strains include the double 'Powder Puffs' and 'Fordhook Giants', and single-flowered 'Indian Spring'. A miniature hollyhock, listed as *Althaea zebrina*, flowers beautifully from September to hard frost at Blithewold Gardens if cut back in July; it does not get rust or need staking, though it is attacked by Japanese beetles. Spider mites can become serious in hot climates and should be controlled. These easy-to-grow plants can provide the strong vertical accents that are so important in garden design.

ALTERNANTHERA FICOIDEA JOSEPH'S COAT *Amaranthaceae* (*Amaranth family*)

Joseph's coat is a low, South American bushy perennial, formerly grown in public gardens by the million as a contrast foliage plant in traditional carpet bedding schemes. It is mostly used in a less formal way today. On a private garden scale Joseph's coat is useful as a foliage accent among annuals and perennials, in containers, or as an edging. The plants are usually propagated by two- to three-inch cuttings taken from established plants; rooting is rapid in warm climates. Where winters are cold, overwinter stock plants under glass to produce cuttings the following spring. When the weather has settled, plant out rooted cuttings four to five inches apart. Soil must be well-drained and of poor to average fertility. Best in full sun; provide noonday shade to avoid bleaching in hot climates. For formal effect, the plants may be clipped to five to six inches high. Interesting variants include *A. f. brilliantissima* with bright red leaves and yellow-leaved *A. f. aurea-nana*.

AMARANTHUS CAUDATUS LOVE-LIES-BLEEDING *Amaranthaceae*

The name *Amarathus* is derived from the Greek amarantos which means "unfading," a reference to the everlasting qualities of the tassellike flowers, which are often dried and used in winter bouquets. This tropical plant is grown as a tender or half hardy annual. In the garden it is used to supply vertical accents, accentuated by the curious, brilliantly colored ropes of chenillelike flowers; they are best positioned to hang over a wall or the side of a container. Some of the best and most available cultivars are 'Hopi Red Dye', 'Elephant Head', and 'Prince's Feather'. These are mostly dusky reddish purple above rather coarse red or purplish leaves, but 'Green Thumb' (two feet tall) and 'Viridis'–which grows five feet tall and works well with *Hibiscus acetosella*– have green to chartreuse flowers. In warm climates, seed directly out of doors, but in colder areas sow indoors six to eight weeks before the last frost, in a temperature of about 0° F. Germination occurs in ten to fourteen days. It is unwise to plant out until the soil is thoroughly warmed as the seedlings will stagnate until conditions are favorable. Soil should drain very freely; they are excellent in coastal gardens. Watering is tricky as they are very fussy, and if rain is scarce, it may be difficult to know when and how much water to apply; overwatering will kill them. Light fertilizing will result in taller plants. An easy old-fashioned plant for

full sun, especially where it is hot and dry. In the region of the Desert
Botanical Garden, it is not only a favorite summer annual, but an important food crop. It is also useful in dried arrangements; try it combined with
sunflowers and zinnias.

AMARANTHUS TRICOLOR JOSEPH'S COAT, TAMPALA *Amaranthaceae*

Joseph's coat is an outstanding plant grown for its bold, tropical-looking
foliage. The upper leaves are brilliantly colored in rosy reds, carmine, and
crimson; the lower are mostly green or brownish. Native to tropical
regions, in this country it is grown as a tender annual. Where summers are
hot and humid it may not survive for the whole season, but is worth growing for the spectacular effect of its leaves. In the garden, *A. tricolor* is a
valuable dot or accent plant, but may be difficult to combine with other
plants. A background of evergreens or a gray fence or wall shows off the
foliage colors well; it combines well with ricinis (castor bean), another tropical-looking plant. Culture is similar to that for *A. caudatus*. *A. tricolor splendens* has yellow and scarlet upper leaves; 'Molten Fire', 'Illumination', and
'Early Splendor' are others offered. The all-green tampala is grown for
food.

AMMI MAJUS BISHOP'S FLOWER *Apiaceae (Carrot family)*

Very similar to Queen Anne's lace, bishop's flower adds a delicate old-fashioned note to the flower border and to cut flower arrangements, both fresh
and dried. It is equally at home in informal or wild gardens, herb garden,
and especially in cottage gardens. This easy annual from the Mediterranean
region of North Africa may be sown directly out of doors just before the
last frost date, or inside in late March or early April. Thin or transplant six
to nine inches apart. Select a sunny or partly shaded place with fertile,
moist soil. Best in cool climates, bishop's flower does not enjoy high heat
and humidity during the summer. It blooms freely, with five- to six-inch-
wide umbels of snowflakelike florets carried aloft on well-branched two- to
three-foot plants. Good effects result from grouping bishop's flower among
and between perennials or annuals to simulate self seeding, or in drifts
through the midsection of the border. Try with *Veronica* 'Sunny Border
Blue' or with *Gomphrena* 'Strawberry Fields'.

AMMOBIUM ALATUM WINGED EVERLASTING *Asteraceae (Daisy family)*

Winged everlasting is an unusual Australian perennial, treated here as a
half hardy or tender annual. Its curiously winged, branching stems may
reach three feet tall, and bear one- to two-inch-wide bright yellow flowerheads surrounded by pure white chaffy bracts. These dry beautifully but
are also attractive in the garden. In spring sow the seeds indoors in a sandy
soil mix, and just press into the medium. Avoid overwatering. Seed sown
directly outside after hard frosts is also satisfactory. In warm climates fall

seeding is recommended. Transplant or thin to eight to twelves inches apart when the weather is settled. Select a sunny place where the soil is light and drains freely. In regions with hot summers, winged everlasting will not last through to the fall, but elsewhere it can be cut the whole summer. In the flower border site winged everlastings so that their rather floppy stems are supported by low shrubs or sturdy perennials; staking is unsightly. For drying, cut whole branches before the flowers are fully mature.

ANTIRRHINUM MAJUS COMMON SNAPDRAGON *Scrophulariaceae* *(Figwort family)*

Found in the wild in the Mediterranean region, snapdragons have been cultivated since ancient times and were a favorite in colonial gardens. Today many improved strains are available, varying in color, height, and flower form. This tender perennial is treated as a half hardy annual and is best started about ten weeks prior to anticipated planting time. Sow indoors or in a cold frame at about 55-60° F.; direct seeding out of doors is seldom satisfactory as the minute seeds are hard to handle and dry out readily. Do not cover the seeds; germination takes eight to fourteen days, at which point exposure to full light will prevent the seedlings from becoming leggy. Be alert for damping off fungus. Plant out seedlings or nursery-grown transplants when the soil has warmed up and plant in a sunny position. The soil must be well-drained and fertile for best results.

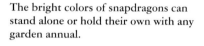

The bright colors of snapdragons can stand alone or hold their own with any garden annual.

AMARANTHUS TRICOLOR (JOSEPH'S COAT) One- to four-foot-tall erect plant with large leaves arranged from the base to the top, usually strikingly striped or blotched. Requires full sun, average soil.

AMMI MAJUS (BISHOP'S WEED) Two-and-one-half-foot-tall loose plant with ferny foliage. Rounded five-inch flowerheads composed of many tiny white flowers. Blooms all summer. Plant in full sun or partial shade in average, well-drained soil.

AMMOBIUM ALATUM 'GRANDIFLORUM' (WINGED EVERLASTING) Three-foot shrubby plant with felty, narrow leaves. One-inch flowerheads with silver white ray flowers and yellow disk flowers that dry well. Borne on long stems. Plant in full sun in average soil.

ANTIRRHINUM MAJUS 'ROCKET PINK' (SNAPDRAGON) Two- to three-foot-tall erect plants with lance-shaped leaves of medium green. Spikes of "dragon" flowers that open from the base upward. Blooms all summer into fall. Plant in full sun to partial shade in well-drained soil.

'Rocket Mix' snapdragons.

Water carefully until the plants are established. In hot, dry areas, they are used as winter annuals, put out as transplants from late September to November and blooming through March. To encourage bushy growth and more abundant flowers, pinch the young plants when they are two to four inches tall. Spacing varies from six to twelve inches apart. The tall strains such as 'Rocket' will reach two-and-one-half to three feet tall, and close spacing (three to six inches) may eliminate the need for staking. Alternatively they can be planted between stronger, bushy plants such as globe amaranth which help to support them. Avoid windswept positions. The tall sorts provide excellent vertical accents in the mid to back of the border or dotted between perennials such as mullein; try them with *Verbena bonariensis*. They make fine cut flowers. The 'Liberty Hybrids' grow eighteen to twenty-four inches tall and the dwarfs such as 'Floral Carpet' are only six to eight inches high. Both are well suited to beds and borders and to container plantings. The dwarf varieties combine well with short grasses and low-growing heliotrope. Snapdragons are best used in solid colors en masse, but a cottagey look is attained with mixed colors. To extend the flowering season, deadhead regularly to encourage the laterals to bloom. In cool summer climates snapdragons will flower until the frost, but in regions of high summer humidity they seldom last the whole season. Rust is a serious fungal disease that attacks snapdragons; choose rust-resistant strains. If you encounter rust, find a new location for snapdragons the following year.

ARCTOTIS STOECHADIFOLIA AFRICAN DAISY *Asteraceae (Daisy family)*

Several different plants from the rich flora of southern Africa are commonly known as African daisies and should not be confused with *A. stoechadifolia*. This is the blue-eyed sort, a tender bushy two- to three-foot perennial with wooly gray-green leaves and white three-inch-wide daisies on long stalks, with a startling blue central disc. *A. s. grandis* has somewhat larger flowerheads. Treat as a tender annual and start from seed indoors in a temperature of 60-70° F. eight to ten weeks prior to the last frost date, or wait until the weather warms and sow direct. Grow on indoor seedlings at 50° F. or so in bright light, and plant out eight to twelve inches apart after frost. Be sure not to overwater; African daisies need very good drainage and light sandy soil. Keep deadheaded throughout the season to encourage more blooms. Excellent as a cut flower and in the mixed sunny border.

BEGONIA X SEMPERFLORENS-CULTORUM WAX BEGONIA *Begoniaceae (Begonia family)*

Wax begonias are surely among the most widely planted annuals in American gardens. They are grown as tender annuals and are derived from the Brazilian *B. semperflorens*. Their single or double one-inch flowers in red, white, or pink are held on succulent stems among shiny bronze or green leaves, providing color in sun or shade from late spring until the frost.

ANTIRRHINUM MAJUS 'SILK'S BRONZE' (SNAPDRAGON) Two- to three-foot-tall plant with lance-shaped leaves of medium green. Spiked "dragon" flowers that open from the base upward. Blooms all summer into fall. Plant in full sun to partial shade in well-drained soil.

ARCTOTIS STOECHADIFOLIA (AFRICAN DAISY) Ten- to twenty-four-inch-tall plant with lobed or slightly toothed one- to four-inch leaves. Daisylike four-inch flowers with creamy-white rays. Blooms June to September if deadheaded. Plant in full sun. Tolerates dry soil and heat.

BEGONIA X SEMPERFLORENS-CULTORUM 'PIZZAZZ PINK' (WAX BEGONIA) Six- to twelve-inch-tall plant with broad waxy green leaves. Single pink flowers are borne all summer. Plant in shade; will tolerate full sun if kept moist. Provide rich, organic soil.

BEGONIA X SEMPERFLORENS-CULTORUM 'SOUTHERN STAR WHITE' (WAX BEGONIA) Six- to twelve-inch-tall plant with broad bright green leaves. Single pink flowers are borne all summer. Plant in shade; will tolerate full sun if kept moist. Provide rich, organic soil.

They even tolerate hot and humid conditions with aplomb. Transplants are often purchased since the dustlike seeds must be started four to six months prior to planting out and take valuable indoor space. Pelleted seed is available. Do not cover the seed, just scatter it thinly or the surface on a very well-drained, fine seed medium and press it in. Cover with glass or plastic until germination occurs. The temperature should be kept 60 -70° F. Keep moist at all times and allow free air circulation after germination. Be alert for signs of damping off. Prick off as soon as possible and harden off before planting out, after all danger of frost is passed. Wax begonias have fibrous, shallow roots and are best grown about one-foot apart in good soil, rich in organic matter which retains moisture; plant closer together if used in containers. A summer mulch is beneficial. Where soil is heavy, raised beds are an advantage; drainage is improved and the soil warms up earlier in the spring. Don't plant out until the soil is thoroughly warm; it will only slow establishment. Water deeply during dry weather and liquid feed throughout the season with 20-20-20. Beware of fertilizing on very hot days as burning can occur. Tried and true six- to eight-inch cultivars with bronze foliage include deep pink 'Gin' and red-flowered 'Vodka'; 'Whiskey' has white flowers over pale bronze-green leaves. These three are sometimes offered as a 'Cocktail Mixture' and are more tolerant of sun than many other wax begonias. The 'Pizzazz' series is another wonderful group, so compact and refined they can even be used in knot gardens. Particularly attractive plants can be propagated vegetatively from cuttings. Wax begonias are ideal for mass plantings, as edging plants, or in containers and windowboxes. Toward the end of the season they can be lifted and potted

Below: **Wax begonias thrive in the shade of a honey locust.**

BEGONIA TUBERHYBRIDA 'NONSTOP APRICOT' (TUBEROUS BEGONIA)
Six- to twelve-inch-tall plants with semidouble flowers.
Flowers in summer. Plant in shade; requires open, friable
soil rich in organic matter.

BELLIS PERENNIS 'POMPONETTE MIX' (ENGLISH DAISY) Four- to
six-inch mounded plant with medium green undulating
leaves. White, rose, or red ray flowers with yellow centers.
Blooms heavily in spring, sporadically through fall. Plant in
full sun to light shade in cool, moist soil.

BRACHYCOME 'BLUE SPLENDOR' (SWAN RIVER DAISY) Nine- to
twelve-inch-tall rounded plant with ferny leaves. Flowers
daisylike with gold centers and deep blue ray flowers.
Blooms all summer. Provide full sun and moist, well-
drained soil.

BRACHYCOME 'WHITE SPLENDOR' (SWAN RIVER DAISY) Nine- to
twelve-inch-tall rounded plant with ferny leaves. Flowers
daisylike with gold centers and white ray flowers. Blooms
all summer. Provide full sun and moist, well-drained soil.

plant selector

Begonia is a huge genus, made up of over one thousand species. In addition to wax begonias and tuberous begonias, many species are useful in summer bedding and in hanging baskets. Many of the *Begonia* species that are used as houseplants are too tender to be brought outdoors, but they will thrive on a sunny patio. Others can be used outside, and their large, striking foliage is a valuable addition to the garden. Another begonia worthy of consideration is the perennial *B. grandis,* which forms a huge, lush mound of dark red leaves dotted with pale pink flowers. *Top*: *B. schmidtiana,* which can be used outdoors. Above: 'Edinburgh brevimosa'.

up for fall and winter bloom indoors. Mildew and botrytis can become serious; leaf spot usually results from overcrowding.

BEGONIA X TUBERHYBRIDA TUBEROUS BEGONIA *Begoniaceae*

Tuberous begonias are unequalled for providing brilliant flower color through the summer months in shaded parts of the garden. Given suitable soil conditions and adequate moisture they thrive even in the difficult areas beneath trees, where competition from roots may be a problem. Although they can be started from seed in a similar way to wax begonias, most home gardeners buy dormant tubers and start their growth or buy started plants in pots. They can be overwintered from year to year in a dry, cool place. Dormant tubers are readily started into growth in a mixture of peat and sand, in a temperature of 70-80° F. Keep the humidity high and young shoots will appear within a week or so. Pot up in loose, highly organic soil. As growth increases the plants must be potted into larger containers to hold until the soil outdoors has thoroughly warmed up. It is folly to try to rush the season, as cold soil will stall growth. Plant twelve to fifteen inches apart in shaded locations, where the soil is open and friable and contains plenty of organic matter; the root systems are deep but not strong and they will suffer in heavy soils. Keep well watered and mulched while vegetative growth is occurring, but foliage is prone to damage, so do not water late in the day when foliage will not have time to dry before nightfall and keep soil off the leaves. Tuberous begonias are greedy feeders and must be fed frequently to bloom abundantly. The 'Non-Stop' strain will flower in four to five months from seeding and is one of the best for garden beds and borders, particularly in the Midwest. It has semidouble flowers in most colors except blue and may be purchased in individual or mixed colors. Smaller-flowered cultivars, such as pale yellow 'Helen Haines', perform better at Blithewold Gardens. There are numerous pendulous or trailing kinds for hanging baskets and planters.

BELLIS PERENNIS ENGLISH DAISY *Asteraceae (Daisy family)*

English daisies are usually grown as biennials and are frequently used to underplant spring bulbs or as edging plants for beds and borders. Occasionally they are planted in rock gardens and make fine additions to tubs, raised beds, and containers for spring color. English daisies are best seeded out of doors in early summer and transplanted four to six inches apart in a sunny nursery bed as soon as they can be handled. Where the summer sun is intense, provide light shade. Late crops can be started from seed in mid-winter at 55-60° F. An average well-drained, fertile soil is fine; keep watered and weeded throughout the season. In cold winter regions, protect with a winter mulch of salt hay or evergreen boughs to avoid sun and wind burn. Plant out as soon as the ground is workable in spring, or overwinter in place in mild climates. The 'Goliath' mix has fully double three-inch flowers in red, pinks, and white on six- to eight-inch stems; the

'Button' mix in red, rose, and white has one-inch double flowers on six-inch stems. Both mixes are available in separate colors.

BRACHYCOME IBERIDIFOLIA SWAN RIVER DAISY *Asteraceae*

This tender annual from the Swan River region of Australia produces masses of one- to two-inch daisylike flowers on delicate, sprawling ten- to fifteen-inch plants. It is a fine addition to rock gardens and is especially attractive in containers and hanging baskets where it can tumble over the edge. It is not as satisfactory on a large scale massed for summer bedding, since the flowering season is relatively brief. Seeds can be sown indoors at 60-65° F. about six weeks before the last frost; germination takes up to fourteen days. Otherwise, seed directly when the weather has settled. Swan River daisies prefer cool weather but do not tolerate hard frost. To extend the flowering time seed at three-week intervals. For fall displays, seed in mid-summer. Nursery-grown transplants are available. Plant out or thin to four to eight inches apart. A sunny place with fertile, well-drained soil on the sandy side is ideal; water during dry spells. Flowering seldom lasts longer than four to six weeks, but regular deadheading and light feeding with 5-10-5 is beneficial. 'Purple Splendor' and 'White Splendor' are popular cultivars, reputed to bloom over a longer period. 'Blue Star' has quilled petals. Support floppy growth with brush if necessary.

BRASSICA OLERACEA ORNAMENTAL CABBAGE *Brassicaceae*
(Mustard family)

Ornamental cabbage hit the market as a novelty item to provide unusual foliage color in the late fall garden. In fact, Galen Gates of Chicago Botanic Garden has documented these plants to maintain attractive foliage to temperatures of -10° F. Their popularity has increased to the point where huge numbers are grown annually for the nursery trade. They are often used in containers but are difficult plants to integrate into a garden setting. Their stiff formal appearance and brilliant colors can be softened by planting with graceful ornamental grasses, or they can he interplanted with low asters, pansies, or chrysanthemums in a complementary color to extend color in the garden into late fall. They are not at their best marching along the edge of a flower border in military fashion. Coloration becomes stronger as the days shorten and nights are cooler, so mid-summer seeding is early enough; at Missouri Botanical Garden, color is delayed or never occurs in warm autumns. Treat as for garden cabbage, sowing directly or into nursery beds in fertile soil. Germination occurs in about three to ten days; when they are large enough prick the seedlings out into nursery packs or thin. Plant in their final places in full sun at least twelve to eighteen inches apart. Keep well watered. Several strains including the 'Tokyo Hybrids' and 'Color Up Hybrids' are available, all with green or greenish-purple rounded and sometimes ruffled leaves enclosing a central rosette of brilliant rosy red, cream, or white. Ornamental kale gives a lacy effect with

A close relative of ornamental cabbage, ornamental kale is used in the same way. It withstands freezing temperatures and is often the last bit of color in the autumn garden.

Right: A dazzling autumn display at The New York Botanical Garden: ornamental cabbages and chrysanthemums.

fringed or feathered leaves, especially in the 'Nagoya' strain. The effect remains until early into the winter.

BRIZA MAXIMA QUAKING GRASS *Poaceae (Grass family)*

This cool-season hardy annual grass from the Mediterranean region is a splendid addition to flower bouquets both fresh and dried and also provides a contrast in shape and texture in beds and borders. The flower stems rise above tufted plants one to two feet tall and are topped with four-inch-long panicles of oval spikelets which dangle on threadlike stems. Sow seed directly in early spring and thin to four to six inches apart or sow in a nursery bed and transplant in a sunny position as soon as they are large enough. Do not allow to dry out while small.

BROWALLIA SPECIOSA BUSH VIOLET, BLUE BELLS *Solanaceae (Nightshade family)*

Bush violets are more often grown as winter-flowering greenhouse plants in containers than in the open garden. However they can be used to good advantage in somewhat shady locations, where the pale blue or white cultivars show up better than the dark blue sorts. Bush violets are excellent subjects for patio urns, planters, and tubs where their bushy but graceful habit shows to advantage; they tolerate semishaded locations. This tropical American perennial, named for John Browall, a contemporary of Linnaeus,

BRASSICA OLERACEA (ORNAMENTAL CABBAGE) Forms heads twelve to eighteen inches across, about one foot high in mid to late fall; survives until frost. Full sun, moist, fertile soil

BRIZA MAXIMA (QUAKING GRASS) Two- to three-foot-tall plant, with rangy habit and grassy foliage. Flowers are spikelets that resemble puffed wheat on wiry stems held above the foliage. Blooms mid to late summer. Plant in full sun and well-drained soil.

BROWALLIA SPECIOSA 'STARLIGHT BLUE' (BUSH VIOLET) Eight- to sixteen-inch rounded plant with one- to two-inch medium green leaves. Starlike flowers from early to late summer. Plant in full to partial shade and somewhat poor soil (over-fertilization causes abundant foliage and few flowers).

CALADIUM X HORTULANUM 'WHITE QUEEN' (FANCY-LEAVED CALADIUM) One- to two-foot upright plant that is grown for its beautiful white leaves, veined in white and often blotched red. Plant in full sun to partial shade and fertile, organic soil. Provide abundant moisture throughout summer.

CALADIUM X HORTULANUM 'FRIEDA HEMPLE' (FANCY-LEAVED CALADIUM) One- to two-foot upright plant that is grown for its beautiful solid red leaves with green margins. Plant in full sun to partial shade and fertile, organic soil. Provide abundant moisture throughout summer.

CALENDULA OFFICINALIS (POT MARIGOLD) One- to three-foot-tall erect plant with medium green sticky leaves. Bright yellow or orange double flowers, composed of all ray flowers. Blooms early summer to late fall if deadheaded. Plant in full sun, well-drained moist soil. Won't tolerate heat.

CALLISTEPHUS CHINENSIS 'ALL CHANGE RED AND WHITE' (CHINA ASTER) Fifteen- to eighteen-inch mounded, somewhat leggy plants with broad medium green leaves. Flowerheads up to five inches across with red or white ray flowers and yellow disk flowers. Blooms in early summer. Plant in full sun or light shade, average soil, not acid.

CANNA 'ARIZONA' (GARDEN CANNA) Upright plant, up to five feet tall, with gray-green leaves and pink-tinged white flowers. Blooms mid to late summer. Plant in full sun with rich soil. Tolerates heat if plenty of moisture is provided.

is treated as a tender annual. Transplants or rooted cuttings may be set out, or seed can be started indoors eight to ten weeks prior to planting outside when the soil has thoroughly warmed. Direct seeding, followed by thinning is another possibility especially on a small scale. Indoors seed will germinate in six to fourteen days in 65-70° F. Do not cover the tiny seeds since they need light to germinate. Keep the soil surface moist by misting often; transplant as soon as possible. Grow on at 55-60° F. and pinch the young plants two or three times to encourage bushiness. A deep fertile soil is ideal but if overly rich, the plants make too much foliage at the expense of flowers. They will bloom in twelve weeks from seeding. Water routinely during dry periods; bush violets resent drying out. Best in regions with long, warm but dry summers. Although they struggle through the heat and humidity of the summer at Missouri Botanical Garden, they look lovely combined with soft pinks such as 'Pretty in Pink' catharanthus and white sweet alyssum in containers. At Brookside Gardens, they are used only in cool conservatory displays. The 'Bells' strain in deep blue, light blue, lavender, and white is popular for container plantings, while the 'Troll' strain is more compact and perhaps better suited for bedding displays.

CALADIUM X HORTULANUM ANGEL WINGS, FANCY-LEAVES
Araceae (Arum family)
The hybrid caladiums available on the market today result from extensive breeding between tropical species. They are grown for their spectacularly colored, angel-wing-shaped leaves which enliven parts of the garden where low-light conditions prevail. They also do well in containers. Sufficiently bold to stand alone, they also make excellent companions for hostas, impatiens, ferns, and other shade-loving plants. A planting of particularly good effect in heavy shade at the Missouri Botanic Garden was a broad swath of white impatiens backed by green and white caladiums, perhaps 'Candidum' or 'White Christmas', which in turn were backed by very dark green hollies. Caladiums thrive on heat and humidity, a difficult combination for many plants. Start as for tuberous begonias; warm soil with bottom heat is very important for good results. Plant outside only when the soil has thoroughly warmed up. Be alert for slugs and keep the flowers removed so that more energy goes into leaf production. There are many cultivars from which to choose. 'White Queen' has white leaves margined in green and veined in red; lower growing than 'White Christmas'. Among the best of the red-leaved sorts is eighteen-inch 'Frieda Hemple' which has solid red leaves edged with green. 'Little Miss Muffet' is an eight-inch dwarf with pale lime green leaves veined and speckled in red.

CALENDULA OFFICINALIS POT MARIGOLD Asteraceae
A favorite during Shakespearean times and long before, this cheerful hardy annual is one of the easiest to grow in sunny but cool gardens. It is well suited

Below: 'Orange', one of the best cultivars of *Calendula officinalis.* Bottom: *Calendula arvensis,* field marigold, is a daintier species.

Canna 'Red King Humbert' has interesting red-brown foliage.

to children's gardens since its large seeds are easily handled, germinate readily, and produce a long display of colorful flowers. It is also grown as a cut flower, in containers both indoors in the winter and outside through the summer, and in flower and herb gardens. The flowers have long been made into ointments used to relieve minor burns and as a skin preparation; in the kitchen the petals may be used fresh to decorate salads or dried to flavor rice, cheese, or egg dishes. Best where summers are not overly hot, pot marigolds come readily from seed sown direct outside in spring or fall where winters are mild. For early bloom for transplants sow indoors at 65° F. eight weeks or so before the last frost. Cover the seeds with one-quarter inch of soil; germination takes ten to fifteen days. Grow in cool areas to avoid lush, weak growth. After hard frost, plant out or thin to six to ten inches apart. A sunny position where the soil is well-drained and of average to poor fertility is best. Avoid overly rich soil, but water during droughts. In hot summer regions, pot marigolds will seldom last the whole season. For bedding purposes and for cutting, mixtures such as the relatively heat-tolerant, eighteen-inch-tall 'Pacific Beauty' mix are popular. It is also available in separate colors of cream, lemon, apricot, gold, and flame. The 'Bon Bon' series in yellow and orange is free-blooming and has double flowers on twelve-inch plants. Protect from slug damage; unsightly mildew attacks the sticky leaves, especially if plants are stressed from drought or if air circulation is poor.

CALLISTEPHUS CHINENSIS CHINA ASTER *Asteraceae (Daisy family)*

China aster is one of only a few annual plants to come from eastern Asia and is one of great beauty. Often grown as a cut flower; American gardeners seem a little shy of using it in the garden, in spite of its glorious range of flower shapes and colors. One reason may be that asters are susceptible to several serious diseases, the worst of which is wilt, but modern strains are largely resistant. However, avoid growing asters in the same place each year, so that soil-borne diseases do not build up. China asters are tender annuals but do best where summers are not unduly hot. For early bloom, start seeds at 60-70° F. indoors about six weeks prior to planting out after frost; germination may be spotty but usually takes six to twelve days. Be careful about watering; the seedlings must not dry out, but good drainage is essential. Grow in full light, twelve hours daily, at about 55° F. until it is safe to transplant, nine to twelve inches apart or more for tall varieties. A deep, fertile soil on the sweet side is best; drainage must be good. Select a sunny position, where air movement is good. Water regularly during dry times; apply a mulch to retain moisture and keep roots cool. Later crops may be seeded directly and thinned; for greenhouse production of pot plants for winter bloom, seed in the fall. Stake the tall sorts; weed and deadhead routinely. Inspect regularly for signs of disease and pests. Remove infected plants and destroy at once; spray against aphids, red spider mites, and leaf hoppers. There are numerous strains varying in height from eighteen to thirty-six inches tall for cutting gardens and beds and borders, to dwarf types only six to ten inches tall ideal as edging plants or for containers. Reds, pinks, lavenders, blues, and white are the usual flower colors; flowers may be single and double, the latter includes sorts with quilled, spider, or crested flowers. Most mixtures are also available in separate colors. Among the talls, the fully double 'Bouquet'['Powderpuff'], 'Pompon', and 'Prinette' mixtures on thirty- to thirty-six-inch stems are popular. The 'Single California Giant' mixture has three-inch flowers on thirty-inch stems. Among the dwarfs, 'Pot 'n' Patio' has a good color mixture of two-and-one-half double flowers on six-inch plants; ten-inch tall 'Dwarf Sparkler Mixture' has spider-type flowers.

CANNA GARDEN CANNA *Cannaceae (Canna family)*

Very few people are lukewarm about cannas; most either love them or hate them. These tall, unquestionably conspicuous plants are native to tropical South America and Asia, and both their large, loose flowers and their bananalike foliage attest to their tropical origins. In recent years, several strains with more restrained colors have been developed making them easier to use. Cannas have stout, erect stems that are sheathed at the base with huge, paddle-shaped leaves, sometimes striped. If used properly, the foliage can be the best part of the part. The flowers are large and flashy and come in brilliant shades of red, yellow, orange, and pink; newer cultivars include some

A common combination: red and yellow cannas, red *Salvia splendens*, bright yellow marigolds; what it lacks in subtlety it makes up in vigor and cheerfulness.

CANNA 'WYOMING' (GARDEN CANNA) Three- to five-foot-tall upright plant with bright green leaves. Bright red and yellow flowers. Blooms mid to late summer. Plant in full sun and rich soil. Tolerates heat but provide plenty of moisture.

CAPSICUM ANNUUM 'FIESTA' (ORNAMENTAL PEPPER) Nine-inch rounded plant with shiny small green leaves. Tiny pale white flowers. Grown for ornamental two-inch fruits that start out yellow and turn bright red in midsummer. Plant in full sun and moist, organic soil.

CAPSICUM ANNUUM 'BLACK PRINCE' (ORNAMENTAL PEPPER) Ten-inch-tall plant with blackish green leaves. Tiny pale lavender flowers. Grown for foliage and for ornamental blackish green fruits that turn bright red in midsummer. Plant in full sun and moist, organic soil.

CATHARANTHUS ROSEUS 'PRETTY IN PINK' (PERIWINKLE) One-foot-tall plants with oblong, glossy green leaves. Starlike pink flowers with darker eyes. Blooms all summer. Provide full sun or light shade and average, well-drained soil.

with paler pink and even white flowers. Among the gaudier hybrids are 'Red King Humbert', which has reddish leaves and scarlet flowers. Cannas have two requirements: water and fertilizer. According to Brian Ward, it is impossible to overwater or overfeed them. Given these two elements, as well as bright sunshine, they will grow quickly and flower abundantly in late summer and fall. In some cases, foliage masks the flowers and needs to be cut back. Although cannas survive winter in Zones 9 and 10, they are treated as annuals in cooler regions, or are brought indoors overwinter and stored in any cool, frostfree area. They need little maintenance other than regular deadheading, watering, and feeding. They can be propagated by division at planting time, or from seed; seed must be soaked or scarified if it is to germinate, and germination takes up to three weeks.

Now that canna is enjoying a resurgence of popularity, some gardeners are practicing restraint, fearful that their flashiness will overtake the garden. Others are enjoying them and using them fully, adding their tropical lushness throughout the garden.

CAPSICUM ANNUUM ORNAMENTAL PEPPER *Solanaceae (Nightshade)*

In general, ornamental peppers are overlooked for the summer flower garden; perhaps they are thought of only for the vegetable garden. However, as foliage plants they assort well with other annual and perennial flowers, and they also decorate the fall garden with their wonderful multicolored fruit. The best cultivar is 'Black Prince', which has attractive blackish green leaves which hold up well in areas of high heat and humidity and are seldom attacked by pests or diseases. The fruits are bright red at maturity (be careful–it is extremely hot and can irritate skin and eyes). At Missouri Botanical Garden, ornamental peppers have been used with dramatic results in combination with silver dusty miller and hemigraphis (waffle plant). At Chicago Botanic Garden, they are placed near dusty miller, pink impatiens, or the pale green leaves of tuberous begonias. At Brookside Gardens, in Wheaton, Maryland, they are a part of the Holiday Display in the conservatory, along with poinsettias. They thrive in containers in late spring at Desert Botanical Garden, and do well with some shade through the summer. 'Jigsaw' has white and purple-splotched leaves and works well in bedding schemes. Seed of this tender tropical annual should be sown about eight to ten weeks before the last frost, at 70-80° F. Germination occurs in six to fourteen days. As the plants grow, pot them up individually and pinch to encourage bushiness. They can be planted outside in full sun nine to twelve inches apart about two to three weeks after the last frost, when the soil has warmed. Avoid planting out too early. A fertile, but not overly rich, soil is best; it should retain moisture well, but not become waterlogged. For winter potplants, start seed in midsummer.

CATHARANTHUS ROSEUS [VINCA ROSEA] ROSE PERIWINKLE
Apocynaceae (Dogbane family)
Rose or Madagascar periwinkle is one of the best annuals for growing in

Rose periwinkle comes in a wide range of colors, from white through all shades of pinks and lavenders to deep magenta. Most have a darker eye, which can be matched to companion plants.

regions where summers are hot and humid or hot and dry; it also tolerates air pollution well. The plants hold up reliably throughout the season and require little maintenance. This Old World native is cultivated as a tender annual in the garden and more and more cultivars are becoming available as its popularity increases. Some of the best include the low-growing 'Carpet' series, ideal massed as groundcover plants. The ten-inch-tall 'Cooler' series is drought resistant; 'Peppermint Cooler' is white with a red eye, 'Grape Cooler' is pink. Early flowering, the 'Tropicana' series comes in various shades of pink and coral on one-foot plants; the 'Pretty in . . .' series is low-growing and suitable for rock gardens. 'Parasol' is one of the taller, and one of the best, varieties, with larger flowers than most. Most rose periwinkles have darker eyes and look particularly good with plants that match their eye color, like cherry red begonias or snapdragons. Most make good container plants and are perfect for city beautification projects or use in street medians. Buy transplants, or start from seed indoors ten to twelve weeks before the last frost, at 70-85° F. Do not cover the seed or allow it to dry out. It usually germinates in one to three weeks, but grows slowly. Do not rush to plant outside early; a cold spell will stunt growth and sometimes the plants never recover. Rose periwinkle thrives in full sun or very light shade in average, well-drained soil. Avoid overwatering. The spent flowers drop cleanly without deadheading. Be alert for slug and snail damage. Occasionally a plant becomes unsightly and yellow, a condition known as the yellows. Remove the affected plant and destroy.

Although it looks like just another pretty flower, rose periwinkle has remarkable medicinal uses. It has been used to control childhood leukemia and to treat sore throats and diabetes.

CELOSIA CRISTATA (CHILDSII GROUP) CRESTED COCKSCOMB
Amaranthaceae (Amaranth family)

These tropical plants are valuable in the summer and early fall garden massed for spectacular effects, as cut flowers both fresh and dried, or grouped as companions for shrubs, perennials, and other annuals. Their tolerance of dry soils and summer heat and general ease of culture, combined with their usually vibrant hot colors endear them to hosts of gardeners (though some people think them quite unsightly). They can be planted as transplants or started from seed indoors or outdoors. Sow indoors about eight weeks prior to the projected planting date. Germination takes only six to ten days; water with lukewarm water to avoid cold shock. This is another plant that will get off to a very poor start if the soil is cold. Do not plant before the soil has really warmed up, two weeks or so after the last frost. If growth is stunted, side shoots will not develop and grow, resulting in tough, thin plants. In a nursery bed out of doors, thin to one foot apart in the rows for cut flowers, or lift and plant where it belongs. Soil should be moisture retentive and fertile for best results although poor soils are tolerated. If the plants are to be pinched, plant about fifteen inches apart and stake after pinching. This results in a very bushy full plant, but they will be susceptible to breakage from wind and rain.

CELOSIA CRISTATA 'JEWEL BOX RED' (CRESTED COCKSCOMB)
Twelve to eighteen inches tall, with matte green, somewhat lobed leaves. Flowers resemble a rooster's comb. Blooms midsummer to fall, for up to eight weeks. Provide full sun and well-drained soil. Tolerant of dry conditions.

CELOSIA CRISTATA 'CENTURY RED' (FEATHER AMARANTH) Twenty-four-inch-tall, eighteen-inch-wide plant with matte green leaves. Flowers in bright red feathery heads. Blooms midsummer to fall (last up to eight weeks). Provide full sun and well-drained soil; tolerant of dry conditions.

CELOSIA CRISTATA 'KIMONO ORANGE' (FEATHER AMARANTH)
Mounded plant, only four inches tall, with matte green, somewhat lobed leaves. Feathery bright orange flower spikes. Blooms midsummer to fall (flowers last up to eight weeks). Provide full sun and well-drained soil. Tolerant of dry conditions.

CELOSIA CRISTATA SPICATA Twenty-four-inch-tall, plant with grasslike leaves and flowers in narrow spikes. Blooms midsummer to fall (last up to eight weeks). Provide full sun and well-drained soil; tolerant of dry conditions.

Otherwise plant about nine to twelve inches apart and do not pinch, probably a better choice for crested cockscombs. Plants so treated will be less full so more plants are required for a given area. In heavy soils it may be difficult to know when to water newly planted stock, but they must not dry out at that stage. The dwarf 'Jewel Box' mixture, which grows about six to nine inches tall, has red, gold, yellow, or pink cockscombs five inches or so across: it is readily available. For those preferring a more subtle flower color, *C. cristata spicata* 'Flamingo Purple' is a must, with its color-coordinated flowers and foliage.

CELOSIA CRISTATA (PLUMOSA GROUP) FEATHERED AMARANTH

Amaranthaceae (Amaranth family)

The feathered amaranths differ from the crested cockscombs in that their

Celosia cristata 'Apricot Brandy', *Salvia farinacea* 'Victoria', and helichrysum. The paler orange of 'Apricot Brandy' is just far enough from the overused red-blue-yellow color scheme.

flowers are arranged in loose plumes. They can be used in similar locations in the garden but are generally more popular than their stiff and tortured-looking relatives. Culture is the same. Both wide and close spacing are satisfactory for feathered amaranths, depending on the desired effect. Several strains are readily available, such as the foot-tall 'Castle' series with red, yellow, or pink flowers. The 'Century Mix' has twelve-inch-long plumes of scarlet, yellow, cream, and rose on sixteen-inch stems. 'Orange Apricot' is a new color at this height. An old but popular cultivar is 'Forest Fire'; it has scarlet flowers on twenty-inch stems above deep maroon foliage. 'Golden Triumph' may reach two feet tall. A relatively new celosia 'Flamingo Feather' is gaining in popularity. Its slender, silver pink to deep rose flowers are arranged in tight spires on two- to two-and-one-half-foot stems; excellent for drying. Paler varieties, such as 'Apricot Brandy', have green/purple foliage and look great with purple *Salvia elegans* or lime green nicotiana.

CENTAUREA CYANUS CORNFLOWER *Asteraceae (Daisy family)*

Affectionately called bachelor's buttons and a staple of cottage gardens, cornflowers are hardy annuals from southeastern Europe. In some parts of the United States they have become naturalized and are often included in meadow seed mixtures. In the garden the tall sorts are effective in mid-border, the shorter ones make good edging plants. They make fine cut flowers. Although transplants are offered in garden centers, cornflowers are very easy from seed and do best if seeded direct. Broadcast seed (in rows in cutting gardens) and cover with one-quarter inch of soil as soon as the soil is workable in spring; later thin to eight to twelve inches apart. For earlier bloom, sow indoors at 60-65° F. about six weeks before planting out; germination takes about eight to ten days. Improved germination results from chilling the seed at 40° F. for five days prior to sowing. Where winters are mild, seed in late summer or fall. Well-drained, average to poor soil is fine, in a sunny position. Among the favorites is thirty-inch-tall 'Blue Diadem' with two-and-one-half-inch intense "cornflower" blue flowers. 'Frosty Mixed', two-and-one-half-feet-tall, has white-tipped flowers in blues, maroon, and crimson. Both may need staking. The 'Polka Dot' strain in separate colors of red, rose, blue, lilac, and white or mixed is a compact grower about sixteen inches tall. Seldom attacked by pests and diseases. Deadhead to extend blooming, which is best in cool summers. Self seeds.

CHRYSANTHEMUM CORONARIUM CROWN DAISY *Asteraceae*

Crown daisies bloom freely with one- to two-inch daisyike flowers in yellow to white; sometimes the flowers are double. At one to three feet tall, crown daisies are well suited to the midsection of flower borders, preferably grouped, and also make good cut flowers. They naturalize freely in meadow gardens. 'Tom Thumb' is a compact one-foot cultivar; semidouble 'Primrose Gem' with yellow-eyed soft primrose flowers and 'Golden Gem' with two-inch golden yellow flowers both grow twelve to eighteen inches tall. Seed directly

Chrysanthemum coronarium.

CENTAUREA CYANUS (CORNFLOWER) Twelve- to thirty-six-inch upright plant with gray, fuzzy leaves. One-and-one-half-inch flowers on tall stems. Flowers single or double in blue, pink, white, or purple. Blooms early in summer, sporadically until frost. Thrives on poor soils in partial or full sun.

CHRYSANTHEMUM CORONARIUM 'PRIMROSE GEM' (CROWN DAISY) Twelve- to eighteen-inch mounds with deeply lobed leaves. Double flowers with primrose yellow ray flowers and gold disk flowers. Blooms midsummer to frost. Plant in full sun and well-drained, average soil.

CHRYSANTHEMUM PARTHENIUM 'AUREUM' [TANACETUM PARTHENIUM] (FEVERFEW) Many-branched plant, two- to three-feet tall, with many small daisylike flowers. Plant in full sun or partial shade, any soil.

CHRYSANTHEMUM X MORIFOLIUM [DENDRANTHEMA X GRANDIFLORA] (GARDEN CHRYSANTHEMUM) One- to six-foot tall, one- to two-foot-wide plant with brightly colored flowers, varying in size, shape, and color. Blooms late summer to fall. Full sun, rich, well-drained soil.

outside as soon as the ground can be worked and cover with one-quarter inch of soil. Alternatively start indoors six to eight weeks before the last frost. Germination takes six to twelve days at 60° F. Thin later to nine to twelve inches apart. As do most daisies, crown daisy needs average to poor but well-drained soil in a sunny position. It is best where summers are not extremely hot and humid. Stake the tall sorts and keep deadheaded. Water deeply during droughts. Low-growing *C. multicaule {Coleostephus myconis}* seldom tops twelve inches, but the plants need as much space sideways. Ideal for edging and containers, 'Gold Plate' covers its six-inch tall plants with masses of semi-double one-and-one-half-inch golden flowers. 'Moonlight' is taller but just as

ANNUAL GARDENING WITH MUMS

Although common garden mums (*Dendranthena* x *grandiflorum,* formerly *Chrysanthemum* x *grandiforum*) are hardy perennials in most areas of North America they are usually treated as annuals. This vast and varied group (divided into thirteen categories by the National Chrysanthemum Society) includes many flower types and colors, some of which are clump-formers, others which are branched and woody. Most gardeners grow garden chrysanthemums from purchased potted plants, which are sold everywhere. They should always be planted before the hottest part of the summer but after all danger of frost has passed; if you don't want to use space in your annual garden for these late-blooming plants, you can plant them in some other area and then transplant them as they begin to bloom. Pinch stems regularly to encourage compact, bushy growth. They do best in full, rich soil.

Left: A mass planting of many varieties of chrysanthemums at The New York Botanical Garden.

Clarkia concinna (Red Ribbons).

floriferous with single lemon flowers. Its uniformity of growth makes it especially useful for summer bedding, edging, and baskets. Baby Marguerite *C. paludosum {Hymenostemma paludosum}* has perky one-inch single white daisies on one-foot-tall plants throughout the summer until frost. Another of the annual chrysanthemums worth growing is *C. carinatum* the tricolor chrysanthemum or painted daisy. It makes bushy plants one to two feet tall, covered with long-stalked, one- to two-inch white, yellow, or red daisies with a contrasting zone surrounding the eye. 'Court Jesters Mixed' is offered. Cultivate all as for crown daisy.

CLARKIA AMOENA [GODETIA AMOENA] FAREWELL-TO-SPRING
Onagraceae (Evening primrose family)

This native Californian wildflower makes a showy addition to midsummer to fall flower beds and is excellent for cutting. Farewell-to-spring is an easy cool weather annual; it does not care for the torrid summers of many parts of the country, remaining vegetative until the days cool. Since it transplants poorly, (sow in pots if necessary), it is best to sow out of doors as soon as the ground can be worked in the spring. In climates where winters are mild, fall seeding is successful. Broadcast in drifts, or in rows if for cut flowers, and later thin to four to six inches apart. Germination takes seven to fourteen days. Full sun is not essential; the plants will bloom freely in light shade usually about two-and-one-half months from seeding. Average to poor soil is acceptable, but it must be well-drained. The plant is self-cleaning and generally low maintenance. Most commonly offered is the 'Grace' series, with single satiny flowers in pinks and rose on two-and-one-half- to three-foot plants. *C unguiculata {C. elegans}*, also from the west coast, is more upright to three feet and bears spires of single or double flowers in purples, pinks, and white; it is excellent massed in the flower border and as fresh or dried cut flowers. A popular doubleflowered strain is 'Royal Bouquet'. *C. concinna* (Red Ribbons) is a narrow-petal version, that is extremely tolerant of heat and drought.

CLEOME HASSLERANA SPIDER FLOWER *Capparidaceae (Caper family)*
Spider flower is one of the few annuals that really mingles well grouped with shrubs, foundation plantings and perennials. Its striking spidery flowers held on tall, strong leafy stems are seemingly unaffected by hot humid summer weather, looking at their best when many a garden begins to look tired. Their lower leaves tend to fall at the end of the summer, and this is covered by companion plants. Try a white one paired with *Artemesia* 'Powis Castle' for a cool effect; for an airy effect, use with *Pennesetum setaceum* 'Rubrum'. Cleomes make excellent cut flowers if they are conditioned by soaking them in very warm water, but their musky scent is not pleasant to everyone; avoid planting close to windows and doors. They are most attractive to hummingbirds. Although cleomes hail from tropical areas of the Americas, for garden use they are treated as hardy or half hardy annuals. They self-seed readily, the seeds remaining dormant until favorable conditions for germination in the

CLARKIA AMOENA [GODETIA AMOENA] (FAREWELL-TO-SPRING) One-and-one-half- to three-foot plant with one- to two-inch-wide flowers. Flowers late summer to fall. Full sun or light shade, average to poor soil, but must be well-drained. Tolerates heat and drought.

CLEOME HASSLERANA 'VIOLET QUEEN' (SPIDER FLOWER) Three to four feet tall, with medium to dark green palmate leaves. Clusters of violet lacy flowers with prominent stamens. Blooms continuously from early summer to frost. Plant in full sun to partial shade. Provide plenty of moisture.

CLEOME HASSLERANA 'HELEN CAMPBELL' (SPIDER FLOWER) Four feet tall, with medium to dark green palmate leaves. Clusters of white lacy flowers with prominent stamens. Blooms continuously from early summer to frost. Plant in full sun to partial shade. Provide plenty of moisture.

COBAEA SCANDENS 'ALBA' (CUP-AND-SAUCER VINE) Vining plant that grows to twenty-five feet or more, climbing by hooked tendrils. Green to purplish leaves and large cuplike flowers. When flowers fade and fall, they leave the decorative light green calyx behind. Plant in full sun and moist soil.

Many plants need to be pinched to achieve their best growth. Removing the newest leaf or leaves with a small piece of the stem encourages a plant to become fuller. Growth points down the stem become activated by pinching, causing more branches to be formed along the main stem.

spring; hybrid strains will not come true. In warm areas sow the seed directly in early spring, but elsewhere start indoors eight to ten weeks before the last frost. They germinate in seven to ten days and take about two months to bloom after setting out. Plant transplants one to two feet apart in sun or light shade in average soil; they will tolerate very dry soils once established, but benefit from watering once a week or so. Staking is seldom necessary, and they are not bothered by pests and diseases. Flowering extends well into the fall or until frost. The 'Queen' series is commonly offered, with flowers in various shades of rose, pink, white, and violet; they grow three to four feet tall. 'Helen Campbell' is arguably the best white.

COBAEA SCANDENS CUP AND SAUCER, CATHEDRAL VINE
Polemoniaceae (Phlox family)
This Mexican vine is indeed underused. It grows fast, climbing by hooked tendrils to twenty-five feet or more and rapidly covering a trellis, arbor, or pergola. It can be planted to scramble over dark evergreen shrubs to interesting effect or try it in a large planter with a wire mesh support (such as a tomato tower); it's a great accent piece for garden parties. In most parts of the country it is grown as a tender annual; in the warm Zones 9 and 10 it becomes woody. In New England, it does not flower until late August or September; fortunately, its foliage is attractive and can even be used in dried arrangements. Sow seeds out of doors after frost or start indoors about eight weeks earlier in freely draining soil at 60-70° F. The large, flat seeds are best sown with the long edge down to minimize rotting. Germination is spotty, but usually takes two to three weeks. Plant out about two feet apart in light shade, in moisture-retentive soil. In northern regions cup and saucer vine thrives in full sun. Do not allow the roots to dry out. Transplants are satisfactory where available. There is a creamy white form, 'Alba'; 'Purpurea' is darker than the species.

COLEUS X HYBRIDUS FLAME NETTLE *Lamiaceae (Mint family)*
This tropical perennial from the Old World makes a stunning foliage display in shaded and partly shaded areas of the garden. Coleus are fine bed or border plants massed or as companions to highlight less showy shrubs or perennials; the dwarf ones are attractive as edging plants. They are also good in containers, and some adapt well to hanging baskets; some cultivars combine well with bedding geraniums. The exotic-looking leaves of coleus range in color from purple, reds, pinks, and salmon through gold, yellow, and brown. Many strains and cultivars are on the market, seemingly more each year. The 'Wizard' strain is available as mixed or solid colors, 'Saber Leaf Mixed' is semi-dwarf at eight inches tall. 'Bellingrath' is one of June Hutson's favorite cultivars; it is red in the sun, chartreuse in shade; although it is slow to bloom, it makes a large hedge by summer's end. Some strains hold their color better in hot sun than others, which tend to bleach out; choose carefully for your own

COLEUS AMBOINICUS (SPANISH THYME) One-and-one-half to three-foot shrubby plant with stout stalks and soft, hairy green leaves. Flowers are insignificant spikes of lavender-pink. Foliage remains attractive from spring to frost. Plant in full sun to light shade. Provide well-drained moist soil.

COLEUS X HYBRIDUS 'BELLINGRATH PINK' (FLAME NETTLE) Ten- to sixteen-inch rounded plant grown for foliage. Small purple flowers insignificant and are usually removed. Foliage remains attractive from spring until frost. Plant in full sun to light shade. Provide well-drained moist soil.

COLEUS X HYBRIDUS 'WIZARD GOLDEN' (FLAME NETTLE) Twelve-inch rounded plant grown for foliage. Small purple flowers insignificant and are usually removed. Foliage remains attractive from spring until frost (does not need frequent pinching). Plant in full sun to light shade—colors more intense in partial shade. Provide well-drained moist soil.

COLLINSIA HETEROPHYLLA (CHINESE HOUSES) Two-foot-tall plant with clusters of bicolored white and deep purple flowers throughout the season. Does best in partial shade and well-drained, fertile soil.

VIEWPOINT
FAVORITE COMBINATIONS

We created a striking display using purple fountain grass, *Rudbeckia* 'Indian Summer', and *Petunia* 'Purple Wave'.
DON BUMA,
BOTANICA, WICHITA

Some combinations that have worked at our garden are:
1. *Ipomoea batatas* 'Blackie' with *Helichrysum petiolatum* 'Limelight'
2. *Nicotiana langsdorfii, Heliotropum* species, and *Perilla frutescens*
3. *Pennisetum setaceum* 'Rubrum', *Petunia* x *hybrida* 'Summer Madness', *Petunia* x *hybrida* 'Velvet Carpet', *Nicotiana* 'Domino Pink', *Hibiscus acetosella* 'Red Shield'
4. *Coleus* x *hybridus* 'Rob Roy', *Petunia integrifolia*, and *Coleus* x *hybridus* 'Buttermilk'
JULIE MORRIS, BLITHEWOLD MANSION AND GARDENS

In most of the following cases, color is the most important factor in the combination:
1.Cleome (purple, pink) with *Verbena bonariensis* and/or tall dahlias
2. *Nicotiana langsdorfii* and *Salvia* 'Blue Bedder'
3. *Tibouchina urvilleana* with dahlias and cleomes and *Verbena bonariensis*
4. *Mandevilla* 'Alice Dupont' in container with *Vinca* 'Color Blush'
5. *Cosmos* 'Sonata White' with *Salvia farinacea* 'Victoria'
KIM JOHNSON, OLD WESTBURY GARDENS

I've used *Portulaca* 'Swanlake' as an underplanting for post- and chain-climbing roses; although each rose is a different cultivar and color, the uniformly white double flowers of 'Swanlake' brought them all together. Because the portulaca is shallow rooted and heat resistant, it didn't compete with the roots of the roses.
MICHAEL RUGGIERO, THE NEW YORK BOTANICAL GARDEN

Above: Coleus x *hybridus* with hostas.

climate. If you find a particular favorite, pot it up for the winter and propagate from stem cuttings the following year. Coleus are usually sown from seed as tender annuals. The tiny seeds are best started inside ten weeks or so before the last frost. Cover lightly and keep the soil surface misted; germination occurs in ten to twelve days. Pinch the young plants to encourage bushiness and plant them out of doors only after the last frost, in light but moisture-retentive soil. Feed occasionally through the season with liquid fertilizer. In order to keep the plants shapely, it is customary to remove the flower buds as they appear. Be alert for slugs and snails, especially where soil is damp.

According to Don Buma at Botanica, in Wichita, coleus can be an excellent full-sun plant, even in Kansas. A large bed of 'Festive Dance' grew to over four-and-one-half-feet tall there, under all-day sun. It does well in full sun in Chicago as well.

Another species, *C. amboinicus* (known as Spanish thyme or Indian borage), has textured leaves.

COLLINSIA HETEROPHYLLA CHINESE HOUSES *Scrophulariaceae*
Chinese houses or pagoda collinsia, sometimes listed as *C. bicolor,* is a seldom-grown half hardy annual of great charm, attractive in mixed borders and as a pot plant. It tends toward floppiness in the Midwest, but is quite attractive when used as a trailer, though for only a short time. It is native in California and in cool summer climates blooms throughout the season. Its clusters of bicolored white and deep purple flowers are carried on two-foot-tall plants.

Transplants are seldom satisfactory; seed directly as soon as the soil is work-able in spring, or fall in mild climates. Thin to six inches apart. Partial shade, especially during the heat of the day, where the soil is well-drained and fertile, is ideal. If necessary stake lightly. Self-seeds. Blue lips, *C. grandiflora,* is some-what smaller but similar. *C. verna,* blue-eyed Mary, is a spring-blooming woodlander from the northeastern states. Best in partial shade where the soil is humus rich and moist; excellent in the woodland garden. Seed in fall for spring bloom. Seed is not widely available but is worth searching for.

CONSOLIDA AMBIGUA [DELPHINIUM AJACIS] LARKSPUR

Ranunculaceae (Buttercup family)

The annual larkspurs may suffer from nomenclatural problems, but there is no quarrel about the beauty of their magnificent flower spikes. *C. ambigua,* branching larkspur or lark's heels, has many low almost horizontal branches, while the eastern larkspur, *C. orientalis,* has few branches, but these are erect. The cultivars and strains offered are probably hybrids of the two. Colors range from white through pinks, reds, and purples to blues and lavender, and flow-ers may be single or double. Larkspurs are cool-climate, hardy annuals; they do not enjoy hot, humid climates. Propagate from seed sown in the fall in mild climates. Elsewhere broadcast seed directly very late just before the ground freezes for earliest bloom or in the early spring as soon as it can be worked. Protect from washing out with a light cover. For cut flowers, sow in rows twelve to eighteen inches apart. Seed may also be started indoors six to eight weeks prior to planting, in six-packs or pots to avoid root disturbance when setting out. Germination is slow and may take up to four weeks. Thin the seedlings to eight to twelve inches apart. Sweet soil that is well-drained and fertile is best, but larkspurs must never dry out; mulch to retain cool damp conditions. Where sun is intense provide light shade, but otherwise an open sunny position is good. The tall sorts are excellent as cut flowers, as well as in meadow gardens and at the middle to back of the flower border. Popular strains include the double-flowered 'Imperial' and 'Giant Imperial' mixtures in a full range of colors on plants up to four feet tall. 'Imperial Blue Bell' and 'Imperial White King' are selections. All need to be staked. At three feet tall 'Blue Picotee' has white flowers rimmed with deep lavender; 'Rosamund' is rose pink. Try interseeding larkspur with pink *Cosmos bipinnatus* and/or *Cosmos sulphureus* 'Diablo'; the last blooms of larkspur will overlap with the beginning of the cosmos, making great use of the same space for long-season bloom.

Low-growing sorts about twelve inches tall include 'Dwarf Hyacinth Flowered' offered as a mixture. Protect plants from slug damage.

CONVOLVULUS TRICOLOR DWARF MORNING GLORY *Convolvulaceae*

Dwarf morning glories come to us from Portugal where they grow in open areas with rather dry soil. They seldom top one foot tall, but the trailing stems spread to make plants about two feet across. Popular in the nineteenth century, they are now coming back into favor in American gardens, perhaps

CONSOLIDA REGALIS 'ROSE' (LARKSPUR) Three- to four-foot erect plant with ferny medium green foliage. Rose-colored spurred flowers. Blooms in spring and early summer. Plant in full sun and well-drained soil. Heat makes them languish.

CONVOLVULUS TRICOLOR 'ROYAL ENSIGN' (DWARF MORNING GLORY) Six-inch-high, twenty-inch-wide dwarf, bushy plant with heart-shaped leaves. Two-inch flowers. Blooms all summer. Plant in full sun in sandy, well-drained soil of low fertility.

COREOPSIS TINCTORIA (CALLIOPSIS) Two- to three-foot mounded plant with long flower stalks. Small, sometimes lobed foliage. Flowers vary from yellow to maroon. Blooms most of summer. Plant in full sun and well-drained soil (will tolerate poor soil).

COSMOS BIPINNATUS 'SONATA' (COSMOS) Twenty-four-inch upright plant with finely cut, ferny, medium green foliage. Daisylike flowerheads with clear white ray flowers and yellow disk flowers. Blooms all summer. Plant in full sun and well-drained somewhat poor soil.

due to their ease of culture, small stature, and abundance of showy two-inch trumpets, arranged in threes. The flowers, which mostly remain open during the day, are typically blue, but the 'Ensign' series has flowers in rose, white, and blue all with a yellow throat; the rose and blue blooms also have jagged white and deeper color zones in the center. These are offered in separate or mixed colors. Some suppliers list the blue form as 'Minor Royal Ensign' and 'Royal Ensign'. Another mixed strain is 'Dwarf Rainbow Flash', which has deep blues, purples, and cherry reds as well as pastel blues and pinks. Sow seed of dwarf morning glories direct after hard frost and thin to one foot apart. For baskets and windowboxes, seed indoors in pots six to eight weeks before the last frost date, at about 60-65° F. Soak or chip the seed prior to planting to facilitate germination, which is usually quick. Where winters are mild, fall sowings for early bloom are successful. Dwarf morning glories are excellent mixed with other annuals in containers of all kinds and make a good splash of color at the front of beds and borders. They tolerate both heat and rather dry soils, and though best in full sun, will provide a good show in partial shade. They seldom last through the summer in Missouri.

Dwarf morning glory spreads rapidly and can be invasive. Planting in containers helps to control its spread.

COREOPSIS TINCTORIA CALLIOPSIS *Asteraceae (Daisy family)*

This American prairie annual deserves a wider following among gardeners. It is excellent in the cutting garden and mingled with perennials and other annuals; a dwarf mixture is compact at one foot tall. Taller varieties make good cut flowers. Colors vary from all yellow to maroon; collect seeds of your favorites to grow the following season. For best results seed directly, as soon as the ground is workable in the spring, or seed in late summer to overwinter. Alternatively sow seed six to seven weeks before the last frost at about 55-60° F. Prick out into peat pots or containers to grow on, so that the taproot will not be disturbed at planting; transplants are difficult. Blooming begins in forty days or so from seed and continues until the fall, except in hot humid climates where their flowering time is curtailed. Stake if necessary. Deadheading prolongs bloom; at Blithewold Gardens, this plant was cut back to half its size and came back beautifully to bloom until frost. Self-sows freely; thin to about six to eight inches apart. Calliopsis (the name means "beautiful eye") is a sun lover, resistant to heat and tolerant of drought, but not of wet soils; be sure drainage is good. However, in dry prairie areas, it does best in areas that are slightly less droughty.

COSMOS BIPINNATUS COSMOS *Asteraceae (Daisy family)*

Named from the Greek *kosmos,* meaning "beautiful thing," cosmos are indeed well named. Easy to grow, they have become one of the most popular annuals and seem to thrive in all parts of the country. Excellent as cut flowers, they also provide a delicate touch in the flower border and the more compact forms make fine container plants; intermingling them with perennial veronicas creates an interesting double vertical effect. The tall sorts can be used to provide a summer screen; they are also at home in the wild or meadow garden. Grow

COSMOS SULPHUREUS 'LADYBIRD MIX' (YELLOW COSMOS) Twelve to fourteen inches tall with ferny, medium green foliage. Flowers semidouble with yellow, red, or orange ray flowers and yellow disk flowers. Blooms all summer. Plant in full sun and well-drained somewhat poor soil.

COSMOS SULPHUREUS 'BRIGHT LIGHTS' (YELLOW COSMOS) Twenty-inch-tall plant with abundant orange-yellow semi-double flowers throughout the season in hot climates. Does best in well-drained, somewhat poor soil and full sun.

CUPHEA HYSSOPIFOLIA (FALSE HEATHER) One- to two-foot dense shrubby plant with glossy, attractive tiny leaves and tiny violet to white stalked flowers. Flowers in winter if brought indoors, in late spring outdoors. Plant in full sun and well-drained soil.

CUPHEA IGNEA (CIGAR FLOWER) Eight- to fifteen-inch mounded plant with dark green glossy leaves. One-inch scarlet flowers are actually tubular calyxes (no petals) with black and white tips. Blooms late summer to fall. Provide full sun and well-drained soil.

or buy transplants or seed out of doors after the last frost. Indoor seeding should be done in a temperature of 60° F., about six to eight weeks before planting out after the last frost. Germination takes five to nine days; flowering occurs ten to twelve weeks from seeding. Plant eighteen inches apart or closer in well-drained, somewhat poor soil for best results; an abundance of fernlike foliage results from too rich a soil. Water infrequently but deeply. After the first flush of bloom, allow to self-seed for a later crop and cut the mother plants down by half their height. These will quickly regain their looks and produce a second flush of bloom. Otherwise deadhead routinely to prolong blooming time, which should last until frost. The tallest cosmos will require staking and are best sited out of the wind (though in Chicago they are strong-stemmed when grown in sun and in soil that is not too rich). Among the best are the two-foot-tall 'Sonata' series available in mixed white, pinks, and reds or in solid colors (they work beautifully with 'Blue Horizon' ageratum, and *Verbena bonariensis*), 'Imperial Pink', a four-foot-tall bright pink, and the semidouble three-foot-tall 'Psyche' series mixed or in red, pink, or white. Pests and diseases are seldom a problem, but goldfinches love them.

Cosmos is used at the Desert Botanic Garden, and throughout the desert region, as a reliable summer annual; many of its colors and its light green foliage look very cooling in a desert garden.

Cosmos sulphureus with white *Gomphrena globosa.*

COSMOS SULPHUREUS YELLOW COSMOS *Asteraceae (Daisy family)*

The yellow cosmos, from Mexico, is somewhat sturdier and may bloom slightly earlier in the season. Culture is as for *C. bipinnatus*. Routine deadheading and removal of unsightly spent flower stems is required, but the parent plants will flower themselves to death and seldom last the whole season in a hot climate. Self-seeded plants will supply bloom until the frost. The 'Lady Bird' series with semidouble flowers bloom early on twelve- to fourteen-inch stems in yellows and oranges; the 'Bright Lights' series also bloom early in yellow, gold, orange, and red at twenty inches. AAS winners include 'Diablo', an eighteen- to twenty-four-inch semidouble with orange-red flowers and single, bright red 'Sunny Red', which reaches fourteen to twenty inches. At Missouri Botanical Garden, seeds of *Consolida ambigua* (annual larkspur) and 'Diablo' cosmos are sown together; the larkspur lingers with the cosmos for a knock-out combination; then the cosmos takes over for a wildflower effect. This species is also very useful in desert areas.

CUPHEA HYSSOPIFOLIA FALSE HEATHER *Lythraceae*

False heather, native of Mexico, is a popular tender perennial in warm Zones 9 and 10, but is used sparingly in colder climates. It is, however, used as a winter-flowering pot plant for garden rooms and conservatories in the North. It is a low-growing shrubby plant with a very neat habit, ideal as a low edging or in the rock garden. Outdoors, its dominant feature is its attractive glossy foliage. Although tender, if left through the cold weather, it becomes a beautiful tan color. Plants may be lifted and potted up before cold weather arrives,

'Gay Princess' dahlia at Old Westbury Gardens in New York. Regular feeding and staking produce spectacular displays of dahlias at Old Westbury. See page 70 for more information about staking dahlias.

and overwintered to produce cuttings for the following year. Otherwise start from seed, with begonias and seed geraniums, very early in the year. Cupheas need a long period to grow and will bloom four to five months from seeding. Germination may be spotty, but usually takes eight to ten days. Plant outside after frost, about nine to twelve inches apart, in a full-sun position in well-drained soil. 'Lavender Lace' has small purple flowers; there is also a white form, not particularly outstanding.

CUPHEA IGNEA CIGAR FLOWER *Lythraceae (Loosestrife family)*

The cigar flower is another Mexican native which is grown in gardens as a tender annual. It is excellent for pots and baskets, but may also be planted outside in a sunny position in the rock garden or flower border. However, massed plants are seldom effective as the one-inch scarlet flowers are often obscured by abundant dark green leaves. It is difficult to combine with other plants and perhaps should be considered a foliage plant with the flowers as a bonus. Culture is similar to *C. hyssopifolia*. Although not common in the Phoenix area, Mary Irish recommends it for shady spots in the desert garden.

CYNOGLOSSUM AMABILE CHINESE FORGET-ME-NOT *Boraginaceae*

Chinese forget-me-not is an apt common name for an east Asian plant with flowers similar to forget-me-nots (myosotis). Although strictly a biennial, plants can be difficult to overwinter in cold climates but they will flower the first year from seed if sown sufficiently early. For earliest bloom sow six to eight weeks ahead of planting time at 70-85° F.; barely cover the seed. After germination (five to ten days) lower the temperature and grow on at 55-60° F. in full light. For midsummer and later bloom, wait until after frost and then seed directly, later thinning to nine to twelve inches apart. Soil for Chinese forget-me-nots should be fertile and well-drained. Although tolerant of drought conditions when established, abundant bloom is encouraged with deep watering in dry times and routine light feeding throughout the season. A position in full sun or partial shade, especially where sun is intense, is fine. Tolerates hot weather if the soil remains moist; apply a summer mulch. Where pure sky blue is desired, Chinese forget-me-nots are difficult to beat. At about two feet tall, they are suitable for the front to middle of beds and borders, and may find a place in the rock garden, although their habit of self-seeding may not be welcome. If used for cut flowers, immediately immerse the stems in water to three-quarter their length to avoid the flowers closing and dropping. The best cultivar is 'Blue Showers' ['Firmament']; 'Avalanche' and 'Snow Bird' have white flowers.

DAHLIA DAHLIA *Asteraceae (Daisy family)*

Long grown by the Aztecs, probably for medicinal use, dahlias have only gained in popularity in American gardens in comparatively recent times. However, they are seldom satisfactory over the long haul in areas with high summer heat and humidity; in cooler climates they are spectacular as cut

CYNOGLOSSUM AMABILE 'BLUE SHOWERS' (CHINESE FORGET-ME-NOT) Fifteen-inch mounded plant with gray-green leaves and abundant tiny sky blue flowers. Blooms all summer. Plant in full sun in well-drained, organic soil.

DAHLIA 'PICCOLO MIXED' (DAHLIA) Two- to three-foot-tall plant with glossy large leaves. Single flowers in many shades of pink, orange, and red with bright yellow stamens. Blooms midsummer to frost. Plant in sun or partial shade and well-drained, moist soil. Deadhead regularly.

DAHLIA 'ROYAL DAHLIETTA ORANGE' (DAHLIA) Shrubby plant, twelve to eighteen inches tall with glossy large leaves. Orange and yellow double flowers. Blooms midsummer to frost. Plant in sun or partial shade and well-drained, moist soil. Deadhead regularly for continued bloom.

DAHLIA 'YELLOW WESTERN' (DAHLIA) Shrubby plant, twelve to eighteen inches tall with glossy large leaves. Yellow double flowers. Blooms midsummer to frost. Plant in sun or partial shade and well-drained, moist soil. Deadhead regularly for continued bloom.

plant selector

Above: Dahlias with caladiums. *Right:* Dahlias with Hybrid Tea roses.

flowers and for sunny beds and borders, extending color well into fall in New England. The tall and medium-height sorts are usually grown from tubers which have been started inside early in the season, as for tuberous begonias. Cuttings may be taken to increase stock. The dwarf types are grown from seed, sown directly in the garden or indoors eight to ten weeks before the last frost. At 60-65° F., the seeds germinate in six to ten days and can be potted individually to be grown on. They will bloom eight to ten weeks later. Do not plant out transplants until the soil has warmed up. Dahlias thrive in sunny positions in well-drained fertile soil which retains adequate moisture. Additional water is necessary during dry periods. Dahlias benefit from regular feeding of liquid fertilizer; they are fed regularly at Old Westbury Gardens

Dahlia 'Gay Princess'.

Dahlia 'Crichton Honey'.

Dahlia 'Walter Hardesty'.

Dahla 'Piccolo Mixed'.

Dahlia 'Snoho Beauty'.

Dahlia 'Royal Dahlietta Orange'.

Officially, there are fourteen types of dahlias, including colarette, cactus, pompon, anemone- and peony-flowered, single, formal and informal decorative, and show types. For the gardeners, the most important factor is not flower shape or form, but height; taller varieties need to be staked, while low-growing ones usually don't.

and they grow large and flower abundantly. Be alert for slug and snail damage, as well as Japanese beetles and red spider mites. Staking is essential for the tall sorts and should be done with stout supports at planting time to avoid impaling the fleshy tubers later on. Deadhead routinely. Blooming lasts until the plants are cut down by frost. To overwinter for the next season, lift the tubers, clean and dry them, and store in a cool, dark, frost-free place in dry peat moss or vermiculite. At Blithewold Gardens, dahlias grow better if allowed to go through a few frosts, then clumps are lifted and allowed to harden on the ground for a few days. They are then cleaned off and stored in peat, at a temperature of 35-50° F.; they are not divided until spring. Many named strains are available, including the two-foot-tall, single-flowered 'Coltness'. 'Rigoletto' has double and semidouble flowers on thirteen-inch stems; the 'Redskin' series has dark bronze green foliage and double and semi-double flowers on fifteen- to eighteen-inch stems. Tall types such as the 'Cactus Hybrids' may reach four feet.

DATURA METELIOIDES DOWNY THORN APPLE *Solanaceae (Nightshade)*
Downy thorn apple, sometimes known as angel's trumpet, is native to Asia. It is cultivated as a tender annual in this country but overwinters satisfactorily in Zones 9 and 10. At Desert Botanical Garden, it is a favored perennial, blooming from June to September and improving with age; several older plants produce up to forty blooms per night. Interestingly, it also overwinters in Chicago if the soil is deep. It imparts a rich tropical look and a bold texture to the garden or patio, which many find appealing. An excellent tub or container plant, it also makes a fine specimen, but must be sited with care since the fruit is very poisonous. It combines well with fall artemesias like 'Silver King'. Growth is slow, and seeds should be sown indoors in midwinter for late summer and fall bloom. Transplant out of doors two to three weeks after the last frost, to a sunny position where the soil has been enriched. The huge trumpet-shaped flowers are often fragrant and may be white, violet, or yellow; some are double. 'Evening Fragrance' grows three feet tall with slate blue foliage and eight-inch lilac-white flowers; 'Rose' has six-inch yellow-rose flowers.

DIANTHUS CHINENSIS RAINBOW PINK *Caryophyllaceae (Pink family)*
Rainbow, Indian, or China pinks are native to China and other parts of eastern Asia and have been cultivated and hybridized for centuries. Although often treated as half hardy annuals, they are in fact biennials or short-lived perennials; under favorable conditions they will overwinter and flower early and abundantly next season. These barely scented but nevertheless charming flowers are excellent for the front of flower beds and borders, in containers or along a sunny path; the taller sorts make good cut flowers. The flower colors include crimson, rose, maroon, salmon, violet, and white, often with a contrasting eye; the crimson cultivars combine beautifully with blue fescue. Rainbow pinks are high-maintenance plants in the garden, needing routine feeding and deadheading, as well as hard pruning once or twice to force

DAHLIA 'CRICHTON' (DAHLIA) Grows to four feet tall if staked. Large glossy leaves. Very double pale apricot flowers. Blooms midsummer to frost. Plant in sun or partial shade and well-drained, moist soil. Deadhead regularly for continued bloom.

DATURA METELIOIDES (DOWNY THORN APPLE) Up to five-foot-tall erect plant with drooping flowers and large, coarse leaves. Yellow-white flowers have a purplish tint on the outside and are trumpetlike, very large, and sweetly fragrant in evening. Grow in full sun and rich soil.

DIANTHUS CHINENSIS 'PRINCESS WHITE' (RAINBOW PINK) Six- to twelve-inch mounded plant with narrow, blue-gray leaves. Two-inch fringed white blossoms. Blooms early summer to fall. Does well in alkaline soils in sun or partial shade. Performs best in cool summers.

DIANTHUS CHINENSIS 'TELSTAR PICOTEE' (RAINBOW PINK) Six- to twelve-inch mounded plant with narrow, blue-gray leaves. Bright crimson flowers with white fringed edges. Blooms early summer to fall. Does well on alkaline soils, give sun to partial shade. Performs best in cool summers.

DIASCIA BARBERAE 'PINK QUEEN' (TWINSPUR) Twelve- to fifteen-inch mounded plant with rounded, simple leaves. Rose-pink spurred flowers on spikes. Grow in full sun and moist soil. Performs best in cooler weather.

DOLICHOS LABLAB (HYACINTH BEAN) Fast-growing vine, grows about twelve feet per year; can be overwintered in warm climate. Purple pealike flowers and bright purple pods. Needs rich soil, sunny location.

DYSSODIA TENUILOBA (DAHLBERG DAISY) Six-inch rounded plant with fernlike leaves. Blooms all summer with gold-orange half-inch daisy flowers. Plant in well-drained soil and full sun. Tolerates heat.

ESCHOLZIA MEXICANA (MEXICAN POPPY) Similar to California poppy; twelve-inch-tall plant with ferny gray foliage and satiny four-petaled flowers in many shades of pink, orange, yellow, and white. Does best in full sun, slightly sandy soil.

another flush of bloom. For this reason, they are more often used in small settings in public gardens rather than massed on a large scale. Treated as biennials they can be direct seeded into a cold frame in late summer and planted out early next spring. More often they are direct seeded outside as soon as the soil is workable or seeded indoors and planted out after heavy frost. Germination takes six to ten days. Soil must be very well drained and neutral to alkaline for best results. Space about eight inches apart. They will bloom in three months from seeding, and if cut back will repeat once or twice before frost. Tall sorts should be staked. Numerous strains and cultivars are available. Some of the best include the six- to eight-inch-tall 'Telstar' strain in solid colors or mixed reds, pinks, and white which is heat resistant, blooms very early, and overwinters well. The 'Princess' strain is also dwarf and heat tolerant. The low-growing, bushy 'Parfait' hybrids have two-inch flowers in scarlet or crimson with a darker eye; they do not rebloom well in Missouri. 'Ideal Violet' is very heat and cold tolerant and carries large rosy violet flowers on one-foot stems. Seldom bothered by pests and diseases.

Dianthus chinensis 'Snowfire', *Dahlia* 'Redskin', *Helichrysum subulifolium,* and *Rudbeckia hirta.*

Dolichos lablab growing with
Thunbergera alata.

DIASCIA BARBERAE [D. CORDATA HORT] TWINSPUR *Scrophulariaceae* *(Figwort family)*

This rather elegant plant from southern Africa has only recently gained acceptance by American gardeners. In strict terms it is a perennial but responds well to treatment as a half hardy annual. While perhaps not at its best massed on a large bedding scale, twinspur is charming in the rock garden and at the front of beds and borders. It is also extremely attractive in baskets and containers, where its six-inch-long racemes of eye-catching salmon pink flowers can be appreciated up-close over a very long period. In hot summers blooming ceases temporarily. A drop in temperature later on seems to precipitate a surge of flowers; a crop timed for the latter part of summer through fall is recommended. For late spring bloom start plants from cuttings taken from overwintered stock or sow seed indoors about eight to ten weeks before the last frost date. With a soil temperature of 60-65° F. germination occurs within two weeks. Nursery-grown transplants are available. After the soil has warmed set plants out six to twelve inches apart in an open position where the soil is well-drained and of average fertility. Direct seeding at the same time and subsequent thinning to six inches apart is satisfactory. Twinspur prefers cool summers; light shade and a summer mulch in hot climates is recommended. Pinch the top two to three inches on young plants especially if they tend toward straggliness; reduce growth by about one-third after the first flush of bloom. If flowering stops through the heat, cut back the plants hard to encourage fall bloom. A hybrid cultivar 'Ruby Fields' is widely offered; 'Rose Queen' and 'Elliot's Variety' are available.

DOLICHOS LABLAB HYACINTH BEAN *Fabaceae (Pea family)*

The hyacinth bean is a very quick-growing vine which is not planted nearly as much as it might be. It can be used in much the same way as scarlet runner beans, to provide a summer screen on a trellis or fence in a very short time. It is quite variable, having outstanding dark foliage and racemes of fragrant, white or purple pealike flowers which are followed by one- to two-incheslong, startlingly purple pods, both decorative and edible. The pods can be used fresh in dried arrangements, but dry an unsightly brown. In a garden setting it typically grows twelve feet or so a year, but where it overwinters it may reach thirty or forty feet. Probably native to tropical parts of the Old World where it is perennial, here hyacinth bean is treated as a half hardy annual. Typical of the pea family, it resents disturbance and is best seeded directly in groups of three to five seeds. Alternatively seeds may be started in peat pots indoors about six weeks before the last frost. Do not hurry to plant out the seedlings as they will be set back if the night temperature drops below 50° F. If planted one foot apart in rich soil in a sunny position, they will rapidly cover their support. Sometimes they are used to provide height, clothing a teepee of stakes in an ornamental setting.

DYSSODIA TENUILOBA DAHLBERG DAISY *Asteraceae (Daisy family)*

This low-growing daisy, native of Texas and Mexico, is one of the best for its tolerance of hot, dry conditions. Its Latin name is derived from the Greek *dysodes*, "stinking," a reference to its pungent leaves, which many people find pleasant. Excellent as an edging or front-of-the-border plant, Dahlberg daisy or golden fleece is also good in hanging baskets. At Chicago Botanic Garden, it has been used to "face" the raised beds in the sensory garden. In the rock garden it is perfectly in scale. Its ability to withstand drought and its informal habit make it an ideal companion for sempervivums and other succulents which need little water but tend to be very stiff; it's a good choice for desert gardens in general, flowering from spring through June. Another species, *D. pentachaeta* (golden fleece), reblooms again in the fall. Early planting is essential for Dahlberg daisies, especially in hot climates. Sow the seeds out of doors in early spring or indoors six to eight weeks prior to the last frost. Germination takes about ten days. Transplants should be planted nine to twelve inches apart in well-drained, average soil in full sun. They tolerate poor soil well, but will rot where drainage is poor. Dahlberg daisies start their long blooming time about four months from seeding, but they peter out in very hot weather. Cut back to rejuvenate or replace. Deadheading is unnecessary; self-seeding often occurs. 'Golden Fleece' is commonly available.

ESCHSCHOLZIA CALIFORNICA CALIFORNIA POPPY *Papaveraceae*

Sometimes listed as *Eschscholtzia* since it is named for the German doctor J. F. Eschscholtz, by any name California poppy is a splendid, brightly colored, free-flowering native perennial treated as an annual. Although each brilliant orange (in the species) poppy is fleeting, routine deadheading and watering ensure that the plants continue their display for many weeks. However, in hot, humid summer climates it really suffers and cannot be relied upon to last the season. Common to other poppies, California poppy resents root disturbance. Wait until the soil is workable and has warmed a little before sowing where the plants are to bloom. Cover the seeds lightly and keep watered; germination occurs in ten to fourteen days. Thin young seedlings to about six inches apart. Transplants are difficult, but early sowings in pots may be successful. In mild climates sow in fall. California poppies prefer a lean, sandy soil that drains freely, and a position in full sun. Reseeds reliably, although seedlings of the cultivars will not come true. One of the breathtaking sights of California is a hillside ablaze with the state flower. In a garden setting use California poppies in the border or as an edging, perhaps with bachelor's buttons or Texas bluebonnets as companions. Many meadow mixtures use these combinations, and massed in a meadow garden the results can be spectacular. Many strains and cultivars are on the market, and these expand the color range. The 'Thai Silk' series in mixed reds, pinks, orange, and gold or pink shades only has wavy-edged, semidouble fluted flowers. 'Double Ballerina' is a little more double. 'Monarch Mixed' has both single and semidouble blooms in pale cream and yellows as well as orange, cerise, and carmine. The Mexican poppy, *Eschscholzia*

Yellow California poppies and blue phacelia growing with a columnar cactus.

mexicana, is similar to the California poppy, though the flowers are slightly smaller.

EUPHORBIA MARGINATA SNOW-ON-THE-MOUNTAIN *Euphorbiaceae*

Sometimes known as ghost weed, snow-on-the-mountain is an easy to grow but underused annual in American gardens today; in the mid 1800s it was highly esteemed. It is native from South Dakota to Texas and thrives in sunny places in average or even poor but well-drained soil; the coloration is more pronounced where soil is not rich or moist. It also tolerates heat and drought well. Snow-on-the-mountain is best seeded directly when the soil has warmed up, or may be started indoors six weeks or so ahead. Germination takes up to three weeks. Plant out or thin to about one foot apart. Be careful when planting out as they often resent being moved. Light staking is sometimes necessary. Snow-on-the-mountain combines well with hot-flowered annuals or perennials such as black-eyed Susans and yarrows, and is striking against the dark foliage of *Berberis* 'Crimson Pygmy' or *Cotinus coggyria* 'Velvet Cloak'. 'Summer Icicle' grows eighteen to twenty-four inches tall. The cool, variegated white and green foliage is also useful for cutting. Sear the base of the stem or dip into boiling water immediately to prevent bleeding. The sap causes a skin irritation in some people. Self-seeds where conditions are favorable. Pests and diseases are seldom a problem.

EUSTOMA GRANDIFLORA PRAIRIE GENTIAN *Gentianaceae (Gentian)*

Recent breeding work has resulted in prairie gentian flowers in white and pinks as well as the usual purplish blue, and double forms are also available. This is a superb cut flower sometimes lasting up to four weeks in water; it is also highly regarded as a container plant, for bedding into the garden, and in formal mixed flower beds. However, prairie gentians are not always easy. In the wild they inhabit damp places in the grasslands and prairies of Texas, New Mexico and as far north as Nebraska. In cultivation they resent disturbance of their taproots, their water requirements are difficult to gauge, and they need an extremely long growing season. In mild climates, seed in fall and overwinter in place; these plants will bloom from April onwards. For transplants—which are really best for this slow-growing plant—sow the tiny seeds indoors at 70° F. about three months prior to the last frost. Germination occurs in one to two weeks; pelleted seed is available for ease in handling. Prick out individually when true leaves appear in six to eight weeks and grow on at 55-65° F., being careful to keep the soil moist but not overly wet. After frost, line out in the cutting garden or plant six to ten inches apart in a sunny or partly shaded position. The soil should be fertile and moisture retentive but porous, slightly alkaline, or neutral. When established prairie gentians tolerate drought conditions and summer heat well. The 'Yodel Hybrid' mixed strain in rose, pinks, lavender, blues, and white grows eighteen to twenty-four inches tall; dwarf 'Blue Lisa' produces its brilliant blue bells early, ideal for pots and the front of the border. The double-flowered 'Echo' strain grows

EUPHORBIA MARGINATA (SNOW-ON-THE-MOUNTAIN) One-and-one-half-foot mounded plant that is grown for its variegated white and green small leaves. Insignificant small flowers with yellow centers. Plant in full sun and average to poor soil.

EUSTOMA GRANDIFLORA (PRAIRIE GENTIAN) Three-foot erect plant that usually needs staking. Gray-green leaves covered with whitish bloom. Large single or double roselike flowers in purple, pink, white, blue. Blooms early summer to frost. Grow in full sun and moist soil. Tolerates heat.

EVOLVULUS GLOMERATUS 'BLUE DAZE' (EVOLVULUS) Nine- to thirty-inch prostrate plant with small gray-green leaves. Rich true blue small morning-glory shaped flowers with white eyes throughout the summer. Plant in full sun and very well-drained soil.

GAILLARDIA PULCHELLA 'YELLOW SUN' (BLANKET FLOWER) One-and-one-half- to two-foot rounded plant with lance-shaped, fuzzy lobed leaves. Very double yellow flowers. Blooms summer into fall. Plant in full sun in average, well-drained soil. Deadhead regularly.

VIEWPOINT

ANNUALS FOR EDGINGS

Lobularia maritima, ortulaca 'Sundial', evolvulus 'Blue Daze', *Zinnia angustifolia*, verbena 'Homestead Purple'.
JUNE HUTSON,
MISSOURI BOTANICAL GARDEN

Dahlberg daisy, spider plant, sanvitalia, *Cuphea hyssopifolia*, 'Universal Mix' violas (if this last selection is planted in the fall, it blooms on warm winter days; it's more heat tolerant than most, and blooms almost to the Fourth of July.
DON BUMA, BOTANICA, WICHITA

Parsley, zinnia 'White Star', marigolds, low-growing ageratum, sweet alyssum, pansies, violas, bellis, torenia, impatiens, *Oxalis triangularis*, *verbena rigida*, petunias, annual vinca, coleus, basil (small-leaved fino-verde, Greek, and colored); in cooler weather ornamental kale and colored lettuce.
KIM JOHNSON,
OLD WESTBURY GARDENS

Bellis perennis, dusty miller, impatiens, lobelia (where there are cool temperatures and/or shade), lobularia (sweet alyssum), pansies, ornamental cabbage, and kale.
GALEN GATES,
CHICAGO BOTANIC GARDEN

Lobelia,, *Dianthus chinensis*, *Ipomoea batatas*, signet marigolds, *Cuphea hyssopifolia*, 'Paramount' parsley, leaf lettuce, especially 'Oakley' and 'Red Sails', dwarf California poppy.
LUCINDA MAYS,
CALLAWAY GARDENS

In sunny, dry situations, I use dusty miller 'Silver Dust', 'New Look', or 'Cirrus', for they are slow growing and their white foliage contrasts with other flowers. In light shade, I use lower-growing 'Elfin' impatiens or lower-growing ageratum such as 'Madison' or 'Blue Danube'. Pansies, French marigolds, and dwarf zinnias are also excellent front-of-the-border plants.
MIKE RUGGIERO, THE NEW YORK BOTANICAL GARDEN

fourteen inches tall and has some bicolored flowers. Recent hybrids include 'Heidi Yellow', which grows eighteen to twenty-four inches topped with sprays of clear pale yellow flowers, and 'Red Glass', twelve to fourteen inches tall, which has bright rosy red blooms. Formerly known as *Lisianthus russellianus*.

EVOLVULUS GLOMERATUS *Convolvulaceae (Bindweed family)*

A subshrubby perennial in its native tropical America, evolvulus has recently gained popularity in American gardens as a tender annual. Its widespread use in hanging baskets, especially 'Blue Daze', has perhaps caused it to be overlooked as a summer bedding plant. However, the remarkable true blue of its flowers is just as welcome at the front of sunny beds and borders, where it assorts well with silver-leaved plants such as *Veronica incana*, or blue-leaved *Festuca ovina glauca* 'Elijah's Blue'. Start from seed indoors and transplant after danger of frost, about twelve to fifteen inches apart. Soil must be well-drained, even on the sandy side. Keep the plants well watered, especially during hot weather, and in active growth with applications of liquid fertilizer. Lift a few plants before they are cut by the frost in the fall and overwinter to produce cuttings for rooting the following spring; it also makes a wonderful indoor pot plant. Very long-blooming, but unfortunately the flowers close in the afternoon. 'Blue Daze' and 'Hawiian Blue Eyed' are readily available.

GAILLARDIA PULCHELLA BLANKET FLOWER *Asteraceae*

There are some fascinating Aztec Indian legends about blanket flowers, the red and yellow colors of which are represented in many Indian blankets. In the wild, the annual *Gaillardia pulchella* grows from Virginia to Florida and New Mexico, in sunny places where the soil tends to be on the lean and dry side. In a garden setting, they are useful for cut flowers and in beds and borders planted among other annuals, perennials, and shrubs. They do not lend themselves well to formal, large-scale bedding schemes. They can be brought into flower for late winter and early spring indoor plants. In regions where winters are warm, seed can be started out of doors in the fall. Elsewhere seeds are sown in early spring outside or indoors at 55-60° F. six to seven weeks before the last frost. Barely cover the seeds, with only one-quarter inch of soil since they require light for germination, which takes fifteen to twenty days. Transplant six to eight inches apart in average, well-drained soil, in full sun. They tolerate dry conditions well but will succumb in wet soils. Too rich a soil promotes leafy soft growth with fewer flowers. Blanket flower starts to bloom about nine to ten weeks from seeding. Deadheading is essential to maintain neatness and extend flowering time. Mildew may become a problem in some areas; be alert for aphid and thrip damage. New strains include the 'Plume' series available with double two-inch brick red ('Red Plume') or yellow ('Yellow Plume') flowers on strong twelve- to fourteen-inch stems. 'Red Plume' looks particularly good with single French marigolds, gazania, or yellow 'Lady Bird' cosmos; all combine well with the nonflowering *Stachys byzan-*

GAZANIA RIGENS (TREASURE FLOWER) Eight- to twelve-inch-tall plants with silvery or gray-green foliage and brightly-colored ray flowers. Needs full sun, well-drained soil. Tolerates heat and drought.

GILIA CAPITATA (QUEEN ANNE'S THIMBLE) Twelve- to fifteen-inch mounded plant with finely dissected dense foliage. One-inch pale blue flowers Blooms in cool weather. Plant in full sun and average well-drained soil.

GLADIOLUS X HORTULANUS (GARDEN GLADIOLUS) One- to five-foot erect plant with sword-shaped, light green foliage. Two- to four-inch flowers in showy spikes of red, orange, pink, white, purple, and picotee. Blooms mid to late summer. Plant in well-drained soil in full sun. Good air circulation prevents disease.

GOMPHRENA GLOBOSA 'STRAWBERRY FIELDS' (GLOBE AMARANTH) Two-foot rounded plant with oblong medium green leaves. Cloverlike bright red flowerheads bloom all summer. Plant in full sun and moist, well-drained soil. Flowers dry well.

Gazania rigens combines well with succulent ice plants, like drosanthemum and lampranthus, above. These plants all tolerate heat and drought.

tina 'Silver Carpet'. The flowers of 'Double Mixed' and 'Gaiety Mixed' range from crimsons, reds, and pinks through cream, yellows, and gold, often bicolored; they may reach two feet in height.

GAZANIA RIGENS TREASURE FLOWER *Asteraceae (Daisy family)*

This wonderful perennial South African daisy is grown as a tender annual in this country, except in frost-free regions. Treasure flowers are valued for the beautiful silvery or gray-green foliage almost as much for their vibrant flowers. These range from orange, gold and yellows through cream to pink and bronzy red, often marked with contrasting colored zones. They show off best in full sun, closing in the evening and often failing to open on cloudy days. For this reason they are not well suited to mass planting, but are superb in intimate settings. Gazanias are fine in containers, dotted around the rock garden or partnered with other sun-loving annuals, perennials, or shrubs as groundcovers or edging plants. They thrive in desert gardens, but resent the heat and humidity of some regions; they do not tolerate the humidity of Brookside Garden's summers. It is wise to get gazanias established early in the season, before intense summer heat. They are typically propagated by cuttings taken in summer and early fall and overwintered, or can be started from seed indoors. These must be sown at least four to six weeks before the last frost in about 60° F. When the soil has warmed up, plant out into well-drained sandy soil about nine to twelve inches apart. They will not tolerate heavy, poorly drained soils, but once established thrive in hot dry conditions. Lift and pot a few plants before they are cut down by frost, to overwinter and provide cuttings for the following season. Seeds are mostly sold as mixed colors; popular strains include the compact, eight-inch-tall 'Mini-Star Mixed', early-flowering 'Daybreak Mix', and 'Talent Mix', also about eight inches in height. Transplants of individual colors are often available.

GILIA CAPITATA QUEEN ANNE'S THIMBLE *Polemoniaceae*

An elegant hardy annual from California and the west coast, Queen Anne's thimble adds a dainty note to beds, borders, and containers early in the season. Try in combination with pansies, calendulas, or tulips for interesting effects. Sow seed outside in place as early as the soil can be worked. Select a sunny position where the soil is well drained or even on the dry side. Rake the seed into the surface soil and later thin to six inches apart. Seed germinates in six to eight days at 55-60° F. In containers allow the plants to drape themselves over the rim. Atop slender stems, the one-inch rounded heads of pale blue or white flowers are borne on two-foot plants, furnished with feathery foliage. Long-blooming where it is cool but short-lived in climates with hot summers. *G. tricolor* (bird's eyes) only reaches twelve to eighteen inches; it has clusters of open, yellow-throated white flowers, edged in pink and with purple eyes. A good filler plant especially in informal or cottage settings.

GLADIOLUS GARDEN GLADIOLUS *Gladioliceae*

Native to South Africa and the Mediterranean, gladiolous are among the most common cut flowers; too often they are seen in less than perfect condition in drooping bouquets. But they make lovely outdoor plants as well, with flowers in just about every color except blue. They are especially striking when planted in masses at the back of the border Gladiolus are grown from corms, which should be planted in full sun; dig holes six to eight inches deep in rich soi–flower will not stand upright if the corm is not anchored–and water generously. Flowering begins after three months; planting can be done in succession. The corm can lifted and stored indoors over winter.

GOMPHRENA GLOBOSA GLOBE AMARANTH *Amaranthaceae*

The cloverlike flowers of globe amaranth are popular for cutting, both fresh and dried. They are also excellent for bedding, as edging plants, and in windowboxes and other containers, resisting summer heat and humidity while blooming over a long season. It performs well at Desert Botanical Garden from spring through April. This tropical plant is treated as a tender annual and is usually started indoors from seed at 60-65° F., eight to ten weeks before the last frost. It is recommended that the seed be soaked overnight and

Large-leaved castor bean, fountain grass, petunias, and gomphrena.

GOMPHRENA GLOBOSA 'LAVENDER LADY' (GLOBE AMARANTH) Two-foot rounded plant with oblong medium green leaves. Cloverlike pale lavender flowerheads. Blooms all summer. Plant in full sun and moist, well-drained soil. Flowers dry well.

HELIANTHUS ANNUUS 'ITALIAN WHITE' (SUNFLOWER) Four-foot-tall erect plant with medium green, bristly leaves. White to cream four-inch flowerheads with black disk flowers. Blooms in summer. Grow in full sun. Tolerates heat, drought, and almost any soil.

HELIANTHUS ANNUUS 'INCREDIBLE' (SUNFLOWER) Four- to six-foot- tall erect plant with very large leaves. Bright yellow eight- to ten-inch flowerheads with green centers. Blooms in summer. Grow in full sun. Tolerates heat, drought, and almost any soil.

HELICHRYSUM BRACTEATUM (STRAWFLOWER) One-and-one-half- to three-foot rounded to erect plant, depending on cultivar. Medium green, smooth leaves. Daisylike flowerheads with glossy, papery bracts that appear as petals of yellow, orange, red, salmon, rose, white, and purple. Blooms mid to late summer. Grow in sun in well-drained soil.

then covered with black paper to improve germination, which takes about ten to twelve days. When the nights stay above 50° F., transplants may be set out in full sun, a foot or so apart, in fertile, moisture-retentive, but well-drained soil. Water during dry spells. Deadheading is seldom necessary, but the taller cultivars such as 'Strawberry Fields' ['Strawberry Fayre'] may need staking. The old favorite 'Buddy' and low-growing 'Dwarf Buddy' both have deep purple flowers. Soft lavender 'Lavender Lady', 'Pomponette Pink', and 'Pomponette White' are about two feet tall, as is 'Strawberry Fields', a hot red. 'Dwarf White' has a clean color and uniform habit, similar to 'Buddy'. June Hutson combines 'Strawberry Fields' with *Verbena bonariensis*, and 'Lavender Lady' with 'Blue Horizon' ageratum. It is considered one of the top ten annuals at Brookside Gardens. For dried flowers cut the stems just before the flowers are in full bloom and hang upside down to dry. Mildew may be a problem if the plants are stressed by drought.

HELIANTHUS ANNUUS COMMON SUNFLOWER *Asteraceae (Daisy)*

With lots of new strains and cultivars on the market, our native annual sunflowers have recently become popular again; with children and birds they have never been out of favor. Sunflowers range in height from about a foot to upwards of six or seven feet. The flowerhead size also varies; in the 'Mammoth' strain they may reach the size of dinner plates, on twelve-foot stems! 'Sunspot' grows only eighteen inches tall with heads a foot across. Both of these are grown especially to attract birds to the garden or for harvesting

A row of sunflowers is a valuable addition to a vegetable garden; not only do they dress up the garden, they also attract pollinating birds and bees.

HELIOTROPIUM ARBORESCENS 'MINI MARINE' (HELIOTROPE) Eight- to twelve-inch tall plants with fuzzy medium to dark green leaves. Clusters of purple flowers. Blooms in summer. Plant in full sun except in areas with very hot summers. Provide fertile, well-drained soil and plenty of water.

HELIOTROPIUM ARBORESCENS 'LEMOINE STRAIN' (HELIOTROPE) One- to two-foot-tall plant with fuzzy medium to dark green leaves. Clusters of purple flowers with a heavy scent. Blooms in summer. Plant in full sun. Provide fertile, well-drained soil and plenty of water.

HIBISCUS ACETOSELLA Five-foot-tall plant that may need staking. Palmate purple foliage and insignificant red flowers. Plant in sun or partial shade and well-drained soil.

HIBISCUS ROSA-SINENSIS 'LUAU' (ROSE OF CHINA) Ten- to fifteen-inch tall plant with glossy green leaves and large yellow and orange flowers.

the seeds for a tasty and nutritious snack. Flower colors are usually in the brown, orange, and yellow range, sometimes with contrasting bands; 'Italian White' has creamy white ray flowers with almost black disks; goldfinches love it. This superb cultivar branches well and grows to about four feet tall. 'Inca Jewels' or 'Color Fashion Mix' are great for mixed darker colors. 'Sunbeam' is the "Van Gogh" looking sunflower, with a yellowish green center; it has no pollen, so is perfect for dried arrangements. The 'Music Box' strain grows under two-and-one-half feet tall with well-branched stems bearing four-inch flowers in yellows and browns. Siting can be difficult especially for the very tall ones. A good background such as an evergreen hedge, outbuildings, or a barn shows them off to advantage and provides protection from the wind; but beware of side shading that might cause them to lean. In any case they will probably need staking. The mid-height sunflowers look well grouped among shrubs and perennials in beds and borders for a cottage garden look; all are excellent for cutting. Sow the large seeds out of doors in spring where they are to flower, and thin to one to three feet apart, depending on the ultimate plant size. For an earlier start, sow indoors, but this is not always satisfactory. Growth is rapid; pot young plants until they can be planted out after danger of frost. Sunflowers do well in rather poor soil on the dry side, in full sun or light shade. It is a summer staple in much of the Southwest, but needs some soil enrichment and weekly watering. Rich soil promotes undesirable lush, weak growth at the expense of flowers. Deadhead to prolong flowering.

HELICHRYSUM BRACTEATUM STRAWFLOWER *Asteraceae (Daisy)*

Strawflowers or everlastings are natives of Australia and are grown commercially in this country for the dried flower market. In the garden they do best in climates where the humidity is low, and thrive in dry soil once established; do not overwater. They are useful as a fresh cut flower as well as for drying; for dried use cut them when the flowers are about half open, bundle them, and hang upside down in a dry, well-ventilated area away from the sun. They are also attractive on a small scale for bedding purposes or grouped among other annuals, perennials, and shrubs in the border. Large-scale mass plantings are seldom satisfactory in much of the country where summers are hot and humid. Where summers are long, sow seed directly in a sunny place after frost and thin to six to nine inches apart. Elsewhere sow indoors at about 60° F. six to eight weeks before the last frost and plant out twelve to fifteen inches apart into very well-drained soil. In dry soil they will self-seed. One of the most popular compact strains is 'Bright Bikini Mixed'. It bears weather-resistant, two-inch semidouble flowers in crimson, reds, pinks, white, and yellows on one-foot plants. 'Swiss Giants Mixture' may reach three feet. Pests and diseases are seldom a problem.

HELIOTROPIUM ARBORESCENS HELIOTROPE *Boraginaceae (Borage)*

Common heliotrope or cherry pie, a reference to its fragrance, grows as a shrub in its native Peru and other warm climates. Its heads of white, lavender,

ANNUALS AS STANDARDS

Annuals "standards" have been considered a particularly intricate art form for many years and are often a testament to the creativity and patience of the grower. A standard is a plant trained on a single stem—usually in a lollipop form, and pruned as a topiary. Annuals that lend themselves well to this type of training are those with strong or woody stems such as angel-wing begonia, fuchsia, geranium, heliotrope, and lantana.

Training a standard takes considerably more maintenance time than growing other annuals, and it will usually take at least a couple of years to develop an attractive plant. The grower must have a place to overwinter the standard where it will receive plenty of light.

To begin training a standard, choose a well-rooted cutting or seedling with a single sturdy stem. Pot the plant in a heavy pot in well-drained, heavy potting mix such as one with plenty of composted bark. The typical mix of peat moss and vermiculite is usually not heavy enough to hold a stake and the developing plant in place. Tie the stem loosely at several intervals to a bamboo or plastic stake using plastic or twist ties, taking care not to cut into the stem.

Pinch off all side shoots, allowing leaves to remain along main stem to help sustain the plant while it is developing. Provide adequate light and water and immediately pinch off all side shoots. When the plant has reached desired height, pinch out growing tip to force side shoots for the main head. As side shoots develop, prune them regularly to achieve the shape you want—whether it be round, square, pyramidal or umbrella-like.

As the plant gains size and becomes more top-heavy, repot into a large, heavy pot. Some growers put stones in the bottom to provide enough weight to prevent tipping. It may be possible at some point to remove the stake if the plant stem can stand on its own.

Heliotrope, zinnias, ageratum, petunias.

or violet flowers bloom over a long period of time and are attractive to butter-flies. Cultivars such as 'Marine' and 'Mini Marine' are ideal as edging plants or may be bedded out on a larger scale; they have intense color, but little fragrance. Trailing ones listed as 'Peruvianum' and 'Peruvianum White' are especially useful in tubs, windowboxes and other containers. Over a period of time, heliotropes can be trained successfully into standards and protected over the winter. These have been used traditionally as "dot" plants to provide height in otherwise low bedding schemes. Try 'Mini Marine' with 'Tahiti Bronze' dwarf snapdragons and *Carex buchanii*. For uniform plants, root cuttings from stock plants early in the year in a temperature of about 65° F. The plants are then potted on for planting outside only after all danger of frost has passed. Seed germination may take a month, so start seed indoors in 70-75° F. about three months prior to the last frost date. Transplants must not be planted out until after the soil has warmed thoroughly; plant twelve inches apart in rich but well-drained soil. In hot climates heliotropes should be shaded from intense sun. Pinch young plants to encourage bushiness and apply liquid fertilizer once or twice during the season. Regular deadheading keeps them looking neat.

HIBISCUS ACETOSELLA *Malvaceae (Mallow family)*
This half hardy annual from east Africa is valued for its purple foliage rather than its small purplish red flowers. These tend to open so late in the season

that in northern climates they may fail to bloom before frost. Well grown, *Hibiscus acetosella* makes a stunning tall accent or "dot" plant underplanted with other annuals; it also makes an impressive standard. Consider growing it with white globe amaranth for example; another dramatic combination is *H. acetosella* with cherry nicotiana and setcreasea. The cultivar 'Red Shield' does well at Brookside Gardens. Start seed indoors at 70-75° F. about eight to ten weeks before the last frost. They take about ten months to flower from seed. Plant out into a sunny or partly shaded place in average, well-drained soil. Staking may be necessary, especially in windswept places; pinching keeps it compact. Be alert for damaging aphids and thrips.

Rose-of-China can be overwintered indoors in a very sunny site; it makes a fussy but beautiful houseplant.

HIBISCUS ROSA-SINENSIS ROSE-OF-CHINA *Malvaceae (Mallow family)*

This popular tropical shrub, thought to have originated in Asia, can impart an exotic feeling to almost any planting scheme. Rose-of-China thrives under hot, humid conditions in the garden as well as in sun rooms and conservatories during northern winters. In the Southwest, it can be grown as a woody perennial with some frost protection. Although the flowers are large and showy, the plants are seldom covered with blooms. It is thought that more flowers result when the roots are restricted in containers. *H. rosa-sinensis* 'Variegatus' has attractive green and white variegated leaves and is a fine foliage plant, frequently trained as a standard. Plants thus trained provide tall accent plants in beds and borders. Bushier, lower-growing cultivars lend themselves to tubs and planters, or can be massed in beds. Numerous named cultivars are on the market with flowers in white, pinks, oranges, and reds, some semidouble. Habit also varies, some being quite bushy to about four to five feet, and others much more upright, reaching fifteen feet or so in height. The ten- to fifteen-foot-tall 'Bridal Veil' has large pure white flowers, blushing white 'Bride' reaches about four feet. Rose red 'Rosea' produces its double flowers freely. Plants are usually started from cuttings indoors in early spring and planted out after the weather has warmed up. Keep bush plants pinched and do not allow to dry out excessively. Soil must be well drained, but fertile. If possible mist or spray with water in dry climates and mulch to discourage bud drop. Susceptible to spider mites and aphids.

From the coastal swamps of Georgia and Florida, *Hibiscus coccineus* is an underused perennial, treated as a tender annual. It flowers the first year from seed, and in mild winters will overwinter in a dormant state. Its showy, scarlet flowers make a dramatic display, especially beside or even in shallow water. Try it with ricinis, cannas, or elephant's ears, or, even better, papyrus. Start seeds indoors early in the season and grow on until the soil has warmed up. Under good conditions established plants will reach four to six feet tall.

HORDEUM JUBATUM SQUIRREL TAIL BARLEY *Poaceae*

This low, tufted grass is often found in the wild in Asia, Europe, and many parts of North America. In the garden it is treated as a hardy annual and may be used as a spring underplanting for taller annuals and bulbs. Its slender stems arch under the weight of its dense, bristly flower spikes, which may be tan, silver, or green. Sow seed in place as soon as the ground can be worked and thin to six to nine inches apart; wider spacing results in a straggly effect because the plants never last long enough to grow together. Sometimes the seeds are covered with plastic to shade out weeds. A full-sun position with dryish soil is ideal. Flower spikes dry well; cut before they are fully mature, bundle, and hang to dry in a dark, dry place. Beware, squirrel tail barley can become a troublesome weed.

HYPOESTES PHYLLOSTACHYA POLKA-DOT PLANT *Acanthaceae*

This tropical and subtropical Old World plant has only recently gained popularity as a garden plant for the summer, although as a houseplant it is better known. Used out of doors, it is a fine foliage plant for shaded places, perhaps under trees, where the soil drains but does not dry out. When hit by strong sun or allowed to dry out, the leaves wilt rapidly and become unattractive. It should be planted in large groups for best effect; other flowers can overwhelm its delicate look. It also works well in windowboxes and mixed planters. Also known as freckleface, polka-dot plant is usually propagated from cuttings, which root readily. Pinch young plants to encourage bushiness and plant outside when the soil has warmed up. The spikes of purple flowers are insignificant; deadheading is not required. Apply a liquid feed once or twice during the season to encourage foliage growth. Before frost, lift one or two plants for stock and overwinter in a sunny place at 55-70° F. 'Pink Splash' has random pink spots all over the leaves; those of 'White Splash' are white. Both grow eight to ten inches tall. Be alert for aphids.

IMPATIENS BALSAMINA GARDEN BALSAM *Balsaminaceae*

Garden balsam grows in the wild in subtropical parts of India and China. It has been grown in gardens for a long time and is often seen planted in cottage gardens. Although not as popular as its showy relative busy Lizzie, the mostly cool-colored flowers—white, cream, pinks, lavender, and crimson—have a less obvious charm. They are carried close to the leafy stems and may be almost hidden by foliage. The double-flowered sorts, such as the two-and-one-half-foot-tall 'Camellia Flowered Mixed', are showier and last longer than the singles. Sow seed of these tender annuals indoors at 70-75° F. some six to eight weeks before the last frost. The seed requires light to germinate, so do not cover with soil. A plastic covering will prevent drying out. Do not allow the young seedlings to be checked; pot on and keep fed until planting time. Pinch when they reach three to four inches tall. Plant out in groups about eighteen inches apart, in a partially shaded place. They are attractive among shrubs, in the flower border, and particularly near a shaded stream or pond. In containers they must not dry out; rich, moist soil is ideal, but slugs may be a problem. Garden balsam self-seeds easily; their seed pods practically explode, making a great show for children.

Cuttings of New Guinea impatiens can be started at the end of summer and brought indoors; they often flower throughout the winter.

HORDEUM JUBATUM (SQUIRREL TAIL BARLEY) Eighteen- to twenty-four-inch tufted grass with five- to eight-inch leaves. Silky three- to four-inch flowers are bushy like a squirrel's tail. Blooms late spring to early summer. Plant in full sun in moist or dry soils. Self-sows readily.

HYPOESTES PHYLLOSTACHYA (POLKA-DOT PLANT) Eight- to ten-inch tall plant with six- to ten-inch-long green leaves speckled with pink; burgundy and white forms also available. Does well in shade; does not perform well in full sun.

IMPATIENS BALSAMINA (GARDEN BALSAM) Branching plant up to two-and-one-half feet tall with six-inch oval leaves and white, yellow, or dark red flowers. Does best in partial shade.

IMPATIENS NEW GUINEA 'TEMPO APRICOT' Six- to ten-inch-tall mounded plant with glossy deep green foliage. Two-inch apricot flowers. Blooms early summer to frost. Plant in partial to full shade in organic, moist soil.

Impatiens wallerana can be planted in blocks of solid colors or mixed together. It forms a neat border, and is often used that way. 'Rosebud', far right, is a relatively new introduction that lives up to its name, with double flowers in pinks, oranges, lavenders, and white.

IMPATIENS NEW GUINEA NEW GUINEA IMPATIENS *Balsaminaceae*

This blanket name includes species, natural hybrids, and their horticultural offspring that have resulted from their introduction from New Guinea in the 1970s. They have attracted much attention in the United States, but they are not well suited to all parts of the country. In parts of the Midwest where summers are very hot and humid, they are not at their best, but they perform well in the Chicago region. They flower much more prolifically late in the season, so in some short-season areas they are used more for their foliage than for their flowers. At Brookside Gardens, in Wheaton, Maryland, they do well in the conservatory, but not outside. Many of the New Guinea impatiens have extremely showy, even gaudy, variegated leaves, and large flowers in brilliant reds, oranges, purples, and pinks as well as sparkling white. Strains such as 'Spectra Hybrids Mixed' ['Firelake Mixed Hybrids'] and 'Tango Hybrid' are started from seed as for *I. wallerana,* but the named cultivars are propagated from cuttings. They root readily at about 60-70° F. in sand, vermiculite, or some other rooting medium. Keep the plants pinched to encourage bushiness. Except where summer sun is intense, a sunny or very lightly shaded spot is recommended; in the South, light shade is necessary, but nowhere do they tolerate the same amount of shade as is usual for busy Lizzies. They must not be allowed to dry out and should be planted in a rich, moisture-retentive but well-drained soil. Excellent for edging or massed planting and for containers. They are popular as winter flowering pot plants, started from cuttings in late summer. Of the numerous named cultivars orange-flowered 'Ambrosia', red-flowered 'Lanai', and salmon 'Sunset' all have green foliage; 'Columbia' has green and yellow variegated leaves and pale pink flowers; bicolored lavender and deep purple flowered 'Tonga' has bronze and green leaves.

IMPATIENS WALLERANA BUSY LIZZIE *Balsaminaceae (Balsam family)*

This East African native is perhaps the most popular of all annuals grown in American gardens today. Easy to grow, busy Lizzies or patience plants require no deadheading or staking, bloom profusely in all colors except true blue, tolerate air pollution, and will grow in sun or shade–what more could you wish? They have received as much attention from the plant breeders as from the gardening public, and hybrid strains abound. Popular ones include the 'Accent', 'Dazzler', and 'Super Elfin' series, all about eight to ten inches in height. The 'Blitz' series may reach fifteen inches tall; the 'Showstopper' series has a cascading habit well suited to hanging baskets and windowboxes. 'Imp Miniature Hawaiian' has recently been introduced, as well as a new true yellow cultivar from Burpee. It is miniature both in stature and in flower size, excellent for the rock garden. All these have single flowers, but the 'Rosebud' series has double flowers on compact plants. Special plants can be propagated from cuttings taken from plants overwintered indoors, but the bulk are started from seed six to eight weeks before the last frost date. Do not cover the tiny seed with soil; cover the flat with plastic to prevent drying out. Seed germinates rapidly at 70-75° F., and the young plants must be pricked off as soon as possible. It is folly to try to plant out transplants too early. The soil must have warmed up to enable the plants to get off to a good start. Plant out about twelve inches apart. Julie Morris of Blithewold Gardens plants four to six of the taller varieties in a twelve- to eighteen-inch pot and feeds them weekly; they make a spectacular display. Well-drained but moisture-retentive rich soil in a lightly shaded position is the ideal. Most strains tolerate deeper shade well, but growth may be taller and less floriferous; the 'Gem' series is more tolerant of full sun. Beware of slugs. In very fertile beds they can reseed themselves to the point of weediness.

IPOMOEA ALBA MOON FLOWER *Convolvulaceae (Bindweed family)*

Moon flower is a wonderful plant for children, who love to watch the flowers open; and for June Hutson, summer isn't really summer until the moon flowers begin to bloom. Moon flowers are one of few that open their flowers at night, at that time releasing a strong perfume (some people liken the scent to cloves, others consider it to be floral) to attract their evening pollinators, especially hawk moths. Typically by midmorning the flowers are closed, but they certainly add exotic interest to the evening garden. This perennial vine from tropical America has escaped in warm parts of the United States; in the garden treat it as a tender annual. The twining plants are very fast growing and cover a fence, trellis, or arbor in a few months. When combined with 'Heavenly Blue' morning glory, the two bloom for double periods, with the moon flower opening as the morning glory closes. Fertilize to promote plenty

IMPATIENS WALLERANA 'DAZZLER VIOLET' (BUSY LIZZIE) Twelve-to eighteen-inch-tall plant with glossy deep green foliage. Blooms early summer to frost. Plant in partial to full shade in organic, moist soil.

IPOMOEA ALBA (MOON FLOWER) Eight- to ten-foot twining vine with heart-shaped green leaves. Four- to six-inch clear white flowers open at night; sweetly scented. Blooms in summer. Plant in full sun and well-drained soil of average or poor fertility. Provide trellis for climbing.

IPOMOEA PURPUREA 'HEAVENLY BLUE' (MORNING GLORY) Eight- to ten-foot twining vine with medium green heart-shaped foliage. Large, clear blue trumpet-shaped flowers. Blooms in summer. Plant in full sun and well-drained soil of average or poor fertility. Provide trellis for climbing.

IPOMOEA BATATAS 'BLACKIE' (SWEET POTATO VINE) Six- to eight-foot drooping vine (doesn't support itself). Grown for its purple-black arrow-shaped foliage. Flowers variegated, resemble morning glories (rarely flowers). Plant in full sun and well-drained soil.

of four- to six-inch white flowers. Start the seeds indoors, two to three to a pot in early spring at about 60-70° F. Soak overnight or chip the seeds to hasten germination, which only takes a few days. Pot on individual plants and set out when the weather warms up. They will bloom about three months from seeding. Self-sows in warm climates. Provide a support at planting time; they may need a little help to begin climbing. They do well intertwined with other vines, like *Mina lobata,* the love vine. Collect seed before frost. Be aware that all parts of the plant are poisonous.

IPOMOEA PURPUREA MORNING GLORY *Convolvulaceae (Bindweed)*

The much-loved morning glory evokes pictures of cottage garden arbors and trellises from grandmother's day. Try it combined with fall-blooming *Clematis maximowicziana {C. paniculata}.* Although from tropical America, this vine performs well as a half hardy annual. Start seeds out of doors where they are to grow twelve to eighteen inches apart in an open, sunny place, after danger of heavy frost is over. Alternatively start seeds earlier indoors in pots at about 65° F.; transplanting may be tricky. Soak the seeds overnight or chip to encourage water absorption necessary for gemination. If planting out of pots, be careful not to damage the roots, which they resent. Not fussy about soil, morning glories will even do well where it is poor, given a good start. Keep well watered until established. So long as the soil is not too rich, they are one of the most reliable bloomers in the garden. The best known cultivar is 'Heavenly Blue', which self-seeds freely. The following year flowers of pink, purple, blue, and sometimes white or bicolored will result. 'Clarke's Early Heavenly Blue' supposedly blooms earlier and the flowers remain open all day in cool or cloudy weather. There are also mixed colored sorts on the market. Kim Johnson of Old Westbury Gardens has used morning glory with *Mandevilla* 'Alice duPont' with great success, though the morning glory's growth had to be kept in check. All parts of the plants are poisonous; the seeds are used as a narcotic in parts of Mexico.

Other species in this genus include *I. batatas,* the sweet potato vine (it's cultivar 'Blackie' has beautiful, divided, almost-black leaves) and *I. quamoclit,* the cardinal vine, which produces one-inch scarlet flowers. Both are underused and of great value.

KOCHIA SCOPARIA F. TRICOPHYLLA BURNING BUSH *Chenopodiaceae*

This tender Mexican annual is a fine foliage plant throughout the season even before it lives up to its common name and turns a brilliant rust or purple with the onset of cold nights. The species itself is seldom grown in gardens, being replaced by the form tricophylla. Its pale green, feathery foliage resembles somewhat that of a dwarf cypress, hence another common name, summer cypress. The two- to four-foot plants look a little like fat green fire hydrants. However, their dumpy habit becomes an asset when planted closely to provide a quick background hedge to a bed of annuals or a young perennial bed; it is a good companion plant in bedding schemes and comes into its own in

Morning glories will scramble up just about any vertical support. Julie Morris of Blithewold Gardens find they are even more floriferous if grown on horizontal supports.

IPOMOEA QUAMOCLIT (CARDINAL VINE) Fifteen- to twenty-foot vines with feathery dark green foliage. Scarlet, one-and-one-half-inch flowers. Blooms in summer. Plant in full sun and well-drained soil of average or poor fertility. Provide trellis for climbing.

KOCHIA SCOPARIA (BURNING BUSH) Two- to three-inch erect, finely branched plant grown for its light green feathery foliage that turns bright red in autumn. Provide full sun and moist, well-drained soil. Tolerant of heat.

LANTANA CAMARA 'LEMON SWIRL' (YELLOW SAGE) Twelve- to eighteen-inch plant with deep green wrinkled leaves with strong scent. Clusters of small, pale yellow flowers. Blooms late spring to mid fall. Grow in full sun and well-drained soil. Performs best in warm weather.

LANTANA CAMARA 'GOLD MOUND' (YELLOW SAGE) Fourteen- to twenty-inch-tall plant with deep green wrinkled leaves with strong scent. Clusters of small bright yellow flowers. Blooms late spring to mid fall. Grow in full sun and well-drained soil. Performs best in warm weather.

the fall, lengthening the season. It combines well with fall asters. Traditionally it is seen marching sedately alongside a path or walkway, but can be employed in imaginative ways in containers, as dot or accent plants, and in mixed plantings. Sow seed indoors at 65-75° F. about six to eight weeks ahead of the last frost date and do not cover; germination occurs in six to ten days. The plants can be set out one to two feet apart (closer for a hedge, wider if accent plants) after the soil warms. Avoid overwatering. Outdoor seeding can be delayed until after frost with good results. A sunny position with light or poor, dry soil is satisfactory; overly rich soil encourages soft floppy growth, which is readily broken and damaged by weather. Until the weather warms up, growth is slow but speeds up as the temperatures rise. If possible plant away from strong winds; in exposed positions stake with a single bamboo cane or shear the plants to maintain their habit. May self-sow. 'Acapulco Silver' is a three-and-one-half-foot-tall introduction with white-speckled foliage. Reputed to cause hay fever.

LANTANA CAMARA YELLOW SAGE, SHRUB VERBENA

Verbenaceae (Vervain family)

Lantanas are tender shrubs, often planted in annual display beds as standards or at ground level for their trailing stems. They are also popular in containers, raised beds, windowboxes, and tubs, where they can spill over the edges and soften the hard lines. Excellent in seaside gardens. It is best to start young plants from cuttings taken from stock overwintered indoors. Cuttings may also be rooted at the end of the previous summer, but must be overwintered indoors, which can be a nuisance. Take and root cuttings twelve weeks or so ahead of planting out time, which is not until after the weather is settled and warm. Rooting is rapid in sand, perlite, or vermiculite at about 70° F. When rooted, pot individually and grow on with a night temperature of 60° F. or so. If for standards, rub out side shoots and grow up a stake to the required height before pinching; for low plants, pinch at three to four inches tall to encourage bushiness. Standards must be very well staked as the branches are brittle and can be badly damaged by weather. The dwarf hybrids come readily from seed started very early. Germination is slow, but given enough growing time they become large enough for bloom throughout the summer. Lantanas grow best in full sun or very light shade where the soil is well drained and fertile, but not overly rich. Too rich a soil encourages abundant vegetative growth at the expense of flowers, particularly when the plants are young. Many public gardens grow lantanas in pots and plunge them pot and all into the ground rather than planting them from the pot. This way the fertility of their immediate soil can be monitored, especially important when they are grown in a bed of mixed plants, many of which require a richer diet. Also, plants still in containers are much easier to lift for overwintering at the end of the season. Keep well watered, especially during dry weather. The typical species has one- to two-inch clusters of yellow and pink flowers; 'Alba' is white-flowered. Some popular cultivars often listed under *L. hybrida* include

Lantana camara 'Radiation', trained on a standard.

Complaints are being registered against the modern sweet pea. It has lost, say the complainers, its original, exquisite fragrance. Today's growers talk of "poise" and "brilliance" in connection with this once simple flower, of "waves" and "frills" and there are some who claim that with every wave and frill some of the old sweetness took wing and that there are now many almost scentless varieties. I do not know. I think I never put any sweet pea to the test that disappointed me.
The Fragrant Garden
Louise Beebe Wilder, 1932

'Gold Mound' and 'New Red'; 'Confetti' has pink, white, and red flowers all on the same plant. 'Lemon Swirl' has variegated foliage. Try 'Gold Mound' in a border with mixed colors of *Zinnia elegans,* or with *Pennisetum setaceum* 'Rubrum'. White fly is a serious problem under glass for overwintering plants.

LANTANA MONTEVIDENSIS WEEPING LANTANA *Verbenaceae*

The weeping lantana, from South America, is treated in much the same way as the shrub verbena. However, for the best standards, run the plants up a stout post and train the shoots to cover an upturned basket. From a distance the resulting growth when in bloom gives the effect of a rosy lavender waterfall and is very beautiful. Keep pruned to shape throughout the season. Feed heavily with liquid feed to encourage a high density of bloom. Very effective in raised beds cascading over a wall or in Victorian-theme gardens. Both this and the above species are excellent plants for cool greenhouses, conservatories, and sun rooms. A white form, 'Alba', is also available.

LATHYRUS ODORATUS SWEET PEA *Fabaceae (Pea family)*

The fragrant, old-fashioned flowers of sweet peas have been a favorite for cottage gardens and as cut flowers for generations. Sadly they do not do well in the torrid summers found in many parts of North America, but where summers are cool they are widely grown. Sweet peas prefer a cool root run in deep, moist soil amended with plenty of organic material. An application of lime to bring the soil pH to about 7 is recommended. Traditionally a trench is dug about two feet deep and filled with a mixture of well-rotted compost, manure, lime, and fertilizer. This is done in fall or as soon as the ground is workable. Sow the large seeds about two inches deep in place, six inches or so apart. Germination may take up to twenty-one days but is hastened by soaking the seeds overnight or nicking or filing the seedcoat to facilitate the uptake of water necessary for germination. Where summer heat comes early, sow in pots indoors six to eight weeks before planting out; germinate at 55-65° F., grow on somewhat cooler. Do not delay planting out; unless there is hard frost, sweet peas thrive in cool weather. Stake the plants, which climb by tendrils, with trellis, netting, or canes arranged so that each plant is supported. In the flower bed, arrange canes or brushwood in a circle to form a "teepee" effect; in the cutting garden plants are best grown in rows up netting or bamboo canes. Where several plants are grown together in a large pot, a cylinder of chicken wire supports them adequately. Keep spent flowers removed; water deeply and feed with liquid fertilizer throughout the season. Be alert for aphids and slugs. The plants will seldom last long after the weather becomes hot. Blooming should begin about two-and-one-half months from seeding. In mild-winter climates, sow in fall and overwinter. Indoor crops for winter bloom are seeded in August. Hundreds of named cultivars have been bred since the eighteenth century. Some are adapted especially for cut flowers, others for high-quality exhibition blooms, while the dwarf types are ideal at the front of the border. Sweet peas come in all colors except yellow; some are

LANTANA CAMARA 'PINK CAPRICE' (YELLOW SAGE) Twelve- to fourteen-inch-tall plant with deep green wrinkled leaves with strong scent. Clusters of small pink and yellow bicolor flowers. Blooms late spring to mid autumn. Grow in full sun and well-drained soil. Performs best in warm weather.

LATHYRUS ODORATUS 'OLD SPICE MIX' (SWEET PEA) Two- to three-foot-tall erect plant with winged stems and olive green foliage and tendrils. Typical pea flowers of yellow, red, purple, white. Blooms in spring. Grow in full sun and well-drained soil. Performs best in cool weather.

LAVATERA TRIMESTRIS (TREE MALLOW) Three-foot or more rounded, open plant with lobed, coarse leaves. Flowers resemble hollyhocks of red, rose-pink or white. Blooms from midsummer to frost. Plant in full sun and rich soil.

LIMONIUM SINUATUM (STATICE) One-and-one-half- to two-foot-tall erect plant with large basal leaves with wavy margins. Tiny flower clusters borne on winged stalks. Grown for brightly colored blue, white, yellow, or pink calyx which remains and dries on plant. Blooms summer to fall. Plant in full sun in dry soil.

Malva sylvestris, another member of the mallow family, has similar flowers.

bi-colored. Many of today's cultivars are American bred. The early-flowering 'Bijou' strain is a twelve-inch bush type excellent for windowboxes and edging. 'Snoopea' has no tendrils and makes neat sixteen-inch plants; it has been largely replaced by the earlier-blooming 'Supersnoop'. Different groups of climbing types include the Early Multiflora Giganteas, which carry many blooms on each stem early in the season usually offered as a mix; the Spencers, Cuthbertsons, Galaxies, and Royals are all offered in mixtures and as individual named varieties. Intermediate types such as 'Jet-Set' grow three feet tall; there are also some heat-resistant mixes. Specialists will select their favorites for flower color, size, and fragrance.

LAVATERA TRIMESTRIS ROSE OR TREE MALLOW *Malvaceae*

This Mediterranean annual with large hollyhocklike flowers is not widely grown in American gardens, probably because it is not happy in high heat and humidity. However, where summers are cool, rose mallows are indispensable in beds and borders of annuals or mixed with perennials and shrubs. The taller sorts make good background screens or add height where needed. A beautiful but fleeting cut flower. For best results sow the large seeds directly, in fall in mild climates or in spring as soon as the ground is workable; cover with one-quarter inch of soil and later thin to twelve to twenty-four inches apart. The plants will bloom in about three months. Alternatively seeds may be started indoors in pots at 70° F., six to eight weeks ahead of planting time. Germination takes up to three weeks. Grow on cool at 50° F. until planting time. Rose mallows do best in sunny positions where the soil is well-drained and of average fertility; additional humus and a summer mulch help to keep the roots cool in warm climates. Routine deadheading is not necessary but does extend the blooming season; staking is seldom necessary. *L. t. splendens* has larger flowers than the species and grows three to five feet tall. 'Loveliness' has deep pink flowers on three- to five-foot-tall plants. Other popular cultivars include bushy two-foot-tall 'Silver Cup', with open two-inch bells in soft pink with darker veins. White 'Mont Blanc' and pink 'Mont Rose' have four-inch blooms and much darker green foliage on two-foot plants. 'Ruby Regis' is cerise.

LIMONIUM SINUATUM SEA LAVENDER, STATICE *Plumbaginaceae*

The annual sea lavender, not to be confused with the perennial *L. latifolium* with the same common name, is grown extensively as a commercial cut flower, particularly for drying. In the garden this Mediterranean import may be planted in sunny beds of mixed annuals and perennials and even in rock gardens, as well as in cutting gardens; even out of bloom, the undulating leaf margins make it an attractive foliage plant. Sea lavender is best sown in place out of doors after the danger of frost has passed, but for earlier bloom sow inside at 65-75° F. some eight weeks earlier. Germination may take up to three weeks. Grow on individually, since sea lavender resents damage to its long taproot. Thin or set out nine to twelve inches apart in a sunny position in

LINARIA MAROCANNA 'FAIRY BOUQUET' (TOADFLAX) Sixteen-inch-tall erect plant with small, linear, flaxlike leaves. Flowers resemble snapdragon flowers in many colors. Blooms spring to midsummer (dies out in hot weather). Plant in full sun or partial shade and well-drained soil.

LOBELIA ERINUS 'WHITE LADY' (EDGING LOBELIA) Four- to six-inch spreading plant with small, rich green leaves. Wiry stems hold abundant white flowers. Blooms in spring. Plant in partial shade in hot areas. Give adequate moisture to keep blooming.

LOBULARIA MARITIMA 'SNOW CRYSTALS' (SWEET ALYSSUM) Six-inch plant that spreads much wider than it is tall. Tiny, fine-textured medium green leaves and bright white flowers. Blooms late spring until frost. Plant in full sun or partial shade in well-drained soil of average to poor fertility.

LOBULARIA MARITIMA 'NAVY BLUE' (SWEET ALYSSUM) Four- to six-inch-tall plant that spreads much wider than it is tall. Tiny, fine-textured medium green leaves. Dark blue flowers. Blooms late spring until frost. Plant in full sun or partial shade in well-drained soil of average to poor fertility.

light but fertile, well-drained soil. Plants do not bloom for two-and-one-half to three months from seeding. They are especially valuable in seaside gardens. Tolerant of dry conditions, but not of wet feet; amend the soil with sand if necessary. Although sea lavender does well in regions with high summer heat, the difficult combination of heat and humidity found in many areas is not ideal. On a large scale in public gardens sea lavender is seldom among the best choices for bedding. Low-growing strains suitable for the front of the border or as edging plants include the mixed 'Dwarf Biedermeier' and 'Petite Bouquet', also available in separate colors; both grow ten to twelve inches tall. The 'Art Shades' and 'Pacific' strains reach two feet tall; the superior two-foot Dutch strain 'Fortress' is available under separate names, such as 'American Beauty Pink' and 'Market Blue'. The Danes and Japanese have new strains worth trying. For dried flowers, cut when good color shows and hang upside down in a dry airy place. Also useful as a winter pot plant.

LINARIA MAROCANNA TOADFLAX *Scrophulariaceae*

This charming, cool-season annual from Morocco is not seen often enough in American gardens, although it would certainly be a welcome addition, especially to cottage-style gardens. The dainty but bushy plants are easy to grow and bear an abundance of miniature snapdragonlike flowers in mixed colors. Available selections include two-foot-tall 'Northern Lights' as well as 'Fairy Lights' and 'Fairy Bouquet', which seldom top twelve inches. Individual colors are not on the market as yet. Broadcast the seed directly as soon as the ground is workable; in the fall in mild-winter areas. Thin to six inches apart. Alternatively seed can be sown indoors six to eight weeks before planting out six to eight inches apart after frost has passed. The plants usually bloom about two months from seeding. Unless the weather is hot, cut them back by about one-third their height after the first flush of bloom. This, coupled with one or two applications of liquid fertilizer, encourages a second flush of growth and flowers. Linarias are not at their best in hot weather and tend to run to seed as the temperature rises; for a fall crop seed in late summer. Especially useful in spring containers, to overplant bulbs, along walkways, or tumbling over the edge of walls or between the cracks in paving stones. Self-seeds into cracks and crevices to beautiful effect.

LOBELIA ERINUS EDGING LOBELIA *Lobeliaceae*

Perhaps rivaled only by delphiniums, edging lobelia provides the most glorious blues so sought after in the garden. Regrettably, this tender, South African annual does not tolerate the torrid summers typical of many parts of the United States, but where summers are cool they are indispensable. Traditionally the fine seed is started indoors ten to twelve weeks prior to the last frost date. Press the seeds into sterile compost or vermiculite (damping off is often a problem); do not cover. Germination takes ten days or more at 60-65° F. night temperature. Lower the temperature and prick off tufts of seedlings to grow on. Nursery-grown transplants are readily available and are

Opposite: Linaria Marocanna 'Fairy Bouquet' at Missouri Botanical Garden.

most practical for home gardeners. When the ground has warmed up, plant out of doors as an edging or in the rock garden, in a sunny or lightly shaded place. Rich, free-draining soil is best; amend with humus to prevent excessive drying out and mulch to keep the roots cool. Blooming usually occurs in two to three months from seeding and continues through the season in cool climates. After the first flush of bloom, it is essential to cut back lightly to shape the plants and encourage more flowers. The compact cultivars, such as the ever-popular, intense blue 'Crystal Palace', light-blue 'Cambridge Blue' and 'White Lady' all grow about five inches tall. Trailing sorts such as the 'Fountain' series in blues, crimson, lilac, and white, and the white-eyed 'Cascade' series, grow twelve to twenty-four inches tall. These are ideal for use in hanging baskets and container plantings, where they can be positioned in partial shade and where frequent watering with cool, potable water keeps them at their best.

LOBULARIA MARITIMA SWEET ALYSSUM *Brassicaceae (Mustard)*

Sweet alyssum is surely among the most popular of annuals, effective in the rock garden, as an edging or underplanting, between pavers or flag stones, as well as in containers of mixed plants. These low, spreading plants, blanketed with masses of tiny, sweet-smelling flowers, remind us of gentler days in

An informal bed of zinnias and marigolds, edged with sweet alyssum.

grandmother's garden. However, under most conditions, this is one easy-to-grow plant. Given a sunny to partly sunny position in well-drained soil of average or even poor fertility, sweet alyssum begins to bloom only five to six weeks from seeding and continues to flower for several months. In climates where summers are hot and humid, the plants may go dormant during the worst of the heat, only to pick up again when cooler days arrive. In these regions consider seeding in midsummer for bloom right through the fall. In Chicago, this plant stops flowering for about two weeks at the end of June but then continues into fall. If plants become straggly, shear them back to encourage fresh new growth; failure to cut back may allow the plant to go to seed and not flower again. Treat sweet alyssum as a hardy annual and sow as early as the ground is workable. It tolerates light frost, but with a soil temperature of about 60-70° F., germination occurs in five to ten days. Broadcast the seed thickly in place, uncovered; nursery-grown transplants may also be set out. Named varieties abound. Pure white 'Carpet of Snow' grows three to five inches tall and ten to twelve inches across; 'New Carpet of Snow' reputedly stays small all summer. Heat-tolerant 'Snow Crystals' has larger individual flowers on six-inch plants. 'Easter Bonnet' is a mix of rose, pale pink, purple, and lavender; the four-inch-tall 'Wonderland' strain comes in cerise, purple, and white. The especially fragrant, deep rose 'Rosie O'Day' blooms early on three-inch plants. Kids enjoy sowing a pinch of seed in a paper cup of soil about six weeks ahead as a Mother's Day gift, to plant out later—one way to encourage a love of growing.

Blue lobelia is mixed with begonias, tansy, and salvia in this planter.

MANDEVILLA X AMABILIS 'ALICE DU PONT' [DIPLADENIA]

Apocynaceae (Dogbane family)

Mandevillas are tender, evergreen vines from the American tropics, and several superior hybrids have become popular as accent plants used in conjunction with annual plantings. Perhaps the best known is 'Alice du Pont' or 'Mrs. du Pont', a hybrid that arose at Longwood Gardens, Pennsylvania. Although of uncertain parentage, 'Alice du Pont' is a strong-growing vine which produces its elegant two-and-one-half-inch pink trumpets freely throughout the warm months. There is also a white-flowering hybrid. In early spring start young plants from cuttings taken from the new shoots of overwintered plants. These root readily in a propagating bed with bottom heat and an air temperature of about 70° F. Pot on into coarse but fertile soil which drains freely; full light is important for sturdy growth. Do not rush to plant 'Alice du Pont' outside; the plants will be set back if the soil is still cold from the winter. Excellent in large baskets or trained up a trellis or fence, mandevillas add a lush tropical note to sunny or partially shaded gardens over several months. Keep the plants well watered and feed regularly through the blooming period. When cold weather approaches, prune back and lift plants to bring inside before the frost. They make attractive additions to bright sunrooms and conservatories through the winter, kept at 70-80° F. As stock plants, allow the plants to die back and maintain in a semi-dormant state until young shoots are needed for propagation.

MANDEVILLA [DIPLADENIA] SPLENDENS 'ROSEA' (MANDEVILLA)
Vining plant with eight-inch-long fuzzy leaves. Flowers are rose pink, funnel-shaped and scented. Blooms all summer. Provide full sun and well-drained soil.

MATTHIOLA INCANA 'CINDERELLA PINK' (COMMON STOCK) Eight- to ten-inch erect plant with gray-green straplike foliage. Pink flowers on tall racemes have spicy fragrance. Blooms early to midsummer. Plant in full sun to partial shade in cool, moist soil.

MELAMPODIUM PALUDOSUM 'SHOWSTAR' (BUTTER DAISY) Ten- to twelve-inch-tall spreading plant. One-inch bright yellow ray flowers bloom all summer. Plant in full sun in moderately fertile, well-drained soil.

MIRABILIS JALAPA (FOUR-O'CLOCK, MARVEL OF PERU) Two- to three-foot-tall plant with one- to two-inch flowers that open in the afternoon. Plant in well-drained soil and full sun.

MATTHIOLA INCANA STOCK *Brassicaceae (Mustard family)*

Stocks are another of the cool-weather annuals underused by American gardeners. The spicy clovelike fragrance of stocks is unforgettable, and they are indispensable plants for old-fashioned and cottage gardens. The species is found in the wild in southern Europe, but has undergone extensive hybridization over the years, so that a full range of colors from white through pale yellows, pinks, and lavenders to deep purples and crimsons is now available, in both singles and doubles. The doubles do not set seed and are generally preferable. As cut flowers stocks are superb both out of doors and under glass for the trade. Elsewhere they are attractive in spring containers, massed as bedding plants, or grouped in the flower border or among shrubs for rapid bloom. Plant under a window to experience their heady fragrance from indoors. Start seeds in early spring at a temperature of about 60° F. Fall seeding is successful in mild-winter climates. Germination takes about ten days; barely cover the seed and keep moist but not wet. After germination lower the temperature to about 50° F. and prick out into porous soil. High temperatures result in failure of the flower buds to set. As soon as the danger of hard frost has passed, plant out in full sun or light shade about twelve inches apart depending on their ultimate height. Close spacing is fine for cut flowers. Feed heavily with liquid fertilizer to avoid potash deficiency. As soon as the day temperatures remain above 65-70° F., stocks begin to turn yellow and decline. In spite of all efforts they are not satisfactory in hot weather. Deadhead below

Melampodium blooms through the summer at The New York Botanical Garden. It is a strong companion to even the showiest annuals, like 'Red King Humbert' cannas, 'Nikki Bright' tobacco flower, 'Cherry Red' zinnias, and castor bean.

Baby blue-eyes has a trailing habit that makes it perfect for hanging over a basket or fence.

the base of the flower spike to encourage lateral spikes. The earliest to bloom is the 'Tryosomic Seven Week' strain, which flowers on twelve- to fifteen-inch plants from seed in seven weeks. This one is the best where summers are hot, since it blooms so rapidly. The one-foot-tall 'Ten Week' strain and two-foot-tall 'Giant Imperial' strain take a little longer to bloom. Other strains abound, especially offered by European seed houses. A wonderful plant for cool-summer regions of the country.

MELAMPODIUM PALUDOSUM BUTTER DAISY *Asteraceae (Daisy)*

Only recently has this New World, half hardy annual become popular in American gardens. Melampodium is a tough, easy-to-grow plant which tolerates summer heat, humidity, and even drought well. It needs no staking or deadheading and usually looks its best; it performs fabulously even in hot and humid summers at Brookside Gardens in Wheaton, Maryland, with as little as six hours of sun per day. The flowering period is long, right up until frost. For earliest bloom it is best to start young plants from seed indoors at 70° F., two months or so before transplanting outside after frost. Later sowings must wait until the soil has warmed up; blooming is only delayed a little. Damping off can be serious if young seedlings are allowed to become overcrowded. Free-draining, moderately fertile soil and a sunny position are ideal for butter daisies; avoid high-nitrogen fertilizers which result in an abundance of foliage but few flowers. This low-maintenance annual is self-cleaning, but growers should be alert for slug damage on young plants. Excellent grouped in the flower or shrub border eight to twelve inches apart or in tubs or other containers. The cultivars 'Medallion' and 'Showstar' are most widely available on the market, but they are very similar. 'Showstar' usually remains only ten to twelve inches tall, while 'Medallion' may reach fifteen to eighteen inches tall. Especially good in areas of high summer heat (though powdery mildew is sometimes a problem in the St. Louis area); it is also a good performer in the Chicago area, providing strong yellow/gold color throughout the season.

MIRABILIS JALAPA FOUR-O'CLOCK *Nyctaginaceae*

Not only are they quaint, but common names often give clues about the plant in question. In this case four-o'clock refers to the flowers which remain closed until late in the day. Alternatively known as marvel of Peru, which indicates the plant's nativity in tropical America. In this country it overwinters as a perennial in mild climates; it self-seeds easily and has naturalized in the South. Elsewhere its tuberous roots must be protected or lifted and overwintered under cover; it is mostly treated as a tender annual. This easy-to-grow plant takes on shrublike proportions by midseason and lends itself to filling gaps toward the back of sunny mixed and perennials borders as well as among shrubs. Start the large seeds indoors four to six weeks before the last frost or outside when the soil has warmed up. With a soil temperature of 70-85° F., germination occurs in seven to ten days. Well-drained soil is best, but four o'clocks tolerate a wide range of soil conditions. When established they with-

MOLUCCELLA LAEVIS (BELLS-OF-IRELAND) Two- to three-foot-tall floppy plant with gray-green, coarsely toothed leaves. Small white flowers appear in summer. Large lime inflated calyxes look like bells and dry on the plant. Plant in full sun with well-drained moist soil.

NEMOPHILA MENZIESII (BABY BLUE-EYES) Low, spreading, trailing plant with fernlike medium green foliage. One-inch sky blue flowers. Blooms spring to midsummer (dies out in hot weather). Plant in partial shade and rich, moist soil.

NEMOPHILA MACULATA (FIVE-SPOT) Three- to six-inch-high trailing plant with small, long lobed leaves. Flowers with blue-veined petals and deep blue spot at the tip of each petal. Blooms summer to frost with adequate water. Plant in partial shade and rich, moist soil.

NICOTIANA ALATA 'STARSHIP WHITE' (FLOWERING TOBACCO) Twelve- to fifteen-inch-tall erect to rounded clumps with leaves of medium green. Starlike white flowers with long tube. Blooms early summer to fall. Plant in full sun or partial shade (in areas with hot summers, the color may fade) and well-drained moist soil.

stand heat, humidity, drought, and pollution with aplomb. They do well at the Desert Botanical Garden in Phoenix, but prefer a somewhat cooled and mulched soil; the top disappears in winter there, but the tuberous root is perennial. It provides a spectacular white display in shaded areas. Blooming seldom occurs until the latter part of summer. The fragrant, tubular flowers range from red and pinks to white and yellows; they self-sow freely. Spotted cultivars are reminiscent of old-fashioned or cottage gardens. An ideal plant for the evening garden. All parts are poisonous.

MOLUCCELLA LAEVIS BELLS-OF-IRELAND *Lamiaceae (Mint family)*

In spite of its common name, this intriguing plant is native from the eastern Mediterranean to India. It is widely sought after by flower arrangers both in its fresh and dried forms, but can also be very beautiful in a garden setting with other annuals, perennials, or even shrubs. Bells-of-Ireland or lady-in-the-bath is not grown for its rather small and pedestrian flowers, but for the half-inch-across pale green, white-veined saucerlike calyces which surround them. It combines well with deep purple flowers like heliotrope or verbena. These are borne in tall spires on branched plants which sometimes reach three feet tall. Although seed may be sown indoors at 60° F. for planting out later, transplants may be less than satisfactory. If conditions allow, much better results may be had from direct sowing in a sunny place. Prepare rich fertile soil as early as possible and press in the seeds; do not cover. Thin to nine to twelve inches apart and provide supports right away, before the plants begin to sprawl. Often reseeds. For drying, cut the stems before the seeds ripen and hang where it is cool and airy; they become very brittle if cut too late. Bells-of-Ireland do not enjoy the summer heat and humidity found in many regions of the United States and often fail to reach their potential.

NEMOPHILA MENZIESII BABY BLUE-EYES *Hydrophyllaceae*

The exquisite clear blue flowers of Californian bluebell or baby blue-eyes earns it a place in cool spring gardens in spite of its brief period of bloom. Regrettably this dainty Californian annual is killed by the late spring and summer heat found in so many parts of the country. In mild-winter areas seed in fall; elsewhere broadcast seed as soon as the ground has dried out. Indoor sowings directly into peat pots are also successful. Germination is rapid at about 70° F. A partly shaded site is best, perhaps on the north side of a building, where there is plenty of light but no direct sun and out of the wind. Soil that is moist and friable, enriched with plenty of organic matter, is ideal although poorer soils will also suffice. Thin plants to six to twelve inches apart. Baby blue-eyes makes an excellent companion for spring-blooming bulbs at the front of the border, in large containers or windowboxes, and in the rock garden. In containers allow its sprawling stems to spill over and soften hard edges. Several cultivars are available. 'Baby Blue Eyes' makes low spreading plants about six inches tall, covered with white-eyed sky blue flowers; 'Pennie Black' sports purple-black flowers edged in pure white. Five-spot,

N. maculata, has larger flowers and is somewhat taller. Each lobe of its icy white flowers is spotted with purple. Try seeding in midsummer for a fall crop outside or seed in fall for pot plants to decorate a sun room or conservatory through the winter. Sometimes self-seeds.

NICOTIANA ALATA FLOWERING TOBACCO *Solanaceae*

Flowering or jasmine tobacco, referring to its fragrance, is perennial in its native South Smerica, but here mostly it is treated as a tender annual. Those on the market today are hybrid strains derived from *N. alata,* which is seldom available but has the best fragrance. In common with many other plants that have been bred for compact habit bearing bigger and more flowers, the modern hybrids have lost much of their charm and wonderful scent so attractive to night-flying moths. However, today's flowers remain open during the day, in contrast to the species which would only open at dusk and on cloudy days. Sow the tiny seed indoors in a temperature of 65-70° F. two to three months before the last frost, or wait until the soil has warmed to sow out of doors. Do not cover the seed; germination takes ten to twenty days. Nursery-grown transplants are readily available. Plant out nine to twelve inches apart according to variety, into fertile, well-drained neutral soil; a little extra lime may be

Nicotiana sylvestris joins delphinium and clary sage in a strongly vertical planting at Old Westbury Gardens.

NICOTIANA ALATA 'MERLIN LIME GREEN' (FLOWERING TOBACCO)
Many-branched twelve- to fifteen-inch-tall erect to rounded clumps with leaves of medium green. Starlike pale green flowers with long tube. Blooms early summer to fall. Plant in full sun or partial shade and well-drained moist soil.

NICOTIANA SYLVESTRIS Four- to five-foot-tall erect flowering stalks with large, rough-textured leaves. Flower clusters are made up of one-inch-long small trumpets that hang down; sweetly scented. Blooms summer to frost. Partial shade in well-drained, moist soil.

NIEREMBERGIA HIPPOMANICA VAR. VIOLACEA 'PURPLE ROBE' (CUPFLOWER) Six-inch rounded plant with small, lance-shaped deep green leaves and clear purple flowers. Blooms all summer. Plant in sun or light shade (in hot areas).

NIEREMBERGIA HIPPOMANICA VAR. VIOLACEA 'MONT BLANC' (CUPFLOWER) Seven-inch rounded plant with small, lance-shaped deep green leaves and clear white flowers. Blooms all summer. Plant in sun or light shade (in hot areas).

beneficial. Select a sunny or lightly shaded position. In hot climates, some shade is recommended to avoid fading, but the intense summer heat and humidity of some parts of the United States are not ideal for flowering tobacco (though they do well in Maryland if cut back). The plants will need to be replaced by midsummer. In cool climates, the plants will continue flowering right up until the frost, especially if cut back; they seem to really do well in cooler weather. Water generously during dry times and fertilize (5-10-10 or similar) on a regular basis for continued flowering. Flowering tobacco is often used in mass plantings in public gardens, but is useful in home gardens grouped in the flower border or rock garden and in mixed containers. Flowers well indoors throughout the winter with bright light. Avoid planting close to tomatoes, eggplant, potatoes, or peppers since virus diseases of the Solanaceae family are easily transmitted. Sometimes attacked by Colorado potato, flea, and cucumber beetles. The most readily available strains include the 'Nicki' series in mixed or solid colors of white, red, rose, pink, and lime green. These make graceful, bushy eighteen- to twenty-four-inch plants; the abundant flowers are lightly scented. The early-flowering, tightly compact 'Domino' series also comes mixed or in the same solid colors, plus purple, salmon, and crimson. Some have a white eye. Slightly smaller the 'Starship' series is similar. Deadhead for neatness and to prolong flowering.

'Nicki Bright' tobacco flower with 'Star White' zinnia.

NICOTIANA LANGSDORFII *Solanaceae*

One of the few green-flowering plants to be grown in American gardens, this native of Chile and Brazil is now gaining wider attention. It is offered as transplants by adventurous nurseries and garden centers and has become popular with flower arrangers as well as garden designers. Its one-inch greenish-yellow, tubular flowers, which bell at the throat, top stems which if well grown can reach four to five feet, but more usually are three feet or so tall. Fine for the middle of the border or among shrubs for an unusual effect. Try as a foil for brilliant rudbeckias and sunflowers, or with large-leaved caladiums, *N. langsdorfii,* and silver mini helichrysums in a semi-shaded bed. It also works well with purple foliage, like that of *Setcreasea* 'Purple Hat'. Staking is seldom necessary. Self-seeds. Seed as for *N. alata.*

NICOTIANA SYLVESTRIS *Solanaceae*

Popular in gardening circles only in the last few years, Argentinean *Nicotiana sylvestris* is now considered to be one of the most desirable accent plants for late-summer borders. Ideally, it should be placed along a path or near a deck or patio where its lingering fragrance can be appreciated. Its massive, rough-textured basal leaves one foot or more long are arranged in a large rosette, above which rises a leafy stalk topped with a heavy cluster of flower buds. These open to reveal pendulous, pure white, tubular flowers which flare at the mouth into one-inch trumpets. At dusk the effect is somewhat akin to shooting stars. Moreover this fragrant display extends through to the onset of cool weather, providing an excellent foil for fall-blooming perennials. Useful in the midsection and at the back of flower borders, especially with cleomes and fountain grass, as well as among shrubs and foundation plantings. A dark background such as a yew hedge or purple-leaved *Cotinus coggygria* 'Velvet Cloak' is dramatic. Does well in partly shaded sites. In windy sites stake early and plant nine to twelve inches apart; where the plants are protected from the wind, wider spacing is satisfactory but staking is still recommended. If you can, give it even more room; it has been known to spread up to three feet across. Removing dead flower stalks contributes greatly to the promotion of new blooms and also improves overall appearance. Start from seed as for *N. alata.* Available as transplants. Aphids can be a major problem.

NIEREMBERGIA HIPPOMANICA VIOLACEA CUPFLOWER *Solanaceae*

A tender perennial from Argentina, cupflower is grown in the North as a half hardy annual, but with good drainage in warm regions it overwinters satisfactorily. Bloom appears to be most abundant when the weather is not extremely hot. During these times fewer flowers are produced, only to pick up again when the temperature drops. The fernlike foliage does not seem to suffer, however, and adds a delicate touch to container or hanging baskets even when out of bloom; it is also nice as an edging, combined with silver foliage plants. Cupflowers are excellent in these settings as well as in the flower bed with annuals or perennials; verbena is one good companion. It is important to keep the plants well fed and watered, especially during hot, dry spells. At the Desert Botanic Garden it is a successful winter annual, though it suffers dreadfully in summer heat. Although the plants can be increased by division or from cuttings, it is most satisfactory to start from seed in early spring, indoors or outside if conditions allow. Germination occurs in six to fourteen days with a soil temperature of 70° F. or more, more slowly at lower temperatures. Harden off thoroughly and plant out six to eight inches apart just prior to the last frost. Nursery-grown transplants are readily available. To encourage bushiness, pinch the plants two or three times. Well-drained but moisture-retentive soil in a sunny or partially shaded place is ideal. The best-known cultivar is 'Purple Robe' which demands extra liquid feeding to do its best. Its deep purple flowers are carried on six-inch-tall plants. The white-flowered 'Mont Blanc' is gaining in popularity and seems to perform better during very hot weather. Its flowers are a little smaller, but the plants grow about seven inches tall. Deadhead to encourage more blooms. Susceptible to slug damage.

NIGELLA DAMASCENA LOVE-IN-A-MIST *Ranunculaceae (Buttercup)*

This buttercup relative with its romantic common name is a charming old-fashioned plant, better suited to sunny cottage gardens than to mass bedding in public gardens. The airy plants self-seed, and crop up in different areas in the garden; they are usually a welcome addition.Treat love-in-a-mist as a hardy annual. Seed out of doors as soon as the ground is workable; in mild climates sow in October and overwinter. Germination takes ten to fifteen days with a soil temperature of 60° F. Transplants are seldom satisfactory due to the long taproot that develops. Thin the seedlings to about six inches apart and feed regularly with a balanced fertilizer for best growth. The soil should be fertile and well drained; additional water during dry times is beneficial. Flowering begins about three months after seeding, but lasts only one to two months. Excellent as fresh cut flowers; sow successive crops for this purpose. The seed pods are valued as dried material and should be cut while still green. Love-in-a-mist prefers cool climates and fades out quickly under hot, dry conditions. May be used to good effect planted closely as a low hedge, perhaps backed by shrubs, or as a companion for strap-leaved daylilies and other perennials in the flower garden. Self-seeds freely. Readily available cultivars include the popular 'Miss Jekyll', which has pale blue flowers on eighteen-inch stems, and its white form, 'Miss Jekyll Alba'. The mix 'Persian Jewels' grows fifteen inches tall and ranges from purple, lavender, and mauve to pinks, white, and blue. There are also dwarf strains.

OCIMUM BASILICUM BASIL *Lamiaceae (Mint family)*

Until recently, this tender annual was confined to herb gardens, but as gardeners have become more sophisticated they have realized how exciting foliage effects can be. New cultivars have become available, and basils are now found in ornamental gardens across the country. 'Spicy Globe' is popular as a formal edging plant and in containers, topping out at six inches or so and requiring no shearing to keep it neat, although this would be a very pleasant, fragrant task; 'Green Ruffles' and 'Purple Ruffles' are much looser plants. They usually reach two feet in height and have large savoyed leaves of brilliant green or deep purple respectively. They make good foliage accents in informal flower gardens and in arrangements, but are generally not pungent

Above: 'Spicy Globe' basil forms a low, compact mound; cinnamon basil bears spikes of purple flowers. *Below left:* Purple basil contrasts with fiery red celosia, while silvery dusty miller acts as a buffer between them.

NIGELLA DAMASCENA (LOVE-IN-A-MIST) Eighteen-inch-tall, erect plant with finely textured gray-green tiny leaves. Blue, white, or pink flowers over an inch wide amid ferny foliage. Grown also for balloonlike spiny seed pods that dry well. Blooms in summer. Grow in full sun and any soil.

OCIMUM BASILICUM 'PURPLE RUFFLES' (PURPLE RUFFLES BASIL) Bushy two-foot-tall plant with ruffled, shiny dark purple leaves and lavender flowers. Blooms in summer. Full sun, well-drained, fertile, moist soil.

OXALIS PURPUREA (WOOD SORREL) Spreading plant, growing six to eight inches tall, with triangular to heart-shaped deep burgundy leaves. Small light pink or lilac flowers appear intermittently throughout summer. Best in partial to full shade.

OXYPETALUM CAERULEUM (SOUTHERN STAR) Eighteen-inch-tall shrubby plant. Long narrow leaves and small, star-shaped blue flowers in summer. Full sun, rich well-drained soil.

enough for culinary use. 'Dark Opal' has strongly aromatic, lustrous, dark purple leaves on twelve-inch plants. Contrast it with a fine-leaved dusty miller and a purple petunia. Basil is a warm-weather plant. Sow the seed eight to ten weeks before the last frost date, by pressing the seed into the soil; do not cover. At a temperature of 65-75° F., germination takes up to two weeks. Direct sowings after the soil has warmed up also do well. Select a position in full sun, where the soil is fertile and well drained, but moist. Space transplants or thin to six inches apart for the dwarf forms, twelve to eighteen inches for the larger sorts. Be alert for damage from slugs and snails; avoid pesticides if the leaves are to be eaten.

OXALIS WOOD SORREL, LADY'S SORREL *Oxalidaceae*

Although closely related to several bothersome weeds such as clovers and shamrocks, some species in the genus *Oxalis* are lovely ornamentals. Most grow from underground bulbs, though they are available in nurseries as transplants. Oxalis will grow in rich soil and partial or even deep shade. Try it in a windowbox with browallia or ivy. *O. purpurea* has triangular, deep burgundy leaves with lighter markings; its foliage is more significant than its delicate pale pink or lilac flowers. Several new species are being researched for use in the Southwest, under extremely dry conditions. Oxalis is easily propagated by bulb division.

OXYPETALUM CAERULEUM SOUTHERN STAR *Asclepiadaceae*

Southern star needs to be enjoyed from up close; its exquisite but tiny, star-shaped flowers don't make much of an impression from a distance. The flowers, which start out as pink buds and turn baby blue and then lilac, are borne on an eighteen-inch shrubby plant with heart-shaped green leaves. It is best used in a smaller hanging basket or a windowbox placed near eye level. Southern star does best in rich well-drained soil; it needs full sun and prefers cool weather. Seeds can be sown indoors six to eight weeks before the last frost; seedlings are planted in the garden after all danger of frost has passed, spaced six to eight inches apart; direct-seeding will produce plants after a year. It has flourished even under humid conditions. Cutting back stimulates new growth. The plant can be dug up and taken indoors for use as a houseplant on a sunny windowsill during the winter.

PAPAVER RHOEAS CORN POPPY, SHIRLEY POPPY *Papaveraceae*

The European corn poppies are easy to grow and have now become naturalized in some parts of this country. They are often seen on the edges of English farmlands, where they are considered a serious weed, but as ornamentals here they are graceful additions to rock gardens, cottage gardens, wildflower and meadow gardens, and are used for cutting. Unlike their close relative the scarlet Flanders poppy (*P. commutatum*), corn poppies also come in pastel yellow, pinks, and white as well as deeper crimson and reds. The 'Mother of Pearl' strain has single flowers, the 'Shirley Re-selected Double Mixture' has double

PAPAVER RHOEAS (CORN POPPY, SHIRLEY POPPY) Two feet tall with a loose habit. Dark green dissected leaves. Three-inch pink, scarlet, crimson, salmon, and white flowers with petals of varied sizes and black centers. Blooms spring to early summer. Plant in full sun and light, sandy soil.

PELARGONIUM X HORTATUM 'TETRA SCARLET' (ZONAL GERANIUM) Twelve- to twenty-inch erect to rounded plant with medium green rounded leaves. Clusters of bright red flowers. Blooms spring to fall. Plant in full sun and moist, well-drained soil.

PELARGONIUM X DOMESTICUM (MARTHA WASHINGTON GERANIUM, REGAL GERANIUM) Two- to three-inch single blossoms in clusters that resemble rhododendron flowers. Rounded, lobed leaves. Prefers partial shade, moist, well-drained soil. Usually bloom early in season; often used in baskets.

PELARGONIUM PELTATUM (IVY GERANIUM) Vining habit with eight- to ten-inch stems and leathery, glossy leaves. Clustered white, salmon, red, or pink flowers. Blooms spring to fall. Plant in full sun and moist, well-drained soil.

and semidouble flowers. The delicate flowers emerge crumpled from hairy buds, but quickly expand to nod in every passing breeze. Poppies develop a strong taproot, which resents transplanting. Sow the minute seeds directly in place, in fall in mild-winter areas, in early spring elsewhere, even on top of melting snow. Cold weather does not disturb them, but the heat and humidity of summer is not to their liking. In such regions of the country, a display of corn poppies is fleeting at best. Select a sunny site, where the soil is light to average, well drained, but moisture-retentive. Germination takes only eight to ten days at 60-70° F. Thin to six to eight inches apart. If seedlings must be transplanted, sow in peat pots or prick off into individual pots at the tiny seedling stage to protect the taproot. Often self-sows. Iceland poppies (*P. nudicale*) are short-lived perennials treated as annuals or biennials. Seed very early in the year in pots or set out summer-sown plants in fall to overwinter and bloom the following season. Reliable and beautiful strains include 'Oregon Rainbows', which has single and semidouble four- to six-inch flowers in an assortment of pastel and deeper colors, and single-flowered 'Sparkling Bubbles' and 'Champagne Bubbles'. If using poppies for cut flowers, sear the base of the stem with a lighted match to seal in the milky sap.

Scented geraniums, from left to right, 'Peppermint', 'Prince Rupert', 'Old Scarlet Unique'.

PELARGONIUM GERANIUM *Geraniaceae (Geranium family)*

Natives of South Africa, geraniums are among the most popular bedding plants; over forty million plants are sold each year. There is an almost endless selection of species and cultivars to suit every taste, including some with lacy and variegated foliage and some with such fragrances as orange, chocolate mint, coconut, ginger, and pine. Zonal geraniums, *P. x hortatum,* are the ones most often used in annual gardening. They are available in white, pink, red, and salmon, with some fancy-leaved varieties available as well; they bloom for a long season and are perennial in Zones 9 and 10. They grow to about three feet, except in mild climates, where, as perennials, they can reach up to six feet. Martha Washington geraniums (sometimes called Lady Washingon or regal geraniums, *P. x domesticum*) have lovely large, single blossoms in clusters that resemble rhododendron flowers, but are a bit more fussy; they prefer partial shade and will quit flowering altogether in hot weather. Ivy geraniums, *P. peltatum,* have small star-shaped flowers and trailing stems; they form a graceful basket and look smashing in stone urns. Scented geraniums are excellent in the border or along walkways, where you will release their fragrance when you brush against them. A sampling of the numerous scents and varieties: almond (*P. quercifolium*); apple (*P. odoratissimum*); apricot (*P. scabrum*); coconut (*P. grossularioides*); lemon (*P. crispum*); lime (*P. nervosum*); nutmeg (*P. fragrans*); peppermint (*P. tomentosum*); rose (*P. capitatum, P. graveolens*). It goes without saying that all make excellent subjects for hanging baskets and windowboxes.

Geraniums do best in climates with summers that have warm and dry days and cool nights. Most do well in full sun or partial shade (the exceptions are the Martha Washington geraniums, which need some shade.) Soil should be well drained and not so rich that it promotes production of foliage at the

expense of flowers. Geraniums are usually purchased as potted plants, but they are among the easiest of plants to propagate from cuttings or seed. Seeds can be sown indoors eight to ten weeks before the last expected frost; seeds will germinate over a period of three to eight weeks. Transplant seedlings to four-inch pots when they begin to show true leaves, and keep them on a sunny windowsill. Tranplant into the garden after all danger of frost has passed, spacing them about a foot apart. Pinch stems regularly to encourage new growth and remove spent flowers and yellow leaves to promote healthy plants. Insect problems include whitefly, aphids, and mealybugs. At the first indication of black areas on the stems or if the leaves look unhealthy, discard the plant to avoid spreading fungal disease. Move whole plants back indoors before fall frost, or take cuttings from them for the next year's flowering plants. When the weather warms up, you can transplant houseplants or set them, pot and all, into the garden.

PENNISETUM SETACEUM FOUNTAIN GRASS *Poaceae (Grass family)*

This perennial grass is mostly grown as a half hardy annual, outside of Zones 9 to 10. Fountain grass makes a fine accent plant in sunny beds and borders and in container plantings; the striking one-inch-long, bristled flower spikes are attractive as cut flowers, both fresh and dried. Cultivars with pink, copper, and red foliage and flower spikes are on the market, but the purple-leaved cultivar 'Rubrum' is particularly handsome. Combine it with *Nicotiana sylvestris* and cleomes for dramatic effect, or try it with *Verbena canadensis* or *Lantana montevidensis*. *P. s. atrosanguineum,* purple fountain grass, provides dramatic color, texture, and "kitty-tail" seedheads that children love. Plant seeds in well-prepared soil six to eight weeks before the last frost and cover with clear plastic, cut with slits to allow germination. Germination occurs in one to three weeks, and the young seedlings must be thinned to fifteen to eighteen inches apart. Pot-grown nursery transplants are often available; plant out in fertile soil in a sunny position. Although it is slow to start, fountain grass takes off in July, especially if deadheaded, and adds immeasurably to the late summer and autumn garden. During growth the plants should be kept moist. If winters are not too severe, plants can be given extra protection, or may be lifted and overwintered indoors; Susan Nolde of Brookside Gardens has noted that they need an indoor temperature of at least 45° F. Galen Gates of Chicago Botanic Garden has observed that they will not survive temperatures below 35° F., so be sure to bring them in before the temperature drops below that point. At The New York Botanical Garden, fountain grass is left in the ground when the summer annuals are removed; they provide a fabulous background for autumn mums that replace the summer annuals. Divide and plant out young plants the following spring. *P. s.* 'Rubrum' can be propagated by cane cuttings as you would a dieffenbachia; cut a section with at least one node and place in a rooting mixture. Pest and disease free. One problem with fountain grass is that in warm climates it reseeds itself practically anywhere and has become a pest; even purported sterile hybrids are not reliably so.

Opposite: Pennisetum setaceum 'Rubrum' with alternanthera, coleus, and begonias at Missouri Botanical Garden.

Pentas lanceolata 'Ruby Glow' with coreopsis.

PENTAS LANCEOLATA EGYPTIAN STAR CLUSTER *Rubiaceae*

This African subshrub has recently found favor as an annual in sunny American gardens, where it imparts a lush, subtropical air. Easy to grow, it blooms over a long period of time once buds have set. Prune lightly and regularly to maintain shapeliness and encourage constant bloom. For early flowering it is best to take cuttings from overwintered plants, in January or February. These root readily at 60-65° F. with high humidity. Pot young plants into larger containers until ready to be set outside when the soil has warmed up. Seed must be started indoors very early for summer bloom. A summer mulch is beneficial to retain soil moisture; extra watering is necessary during dry spells. Egyptian star cluster is an excellent plant for containers throughout the summer, either on its own or in combination with other plants. Butterflies love it. Lift established plants before frost to provide cuttings for next year. The best-known cultivar is 'Pink Profusion', which is a good, strong pink. Others in the pink/red range are available.

PERILLA FRUTESCENS BEEFSTEAK PLANT *Lamiaceae (Mint family)*

Kin of coleus and basil, perilla is a tender annual plant from India and eastern Asia, where it is widely cultivated for food. As an ornamental, its rise in popularity as an accent foliage plant has paralleled that of purple-leaved basil, with which it may be used interchangeably. It is excellent at the back of the border, where its dense three-foot-tall stems, heavily clothed in dark purplish-green leaves, provide a foil for bright annuals or dainty perennials, such as *Gaura lindheimeri* and baby's breath. It is also sufficiently sturdy to make a low hedge and can provide light support for fall-blooming asters. Sow seed uncovered indoors at 65-75° F. some six weeks before the last frost date or direct seed when the soil has warmed. Cool temperatures delay germination, which normally takes two to three weeks. Plant out or thin fifteen to eighteen inches apart, more widely if the plants will be pinched to encourage bushiness. Cuttings root readily. Perilla thrives in full sun, where the soil is fertile and kept moist, but it tolerates poor soil well. Having once grown perilla, it self-sows so freely that you will never have to seed again. The spent flowers are attractive for dried arrangements, but to avoid self-sowing, deadhead routinely or pinch out flower buds as they develop. It also makes a superior vinegar.

PETUNIA X HYBRIDA PETUNIA *Solanaceae (Nightshade family)*

How many million petunia seedlings are raised in this country each year? Petunias top the list of popular annuals to grow in home gardens, however humble, and many millions more must be planted out in public and grand estate gardens across the nation. Their enormous popularity has made petunia breeding a big business, with most of the hybrids being derived from *P. axillaris* and *P. violacea*. Almost every flower color is available, some bicolored, on bushy plants, cascading plants, taller plants, and more compact plants, some with single flowers, others double-flowered, ruffled, fringed, fluted, or with contrasting veins. Closely related to tobacco (in fact, its name is derived from

PENNISETUM SETACEUM 'RUBRUM' (RED FOUNTAIN GRASS) Two-to four-foot upright arching plant grown for its reddish-purple leaves. Three- to six-foot reddish-purple soft inflorescences. Blooms summer to frost. Plant in full sun to partial shade in moist, well-drained soil.

PENTAS LANCEOLATA 'PINK PROFUSION' (EGYPTIAN STAR CLUSTER) One- to two-foot erect or spreading plant with dark green lance-shaped leaves. Strong pink star-shaped flowers. Blooms throughout summer. Full sun, moist soil.

PERILLA FRUTESCENS 'ATROPURPUREA' (BEEFSTEAK PLANT) Many-branched plant, one to four feet tall. Deeply textured dark purple leaves, small spikes of lavender flowers. Full sun, rich, well-drained soil.

PETUNIA X HYBRIDA [MULTIFLORA] 'TOTAL MADNESS' (GARDEN PETUNIA) Ten-inch-tall spreading plant with medium green fuzzy, sticky leaves. One- to two-inch flowers in many colors. Blooms all summer. Plant in full sun to partial shade in light, well-drained soil. Deadhead regularly.

Petunia x *hybrida* 'Azure Pearls' (multiflora).

Petunia x *hybrida* 'Polo Red Target' (multiflora).

Petunia x *hybrida* 'Polo Orchid Vein' (multiflora).

Petunia x *hybrida* 'California Girl' (grandiflora).

Petunia x *hybrida* 'Big Daddy' (grandiflora).

Petunia x *hybrida* 'Purple Pirouette' (grandiflora).

Petunias are excellent candidates for all sorts of baskets and containers.

a South American word for tobacco), this Argentinean native blooms in sunny positions throughout the summer and fall until the frost cuts it down. Start the seeds indoors nine to twelve weeks before the last frost date. Scatter the tiny seeds on the surface of a sterile seed medium (vermiculite is best for the F1 and F2 hybrids), and press in without covering; petunias need light to germinate. Keep the soil moist and at about 65-75° F. Germination takes six to ten days for the dwarf and bedding varieties; the large and double-flowered sorts are a little slower. As soon as they can be handled, prick off the seedlings to give more space and lower the temperature to 60° F. or so. Seedlings in close quarters are very susceptible to *Botrytis* fungus. Plant outside six to ten inches apart about when the last frost is anticipated. Do not be in too much of a hurry to plant out, although the garden centers will be brimming over with plants. If you must, buy and keep in a sunny protected place for a few days, so that you can cover the plants in case of a sharp freeze, although petunias are less tender than impatiens or begonias. Blooming takes two to three months from seed. Plant out into any well-drained soil in a sunny position; a shaded site discourages flowering. Be alert for slugs and snails, which do enormous damage, as well as aphids on the succulent new growth. Tobacco mosaic may be a problem; avoid having smokers handle the plants and remove affected plants promptly and burn. To encourage free-flowering, pinch young plants and keep well watered throughout hot weather. Blooming often stalls after the first flush, especially in hot climates. Shear the plants to two inches or so from the ground, water, and fertilize heavily with a balanced fertilizer, such as 20-20-20; you will be rewarded with another flush of flowers on neat, compact plants within a few weeks. Do not be afraid to cut back lanky or untidy growth.

PHLOX DRUMMONDII 'CECILY' (ANNUAL PHLOX) Two- to three-foot-tall round plant with clasping medium green leaves. Flowers in pink clusters. Blooms summer to frost. Plant in sun to partial shade in well-drained moist soil.

PHLOX DRUMMONDII 'DWARF BEAUTY' (ANNUAL PHLOX) Two- to three-foot-tall round plant with clasping medium green leaves. Flowers in clusters of rose, crimson, scarlet, violet, white, or yellow. Blooms summer to frost. Plant in sun to partial shade in well-drained moist soil.

PHORMIUM TENAX 'ATROPURPUREUM' (NEW ZEALAND FLAX) Six- to ten-foot clump with bronze-purple sword-shaped leaves. Flowers insignificant. Foliage attractive all summer.

POLIANTHES TUBEROSA (TUBEROSE) Two- to three-foot-tall plant for containers or in-ground planting. One-foot-long glossy, grasslike leaves. Waxy white tubular flowers with rich spicy scent. Blooms midsummer to frost. Plant in full sun in rich soil.

At The New York Botanical Garden, petunias are not sheared; rather, they are randomly pruned back after the first flush of flowers, with some pruned each week. After a few weeks, all have been pruned; Mike Ruggiero reports that this produces flowers all season, not just in spurts between shearings.

Petunias are generally divided into two sorts: the grandiflora types, which have very large flowers, both singles and doubles; and the smaller-flowered multiflora types. The latter tend to stand up better to adverse weather conditions and flower profusely. Where summers are hot and humid, one of the best of the multifloras is the 'Madness' series, available in solid colors as well as the 'Total Madness' mixture. The 'Polo' series grows a little more upright. Of the single grandifloras the 'Cascade' and 'Supercascade' series are especially well adapted to growing in containers and windowboxes; grandifloras need deadheading for profuse bloom. The 'Flash' series in solid colors on ten- to twelve-inch plants and the 'Falcon' mixture in solid colors are both popular. The grandiflora doubles include the 'Tart' series, named for fruits such as coral and red 'Apple Tart' and rose and white 'Cherry Tart'. The new 'Floribunda' hybrids have double flowers. 'Purple Wave', a 1995 All-America Selection is wonderful in hanging baskets or windowboxes, or as a groundcover; the intense purple color is almost intoxicating. *Petunia integrifolia* var. *integrifolia* is great in containers and is less fragile than most other petunias. There are countless named varieties to suit everyone's taste in both groups, especially in the doubles. Petunias are valuable in the garden, providing color en masse as well as in the rock garden, in flower beds and borders, as edging plants, and of course as container plants for tubs, planters, and hanging baskets. Excellent in seaside gardens and anywhere that has sun for at least half the day.

Petunia integrifolia var. *integrifolia* forms a dense mass and never stops flowering; it is great both as groundcover and in baskets.

PHLOX DRUMMONDII ANNUAL PHLOX, TEXAS PRIDE *Polemoniaceae*

This native Texan is not as widely grown as it deserves. Hardy and easy to grow, annual phlox blooms right through the hot days of summer and is sufficiently reliable for massed plantings (though June Hutson finds it does not tolerate the humidity of St. Louis). It is also charming in cottage gardens, as an edging, or grouped among annuals and perennials in mixed borders, containers, or windowboxes. The taller sorts make good cut flowers. Outdoor sowings can be made in early spring when the ground becomes workable; later sowings will extend the season. For early bloom or where the season is short, start seeds indoors at about 60° F., two months or so ahead of the last frost. Germination takes ten to twenty days; as it is most uniform in darkness, cover the flats with black plastic and keep out of the sun. If the temperature rises to 75° F., germination will be inhibited. Transplant or thin to eight to twelve inches apart. A rich, well-drained soil, slightly on the acid side, is ideal; annual phlox do not thrive in poor, dry soil. Apply a summer mulch and keep watered during hot weather. Mildew is a problem in dry soils. Fertilize once or twice during the season. Deadhead routinely to extend flowering. Popular strains include compact 'Twinkles', six to eight inches tall, which has small star-shaped flowers in a full range of white, pinks, lavenders, blues, reds, and purple. The Dutch 'Palona' strain grows six inches tall and blooms early in a full color range with many bicolored flowers; 'Globe' is similar but is reputed to transplant more easily than some. The 'Grandiflora' strain grows fifteen inches tall for cutting. Plants will be in flower in two to two-and-one-half months from seeding.

PHORMIUM TENAX NEW ZEALAND FLAX *Agavaceae (Agave family)*

New Zealand flax has become popular as a stiff, striking accent plant or foil for looser annuals and perennials in open borders. Its upright, sword-like leaves vary from various shades of brownish or purplish red to maroon-flushed dark green; some are variegated. There are numerous cultivars and hybrds including the semi-dwarfs 'Bronze Baby' and 'Yellow Wave', which is yellow-variegated, and the huge purple 'Purple Giant'. Height varies from six to twelve feet according to the cultivar. *P. colensoi* is smaller. Propagate the cultivars by division in spring; seed germinates readily, but young plants are very variable. In regions colder than Zone 8, phormiums must be maintained indoors at 45-50° F. through the cold months, to be set outside again as soon as the danger of frost has passed. They are decorative additions to sun rooms and cool conservatories, where they are usually grown in containers for ease of handling. Plant New Zealand flax in a moisture-retentive, fertile soil and feed regularly with a dilute liquid fertilizer. Low-maintenance except for the removal of occasional damaged or dead leaves, they are seldom bothered by pests or diseases, except for mealybugs indoors. Full sun or partial shade is fine in most regions, although the variegated sorts in particular appreciate light shade from

New Zealand flax with petunias and hibiscus.

intense noonday sun. The curious flowers are borne on tall, naked stems above the foliage, but it is the leaves that are prized for their architectural form in the garden.

POLIANTHES TUBEROSA TUBEROSE *Agavaceae (Agave family)*

The tuberose is grown extensively for the commercial market, for use as a cut flower and as a source of perfume. The delicate waxy white flower, available in a double form, is a nice accent for a smaller border or a hanging basket; it would get lost among bolder, showier plants. Tuberose grows to three feet, with long narrow leaves. It grows from rhizomes, which can be set out in the garden in late spring or early summer and covered with about an inch of fine, light soil. Rhizomes can be dug up before frost and stored over winter in a cool, dry place; although it usually flowers in late summer and early fall, it can be forced indoors in spring or even in early winter.

Portulaca is loved for the intense colors of its flowers and its easy culture; it tolerates almost every situation. *Above:* 'Sundial Yellow'.

POLYGONUM CAPITATUM KNOTWEED *Polygonaceae (Buckwheat family)*

Native to the Himalayas, knotweed is a trailing plant with many-jointed stems and tiny pink flowers in dense, round heads. A perennial treated as a half hardy annual, it can be started from seeds sown in warm soil in early spring and transplanted to a sunny location into average soil after all danger of frost has passed. It reseeds tenaciously, and some species in the genus, like *P. polystachum,* are a terrible nuisance because their roots form a tangled network that is almost impossible to remove. It exudes a sweet perfume. Another species, *P. orientale*, or kiss-me-over-the-garden-gate, produces flowers in dense spikes up to three inches long.

PORTULACA GRANDIFLORA MOSS ROSE *Portulacaceae (Purslane family)*

Moss rose is one of the best low-growing annuals to provide summer color in those difficult sunbaked, dry places of the garden. It is ideally suited to growing alongside walkways, on exposed banks, or in the rock garden, and it also thrives in patio planters. This Brazilian native has fleshy, succulent foliage and an abundance of one-inch-wide single or double flowers in vivid colors of almost neon intensity. Regrettably the flowers are very sensitive to light and fail to open on overcast or rainy days. Sow the tiny seeds indoors about six to eight weeks before the last frost, or wait until the soil has warmed up outside and mix the seed with dry sand and broadcast where the plants are to flower. Germination occurs in five to ten days; thin to six inches apart. At The New York Botanical Garden, seeds are sown in plugs, with about ten to twenty seeds per plug. Nursery-grown transplants are readily available, especially the 'Sundial' series in individual colors of cream, fuchsia, yellow, pink, and scarlet, and the 'Cabaret' mix in a similar range of colors. 'White Swan' is a smashing, double, white form; it looks wonderful with roses, producing a white carpet that does not clash or compete with the roses' colors. The 'Cloudbeater' mix is reputedly less sensitive to low light intensity. Blooming begins about forty to

POLYGONUM CAPITATUM (KNOTWEED) Six inches high, trailing to ten inches long. Small leaves sometimes dotted with brown or pink spots. Small pink flowerheads borne in mid-summer. Plant in full sun. Tolerant of wet or dry infertile soil.

PORTULACA GRANDIFLORA 'SUNDIAL PEPPERMINT' (MOSS ROSE) Six to eight-inch spreading mound with small succulent gray-green leaves. Double crepe flowers. Blooms from early summer to frost. Plant in full sun in poor, dry soil. Very tolerant of heat.

PORTULACA GRANDIFLORA 'SUNDIAL PINK' (MOSS ROSE) Six to eight-inch spreading mound with small succulent gray-green leaves. Double crepe flowers. Blooms from early summer to frost. Plant in full sun in poor, dry soil. Very tolerant of heat.

RHODOCHITON ATROSANGUINEUM (PURPLE BELL VINE) Vining plant that hangs three to four feet. Flowers with spreading fuchsia calyx and two-inch-long bell-shaped purple-black flowers. Blooms summer to frost. Fertile, moist, well-drained soil. Full sun, some shade in hot areas.

fifty days from seeding and continues until frost, although toward the end of
summer the plants often decline dramatically. Dry, poor, even gravelly soil is
fine–in fact it is preferred–in a very sunny position. Self-sows. Water only if
severe drought. Portulaca does not need to be deadheaded; it seems to clean
itself almost magically.

RHODOCHITON ATROSANGUINEUM PURPLE BELL VINE
Scrophulariceae (Figwort family)

Purple bell vine, sometimes listed as *R. volubile,* is an unusual perennial vine
from Mexico, grown here outside Zones 9 and 10 as a tender annual. Its
slender stems carry small heart-shaped leaves on twining petioles that scramble up whatever supports it can find to a height of six to eight feet. Purple
bell vine needs a long season to do its best. Start seed, fresh if possible, three
to four months ahead of the last frost date, in individual peat pots at 65-70°
F. Germination is spotty and may take two to six weeks. The soil must be
fertile and free-draining; add sand or perlite if drainage is questionable.
Grow on in a sunny position without checking at 65-70° F.; applications of
dilute liquid fertilizer help maintain rapid growth. When the pots are full of
roots, transfer plants to four- to five-inch pots and grow on until the soil has
warmed outdoors. During this time, the plants will need to be trained up
strings or wires which can be planted out later along with the plants.
Transplants are available. Do not rush planting out; a warm sheltered position is ideal. Where summers are hot, provide light shade. Keep well
watered; growth is rapid. Excellent for hanging baskets, trained up arbors or
trellises, or even teepees in the flower garden. The deep purple, tubular flowers, each framed by a cloaklike fuschia-colored calyx, do not appear until the
latter part of the summer, but continue into the fall until cut down by frost.
A white form is also available.

RICINUS COMMUNIS CASTOR BEAN *Euphorbiaceae (Spurge family)*
Widely naturalized throughout warm parts of the world, castor bean has decorative value and is also of great economic importance, but it requires caution,
for its oily seeds are encased in an attractive but **deadly poisonous** skin. In
the garden **be certain that castor bean plants are not accessible to children** who might ingest the seeds. Even handling seeds that have been soaked
can cause a serious reaction. Remove the spent flowerheads for safety. This
massive, shrublike plant with three-foot-wide palmate leaves adds a strong
subtropical atmosphere to the garden, particularly when combined with cannas, cleomes, and pennisetums. Don Buma of Botanica in Wichita uses it
with the yellow, fall-blossoming *Cassia alata,* which grows to eight feet tall; it
is especially impressive as a mass planting seen from height. It makes a fast-
growing screen and is good in large containers, but is especially effective
reflected in the surface of formal water gardens. In warm regions seeds can be
sown direct; elsewhere sow individually indoors six to eight weeks before the
last frost. At 70-75° F., germination takes fifteen to twenty days. Plant out

Ricinus is grown for its dramatic,
huge leaves, but its flowers are also
interesting. This plant is extremely
poisonous and should not be planted
where it can be ingested by children
or pets.

RICINUS COMMUNIS 'CARMENCITA' (CASTOR BEAN) Six-foot-tall, erect plant grown for its elegant bronze-brown leaves. Flowers without petals, not particularly attractive. VERY POISONOUS. Plant in full sun in rich, organic soil.

RUDBECKIA HIRTA 'BECKY MIX' (BLACK-EYED SUSAN) Eight- to ten-inch-tall erect to round plant with hairy foliage. Lemon to bright orange ray flowers, darker near center, and dark brown disk flowers. Blooms in summer and fall. Plant in full sun and rich, well-drained organic soil (will tolerate dry soils).

RUDBECKIA HIRTA 'DOUBLE GOLD' (BLACK-EYED SUSAN) Thirty-six-inch-tall erect to round plant with hairy, medium green foliage. Golden double and semidouble ray flowers and dark brown disk flowers. Blooms in summer and fall. Plant in full sun in a rich, well-drained organic soil (will tolerate dry soils).

RUDBECKIA HIRTA 'GLORIOSA DAISY' (BLACK-EYED SUSAN) Thirty- to thirty-six-inch-tall erect to round plant with hairy, medium green foliage. Bronze, chestnut, mahogany, or golden ray flowers and dark brown disk flowers. Blooms in summer and fall. Plant in full sun in a rich, well-drained organic soil (will tolerate dry soils).

four to six feet apart in full sun in rich soil high in organic matter. Abundant moisture is necessary as well as routine feeding for best results. The plants will grow four to fifteen feet tall, depending on the cultivar and conditions, perhaps to thirty feet in the tropics; stake early and avoid windswept sites. Cultivars are available with green, bronze, or red foliage. 'Carmencita' is well known; it has bronzy brown leaves on six-foot-tall plants. 'Sanguineus' has dark red stems, foliage, and fruiting clusters. 'Zanzibariensis' has purple/burgundy leaves and stems and can grow twelve to fifteen feet in one season. 'Impala' has particularly handsome leaves, with a heavier texture than the species. Said to repel moles, but attractive to Japanese beetles.

RUDBECKIA HIRTA BLACK-EYED SUSAN *Asteraceae (Daisy family)*

During the summer and early fall, our native black-eyed Susan is a familiar sight along the highways and byways of this country. Once confined to the prairie states, it has now become widespread and exhibits a great deal of variation from one population to another. Biennial in the wild, black-eyed Susan comes from seed to bloom in the first year and is mostly treated as an annual. Named varieties include eighteen- to twenty-four-inch-tall 'Marmalade', perhaps better known as 'Orange Bedder', since the four-inch flowers are brilliant golden-orange with a dark brown center cone; it is especially recommended for mass bedding purposes. 'Rustic Colors' ['Rustic Dwarfs'] has slightly smaller flowers in a range of yellow, orange, brown, and mahogany on two-foot plants. 'Irish Eyes' is unusual for its green centers. The 1995 All American Selection 'Indian Summer' is more floriferous, longer-blooming, and more weather-tolerant than other cultivars; it has six- to nine-inch flowers on thirty- to thirty-six-inch stems. The semidouble and double-flowered 'Gloriosa Daisy' strain has larger flowers; some are tetraploid, their flowers reach six inches or more across. Among the most popular are 'Double Gold', with four-inch flowers on three-foot stems, and neat fifteen-inch-tall 'Goldilocks', which has flowers three to four inches across. The taller sorts make excellent cut flowers but need staking. All are useful to enliven a shrub border or tired ho-hum flower bed in the late summer, especially in informal parts of the garden. Sow the seed out of doors in early spring. Where the season is short, sow indoors at about 60° F. eight to ten weeks before the last frost. Nursery-grown transplants are readily available; many nurseries list them in the perennial section. Full sun and rich, well-drained soil produce the best results, although black-eyed Susan tolerates poor, dry soils well. Additional organic matter is beneficial during soil preparation. Water during dry weather; mildew causes the coarse foliage to become unsightly if the plants are unduly stressed from drought or poor air circulation. Hot, dry weather is to their liking. Bait for slugs and snails; aphids can be a major problem. Deadhead to avoid abundant self-seeding and for neatness.

SALPIGLOSSUS SINUATA PAINTED TONGUE *Solanaceae (Nightshade)*

This charming Chilean native has been hybridized to bloom in the most glorious color combinations. The large, funnel-shaped flowers have the texture of

Painted tongue with grandiflora petunias and calceolaria.

velvet, in clear yellows and white as well as dusky brown, purples, red, and blues, all veined in contrasting colors. Salpiglossus deserves a much wider audience in residential gardens as a cut flower, in the flower border toward the back, and as a cool greenhouse or conservatory plant. The old cultivars are not ideal as bedding plants on a large scale, which may explain its unfamiliarity; newer strains are more compact. Start the extremely fine seed indoors at 70-80° F. about eight weeks before the last frost dates, uncovered but in total darkness. Germination takes up to three weeks. To facilitate even sowing, mix the seed with fine sand. Prick out into individual pots to avoid transplant shock; pinch to encourage bushiness. Alternatively, broadcast seed in place as soon as the ground is workable and cover with one-eighth inch of fine soil. Thin or set out twelve inches apart; transplants are available. Plant out into a sunny position where the soil is fertile and well drained. Add plenty of organic material to retain moisture in the hot weather; a summer mulch is beneficial. Keep deadheaded and watered during summer heat. The tall sorts will need to be staked or planted among stronger-stemmed companions. Salpiglossus generally comes in mixed colors. Good strains include the F2 'Bolero Hybrids' and F1 'Splash' mixture, both about two feet tall. The F1 'Casino' strain is a more compact eighteen to twenty-four inches tall. Best in regions with cool summers.

SALVIA SAGE *Lamiaceae (Mint family)*

This huge genus includes shrubs and perennials as well as biennials and annuals, many of which are becoming widely accepted for their decorative flowers or foliage as well as for herbal use. For example, the subshrubby culinary sage *S. officinalis*, long a staple in herb gardens, is becoming increasingly popular with sophisticated gardeners as a contrast foliage plant, especially in its purple-leaved and tricolor forms. Many of the warm-climate shrubby sages, such as *S. leucantha* and *S. involucrata*, are now cultivated as annual ornamentals in cool parts of the country; *S. leucantha* is used for its foliage in spring and for its flowers in fall at The New York Botanical Garden. The red-flowered, deliciously fragrant pineapple sage (*S. elegans*) earns a place in both the herb garden and the flower bed, as do the biennial clary sage (*S. sclarea*) and its showy variety *S. s. turkestanica*. Wooly-leaved sage (*S. argentea*), also a biennial, is gaining popularity as a foliage accent plant for its bold rosette of white wooly leaves; the tuberous-rooted perennial *S. patens*, with its glorious gentian blue flowers, is increasingly available. Perhaps better known to American gardeners is the stocky scarlet sage (*S. splendens*), the backbone of many a Victorian public bedding scheme. This tender Brazilian perennial has been acutely overused, too often massed in garish combinations almost always in its usual strident scarlet form. Cultivars abound, differing little except in height and time of flowering. At twenty-six inches in height, 'Bonfire' is one of the tallest; 'Red Hot Sally' is a ten-inch dwarf, reputed to bloom by June 20 in the Northeast. 'Flame' lives up to its name and cries out for the cooling effect of a silver-leaved companion or graceful grasses. The uniform twelve-inch-tall

SALPIGLOSSUS SINUATA (PAINTED TONGUE) Eighteen- to twenty-four-inch-tall upright plant with sticky leaves and stems. Flowers are trumpet-shaped in gold, yellow, blue, and red with variations in color patterns. Blooms throughout summer in cool climate. Plant in full sun and well-drained soil.

SALVIA SPLENDENS 'FLAME' (SCARLET SAGE) Twelve- to eighteen-inch-tall plant with large dark green leaves. Bright red flower spikes with distinct calyxes. Blooms summer to frost. Plant in full sun or partial shade in well-drained soil.

SALVIA COCCINEA 'CHERRY BLOSSOM' (TEXAS SAGE) Twelve- to fifteen-inch-tall upright, slender plant. White and salmon irregular flowers. Flowers early summer to fall. Plant in full sun or partial shade in well-drained moist soil.

SALVIA GREGGII (AUTUMN SAGE) Three to five feet tall, with small oval leaves and magenta flowers; other colors also available. Full sun. Tolerates heat and dry conditions; one of the best salvias for the Southwest.

Red *Salvia splendens,* blue *Salvia farinacea* 'Victoria', red zinnias and silver
dusty miller.

'Empire' series includes light salmon, lilac, purple, and white-flowered plants.
These colors are easier to use in combinations in the garden, but their habit is
still blocky and awkward. Try the dark burgundy form with the mealy-cup
sage, a stunning combination accented with silvery artichoke foliage and bordered by a lime-green hedge of coleus at Wave Hill. Texan mealy-cup sage (*S.
farinacea*) has a much looser and less self-conscious habit. Attractive as a forage
plant for bees, it is also visited by butterflies and hummingbirds. It makes a
fine cut flower and holds its color as dried material. This low-maintenance
plant does not really need deadheading and holds up well in spite of hot,
humid weather. In its native habitat and in mild climates, mealy-cup sage is
truly perennial, but elsewhere it adapts well to treatment as an annual, sometimes self-seeding. The 'Victoria' series is widely grown. It comes in mid-blue
and a silvery white on eighteen-inch stems; try it with yellow snapdragons of
the same height. 'White Porcelain' is another reliable eighteen-inch-tall white.
'Blue Bedder' reaches two feet in height, while 'Mina', a brilliant blue-purple,
grows one foot tall. All have attractive mealy or silvery foliage. New cultivars
of the Texas sage *S. coccinea,* a native of the southern United States, Mexico,
and Brazil, have recently been introduced. 'Lady in Red', an AAS winner,
grows one to two feet tall with a much looser habit and flowers of a more subtle red than scarlet sage. Perhaps not as eye-catching in a mass planting, this
one is better used as an accent or dot plant in bedding schemes; much easier
to integrate into a mixed flower border. 'Pink Glimmer', two to three feet tall,
and 'Cherry Blossom', twelve to fifteen inches tall, are both new, free-flowering cultivars with white and salmon flowers. *Salvia* 'Indigo Spires' is another
favorite in many botanic gardens; at Blithewold Gardens, it blooms through
October with the tail end of perovskia and the full bloom of *S. pitcheri;* purchase as staked cuttings from specialty nurseries, and don't overlook them
because they seem unimpressive when young. South American *S. guaranitica*
is a three- to five-foot subshrub, now being grown as an annual in many parts
of the country. Its indigo blue flowers borne on bushy plants are regularly visited by hummingbirds. This again is not a plant to mass, but is a fine accent
plant or gives good effect planted in drifts in the flower bed. Its loose, airy
habit allows a view of shorter plants behind. Thrives in the high heat and
humidity of midwestern gardens; often overwinters satisfactorily. At
Brookside Gardens in Wheaton, Maryland, it is perennial and forms a solid
mass rather than an airy drift; it is, however, floppy and requires staking. *S.
viridis,* more often listed as *S. horminum,* is a true annual. This fast-growing
native of southern Europe is grown not for its rather insignificant flowers but
for the pairs of brightly colored bracts that subtend them, on the upper third
or so of each branch. The bracts may be pink, blue, or a greenish white, all
patterned with darker veins. The plants typically reach about eighteen inches.
'Tricolor' mix has a good blend of colors, and 'White Swan' is chalky white. A
shorter, better-branched strain named 'Claryssa' is available as a mixture or in
solid colors of blue, actually deep violet, pink, and white. This species does not
do well at Missouri Botanical Garden, becoming lanky in the humidity. All

Salvia leucantha.

Salvia officinalis 'Purpurea'.

Salvia splendens 'Carbinierre Blue'.

Salvia coccinea 'Lady in Red'.

Salvia farinaceae 'Porcelain'.

Salvia uliginosa.

SALVIA FARINACEA 'VICTORIA' (MEALY-CUP SAGE) Eighteen-inch-tall dwarf plant with rich green, lance-shaped leaves. Tiny deep violet-blue flowers are borne on tall slender stems. Blooms midsummer to frost. Plant in full sun in well-drained moist soil.

SALVIA PATENS (GENTIAN SAGE) Three-foot open loose plant with large, deeply veined deep green foliage. Blue flowers in pairs. Bloom in mid to late summer. Plant in full sun or partial shade in well-drained soil.

SALVIA OFFICINALIS 'BICOLOR' (GARDEN SAGE) Two-foot-tall upright spreading plant with rough-textured gray-purple-green leaves. Violet-blue flowers appear on spikes late in summer. Plant in full sun or partial shade in well-drained soil.

SANVITALIA PROCUMBENS 'MANDARIN ORANGE' (CREEPING ZINNIA) Twelve- to sixteen-inch-tall spreading plant with small medium green leaves. Orange daisylike one-inch-wide semidouble flowers with dark purple disk flowers. Blooms early summer to frost. Plant in full sun and loose, well-drained soil. Tolerant of drought and humidity.

salvias are excellent as cut flowers, both fresh and dried, and combine well with perennials and other annuals in the flower bed. Self-seeds freely. Many salvias do well in dry climates; Mary Irish of the Desert Botanical Garden recommends *S. horminum,* and *S. coccinea,* as well as *S. clevelandii, S. ballotaefolia, S. pitcheri, S. leucantha, S. greggii,* and *S. microphylla.*

Seedlings of annual and biennial salvias are readily available as transplants in the nursery trade. They are seeded indoors about ten weeks before the last frost and set out when all danger of frost has past. For later bloom, seed directly when the soil warms up. Set out young plants into average well-drained soil in a sunny or partly shaded place. Where the sun is intense, a little shade is desirable to avoid fading. Pinch young plants to encourage bushiness. Provide plenty of water during hot, dry spells. The shrubby sages are started from cuttings of new growth from plants overwintered with protection. Keep the rooted cuttings pinched and plant out after frost. Many salvias are susceptible to whitefly; be sure to check new plants carefully before you plant them out.

SANVITALIA PROCUMBENS CREEPING ZINNIA *Asteraceae (Daisy)*
Sanvitalia is a wonderful low-growing annual from Mexico that thrives on the summer heat and humidity typical of some parts of the United States; it has been singled out for praise by experts in Northeast, mid-Atlantic, Southwest, Midwest, and Great Plains gardens. It is easy to grow and dependable, excellent as a uniform edging plant, alongside hot sidewalks, in hanging baskets or containers, as well as in the rock garden. For early color sow sanvitalia indoors, but direct, outdoor seeding after the soil has warmed up gives much better results. Transplants are seldom satisfactory, which may explain why it is not grown more in home gardens. With soil temperatures about 70-85° F., germination takes only three to seven days; for best results, do not cover the seeds. Thin to five to six inches apart. A spot in full sun where the soil is light and even sandy is ideal; avoid wet, poorly drained or rich soils. The best-known cultivars are orange-flowered 'Mandarin Orange', which starts early and lasts long, and 'Gold Braid', which has clear pale yellow flowers, both with brownish purple centers. 'Double Sprite Yellow' is especially well suited to hanging baskets.

SCABIOSA ATROPURPUREA PINCUSHION *Dipsacaceae*
Pincushion, sweet scabious, or mourning bride all refer to the same old-fashioned plant so dear to cottage gardeners and flower arrangers. This charming plant is native to southern Europe but is just as welcome in American home gardens. Sweet scabious is indispensable in the cutting garden, but also earns its place in the rock garden, in the flower border, and especially in cottage gardens, where it attracts countless butterflies. Seed indoors in small pots or in a cold frame five to six weeks before the last frost at about 55-60° F. and harden off thoroughly before planting out eight to twelve inches apart. Nursery-grown transplants are available, but care must be taken to avoid

But in midautumn there comes a day to return to the study window and the partial vision of a garden and of gardening that it affords. . . Finally pineapple sage (*Salvia rutilans*) is in bloom. I cannot smell the sweet and fruity perfume of its leaves, but I can see in late afternoons the uncanny incandescence of its slender scarlet torches of flowers, aglow with the sun behind them. I also enjoy another salvia nearby, *S. involucrata* 'Bethellii'. Its deep rose flowers are pleasant enough, but its leaves own my heart, for they are a pale green, velvety even from this distance with some trick, like stained glass, that makes them so glow from within that one could imagine that they would look the same on a dead planet no longer lit by its cold star.
ALLEN LACY, *THE GARDENER'S EYE,* 1992

breaking the strong taproot. Otherwise, sweet scabious can be seeded directly in early spring and thinned. Germination may take up to four weeks. In the South and for indoor bloom in winter and spring resow in late summer. The plants begin to bloom about three months from seed and continue to flower until frost; deadhead routinely to prolong the display. The flowers range in color from deep purple and violet to pale blues, pinks, and white. Mixed seed strains include three-foot-tall 'Giant Double' and eighteen-inch-tall 'Dwarf Double' mixes. Julie Morris of Blithewold Gardens uses the 'Dwarf Double' mix variety in the cutting garden; the stems were long enough for cutting, and, with deadheading, the plant stayed attractive without staking while taller varieties flopped over and became unruly. Scabiosas adapt well to soils of average fertility but seem to prefer it on the sweet side; a light dressing of lime at planting time is recommended. Select a sunny position and water routinely throughout the season. Brush stake with twiggy sticks and keep well weeded. Red spider mites can be serious during hot, dry weather; a virus disease, aster yellows, sometimes becomes a problem.

SCAVEOLA X 'BLUE WONDER' FAN FLOWER *Goodeniaceae*

This hybrid has become an overnight sensation in eastern gardens, although 'Mauve Clusters' is known in California. In frost-free climates, they are perennial, but elsewhere must be treated as tender annuals. The fleshy plants are excellent for large hanging baskets, where the stems will hang down three feet or more below the container. In the garden, they make colorful, matlike covers–an unusual plant for massed bedding. In bloom from late spring until the frost, the plants are covered with bright blue fan-shaped flowers, one inch or so across. Scaveola is usually started from cuttings taken from stock plants in early spring. These root readily at 70-75° F. Grow on at 65-70° F.; pinch to promote bushiness. Keep the plants well watered to avoid a check in growth. When the soil has warmed up outside they can be planted fifteen to eighteen inches apart, into very well-drained, fertile soil. They grow rapidly to form a dense mat and bloom profusely throughout the season. Water routinely during dry spells. Before frost, lift one or two plants and cut back to induce young growth for cuttings the following year.

SCHIZANTHUS PINNATUS BUTTERFLY FLOWER *Solanaceae*

Butterfly flower, or poor man's orchid, is a tender annual from Chile, grown mainly as a cool-season container crop in greenhouses. In areas with moderate summer temperatures, they may be satisfactory as outdoor bedding plants, and even where it remains cool, other annuals are superior for summer color. In spite of this, butterfly flowers have a charm and beauty of their own. They are long-lasting as cut flowers and make elegant, even exotic pot plants for sun rooms and conservatories, and out of doors. Start seed early in the year for bloom in containers by late spring. Press the tiny seed into the soil surface and germinate at 60-65° F. in total darkness. Germination takes about ten to twenty days. For planting outside, sow eight weeks before the last frost date;

SCABIOSA ATROPURPUREA (PINCUSHION) One- to three-foot-tall plant with oblong soft green basal leaves. Pink, lavender, purple, maroon, red, yellow, or white mumlike flowers borne on tall stems from early summer to frost. Plant in full sun and fertile, well-drained soil.

SCAVEOLA X 'BLUE WONDER' (FAN FLOWER) Plant will hang over container or form a matlike groundcover. Blue fan-shaped flowers, one inch across, from late spring to frost. Full sun, very well-drained fertile soil.

SCHIZANTHUS PINNATUS (BUTTERFLY FLOWER) Three- to four-foot-tall pyramid-shaped plant with light green, finely dissected foliage. Small, delicate flowers in lavender, rose, and brown. Cool-weather annual blooms in spring and fall. Plant in full sun to light shade; rich, moist, organic soil.

SENECIO CINERARIA 'CIRRUS' (DUSTY MILLER) Six- to eight-inch-tall rounded plant grown for its compact round silvery leaves. Flowers yellow or cream and borne above foliage (usually removed). Grow in full sun. Performs well in poor, dry soils.

SENECIO CINERARIA 'SILVER LACE' (DUSTY MILLER) Six- to eight-inch rounded plant grown for its lacy, delicate silver leaves. Flowers yellow or cream and borne above foliage (usually removed). Grow in full sun. Performs well in poor, dry soils.

SETCREASEA PALLIDA 'PURPLE HEART' (PURPLE-HEART) Eight- to ten-inch tall plant with dark purple jointed foliage, will hang over sides of containers. Small pink flowers in early summer to fall. Moist, well-drained soil, full sun.

SILENE OCULATA 'ROYAL ELECTRA' (CATCHFLY, ROSE-OF HEAVEN) Fifteen-inch-tall plant with sticky green leaves. One-inch, upward-facing cup-shaped flowers in red, pink, purple, blue, or white. Full sun, well-drained soil.

SOLANUM JASMINIODES (POTATO VINE) Shrubby climber, growing about eight feet per season. Bright green leaves, small white flowers with yellow centers. Fragrant. Needs sun, with some protection, and well-drained, fertile soil.

for the cutting garden, delay outdoor sowing until hard frost has passed. Supplement winter light if dull overcast weather is prolonged. For winter flower in frost-free regions, broadcast seed directly in early fall. Butterfly flower only blooms for about four weeks, so make successive sowings to extend the season. Plant outside in a lightly shaded position about twelve inches apart; pinch for bushier plants. The stems are very brittle and tall plants must be staked; avoid windy sites. Grow butterfly flower in rich, well-drained soil, amended with organic matter. Mulch out-of-doors. Avoid watering plants in large containers or raised beds; the soil must not become waterlogged. Several mixed strains are available, probably correctly called *S.* x *wisetonensis, S. pinnatus* x *S. retusus* 'Grahamii'. 'Star Parade' forms compact eight-inch plants with pink, blue, and lavender flowers; 'Hit Parade' is a more vigorous strain, one foot in height. An F2 hybrid, 'Disco' may be the best for growing outdoors; it grows twelve to fifteen inches tall.

SENECIO CINERARIA DUSTY MILLER *Asteraceae (Daisy family)*

The cut silvery leaves of dusty miller add impact to any summer color scheme. This foliage perennial from the Mediterranean region is treated as an annual in most parts of the country, started either from cuttings or from seed. Sow seed or root cuttings from overwintered stock indoors early in the spring at about 65-70° F. Do not cover the seed, which will germinate in seven to twenty-one days. Nursery-grown transplants are readily available. Plant out of doors two to three weeks before the last frost is expected; dusty miller tolerates cool temperatures, but as the weather warms up growth will accelerate. A sunny or very lightly shaded position where the soil is light and well drained is best. It is best to remove the flower buds as they appear and to prune to shape periodically. Overly rich soils result in weak, rank growth, susceptible to fungal diseases; poor drainage encourages root rot—entire beds can be damaged by this. Do not overwater; tolerant of drought conditions, but susceptible to leaf hoppers. Mike Ruggiero of The New York Botanical Garden finds that dusty miller will sometimes overwinter in well-drained soils.

Dusty miller is indispensable in the flower border as a formal edging plant, grouped as a foil for brighter colored annuals and perennials, in the rock garden, and in containers. The felted silver leaves quiet down strident oranges and scarlet but enliven pinks, purples, and blues; the contrast with deep purples like 'Mini Marine' heliotrope is splendid. It works well in complex combinations; a sensational planting at New York's Rockefeller Center combined delphiniums, white begonias, and dusty miller. It is also useful as an edging in an herb garden. Galen Gates of the Chicago Botanic Garden likes to use dusty miller in the far reaches of the garden, particularly for people who can only view their landscape late in the evening; the silver foliage reflects the final, dim rays of the sun, and it is the last plant to be seen. Best-known of the cultivars is 'Silver Dust', which has deeply cut leaves on plants eight to twelve inches tall; 'Silver Queen' is similar. The foliage of 'Cirrus' has rounded lobes;

Silvery dusty miller cools down the intensity of this combination of basil, perilla, and celosia.

it is especially resistant to rain damage and frost. 'Diamond' grows about ten inches tall. The cultivar 'Silver Lace', which has dissected leaves, is often offered under dusty millers. It correctly belongs with *Tanacetum {Chrysanthemum} ptarmiciflorum),* which does nothing to detract from its value.

SETCREASEA PALLIDA PURPLE-HEART *Commelinaceae*

A relative of the wandering Jew, purple-heart is usually grown for its long, narrow, deep burgundy leaves that combine well with silver or gray plants. It shows its best color if grown in full sun but will tolerate partial shade. It also produces small pale pink, white, or lilac flowers, usually at the end of the season and sometimes not at all. It is a fast-growing plant, with short, sometimes brittle stems and a trailing habit; it makes a lovely hanging basket. Although perennial in Zones 9 and 10, this plant is frost-tender and is usually grown as an annual. It is sometimes indoors for the winter, but it loses some color there. It roots very easily from cuttings taken at the end of the season, and does best in rich soil. Don't overwater it.

SILENE OCULATA CATCHFLY *Caryophyllaceae (Pink family)*

Although somewhat rare in this country, long-flowering catchflies are useful in beds, borders, and rock gardens; they are more frequently seen in British garden catalogs. *S. armeria* (none-so-pretty, sweet William catchfly) grows to about fifteen inches tall, with clusters of small pink flowers and green leaves that are covered with a sticky fluid that explains the plants common name. *S. oculata,* rose of heaven, is even grows to about a foot tall; the flowers come in many colors. Seeds are usually direct-sown. Choose a sunny spot with well-drained soil and space six to nine inches apart. Seeds sown in the fall will flower in early summer; those sown in early spring will provide midsummer flowers.

SOLANUM JASMINOIDES POTATO VINE *Solanaceae (Nightshade family)*

Potato vine, or jasmine nightshade, is a shrubby Brazilian climber, hardy here only in Zones 9 and 10, where it is semievergreen. Elsewhere it is treated as a tender or half hardy annual and young plants are started each year, usually from cuttings. These are taken in early spring from overwintered stock plants, lifted the previous fall before frost. Alternatively fall cuttings are rooted and overwintered in a sun room or conservatory and groomed for planting out the next season. Seed is sown around the turn of the year at 60-65° F. degrees; potato vine needs a long growing season. Plant out only when the soil has warmed, as you would its relatives, tomatoes and eggplants. Potato vine likes an open, sunny position but protection from intense midday sun. Soil must be well-drained and fertile; water routinely during dry weather and feed container plants to avoid checking growth. This interesting plant is excellent for containers, either spilling over the edges or trained up a framework of some sort. It also makes a fine clothing for trellises and arbors, especially those where the enticing fragrance of the flowers can be appreciated. Young plants will grow about eight feet or so tall and usually begin to bloom from midsummer on. Where they are hardy, vigorous plants may reach fifteen to twenty feet in a season; do not be afraid to prune as necessary. A variegated cultivar *S. j.* 'Variegata' with deep gold and bright green leaves is also available. Be alert for white fly attacks under glass.

STROBILANTHES DYERANUS PERSIAN SHIELD *Acanthaceae*

Persian shield has long been grown out of doors in frost-free zones and in greenhouses, but only recently has it become popular as a summer bedding plant and in containers. This Burmese native has striking eight-inch-long leaves, iridescent blue and lilac on top, purplish maroon beneath. Persian shield is usually started from cuttings taken in the fall or from plants lifted and overwintered under glass. Take cuttings from young growth from late January onwards; it is easy to build a large stock quickly. After rooting, grow the plants on under warm humid conditions, with a night temperature of at least 60-70° F. Protect the plants from intense sun to avoid leaf scorch. Use a rich, well-drained potting soil; to maintain rapid growth, do not allow the plants to dry out. Pinch at least twice before planting out to encourage bushinesses. Set out plants fifteen to eighteen inches apart only after all danger of frost has passed. Keep pruned if growth becomes straggly. This tropical plant thrives in the hot humid conditions found in many parts of the country during the summer.

Above: Setcreasea's jointed stems make a perfect plant for a hanging basket. Below left: Marigolds, tall and short, with pansies, zinnias, dusty miller, and fountain grass

Marigolds are bright and beautiful if, like cousins, you don't have too many of them at once.

Hardly any flower makes sense when bedded by the thousands, though that is the way you commonly see flowers used in parks. Nobody expects much imagination or thought in public plantings; the theory, as I understand it, is that if you're driving along at seventy miles an hour, it makes no great difference what the flowers are or how they are grouped.

But in home gardens, needless to say, there is no reason to mass flowers of the same kind endlessly–there is no reason to have solids beds or (here I commence to meddle) solid edgings of a single brassy flower. The mere fact that you get a lot of seeds in a packet doesn't mean you have to plant all of them. They keep quite nicely for next year. A handful of marigolds, stuck in here and there among violets or blue or yellow petunias can be festive, whereas a solid mass of marigolds, apart from being overwhelming, can be dull.

HENRY MITCHELL, FROM
THE ESSENTIAL EARTHMAN.

TAGETES MARIGOLD *Asteraceae (Daisy family)*

This hugely popular group of plants has been hybridized extensively to produce a range from three- to four-inch-tall plants with one-and-one-half- to two-inch flowers to three-foot-tall plants with mophead flowers five or six inches across. The major parents in this hybridization program have been *T. patula,* commonly known as the French marigold, and *T. erecta,* known as the African marigold. *T. tenuifolia,* the signet marigold, and *T. lucida,* sweet marigold, have also contributed. The modern triploid marigolds result from a direct cross between the French and African types. In spite of their common names, all these species are native to Mexico and Central America; some are calling the *T. erecta* types American marigolds. All are very easy to grow and are readily available in a bewilderingly wide assortment. Colors range from the much-heralded white marigold, such as 'French Vanilla' and 'Snowdrift', in fact creamy white, through lemon and brassy yellows, oranges, scarlet, and burgundy to maroon and brown, often bicolored. The foliage of most has a pungent odor, but some are more pleasantly fragrant; 'Lemon Gem', for example, has a strong, refreshing citrus scent. They are often planted around vegetable gardens to repel insects; herbalists used them to repel moths in clothes closets. Sow seed indoors at 65-70° F. five to six weeks (six to eight weeks for the triploid types) before the last frost or wait and seed direct when the soil has warmed; cover with one-quarter inch of soil. Germination is rapid, usually four to five days. The seeds are large enough for children to handle easily. This, combined with their speed of germination and bright flowers over a long season, makes them a favorite for children's gardens. Don't try to rush the season with marigolds. They should not be planted out until two to three weeks after the last frost at the earliest. Garden centers tend to put out young plants already in flower far too early to attract customers, but once planted in the home garden there will be little root growth until the soil warms. Few tolerate frost. Thin or transplant six to fifteen inches apart according to variety. Low-growing sorts suitable as edging plants, such as the signet and single dwarf French 'Disco' series, can be planted four to six inches apart. The tall African types, excellent as cut flowers, such as the 'Climax' series, should be no closer than fifteen or even eighteen inches apart to do their best. Site marigolds where they will get sun for most of the day. High summer heat may cause stalling of flowers, so in regions of intense summer heat, some afternoon shade is preferable. One of the best African types is 'Primrose Lady', recommended by The New York Botanical Garden for its pale primrose yellow flowers on twelve- to sixteen-inch stems. The triploid types continue to bloom in spite of the hottest weather. Average, well-drained soil is fine; overly rich soil promotes lush vegetative growth at the expense of flowers. Drought tolerant. Deadhead to prolong blooming and for neatness. Red spider mites can become serious; be alert for slugs and beetles. The virus disease aster yellows sometimes attacks marigolds; remove affected plants at once. Some of the best-known varieties include the dwarf French semidouble 'Queen Sophia' and 'Aurora' series, both available in solid or mixed colors. 'Spice Saffron'

STROBILANTHES DYERANUS (PERSIAN SHIELD) Eight-inch-long leaves, iridescent blue and lilac on top, purplish maroon beneath. Full sun or partial shade; rich, well-drained, moist soil. Thrives in humidity.

TAGETES ERECTA 'EXCEL PRIMROSE' (AFRICAN MARIGOLD) Erect plant to three feet tall with ferny, toothed fragrant leaves. Blooms from early summer to frost. Plant in full sun and average well-drained soil.

TAGETES PATULA 'FRENCH VANILLA' (FRENCH MARIGOLD) One-and-one-half- to three-foot-tall plant with ferny, deep green foliage, creamy white flowers. Blooms early summer to frost. Plant in full sun. Tolerant of dry soil.

TAGETES PATULA 'QUEEN SOPHIA' (FRENCH MARIGOLD) Fourteen-inch rounded plants with ferny, deep green leaves. Red flowers edged with bronze. Blooms early summer to frost. Plant in full sun. Tolerant of dry soil.

Above: A monochromatic scheme, with yellow marigolds and tobacco flower. *Right:* 'Voyager' marigolds and 'Red Flame' salvia. *Far right:* Red fountain grass and orange marigolds.

flowers until November in one of the dryest and hottest locations at The New York Botanical Garden. The signet types, such as the eight-inch-tall lemon, gold, and orange 'Gem' series and lemon yellow 'Lulu' (a Blithewold favorite), all have one-half- to one-inch flowers; these have almost feathery foliage, attractive even when not in bloom, and are great for edgings and rock gardens. Space the triploids, such as the twelve-inch-tall 'Nugget' series, about ten inches apart; their two-inch flowers in solid yellow, gold, orange, and red are fully double. In the Chicago Botanic Garden, this series is used in raised beds in the Sensory Garden, where the fragrant flowers are readily appreciated and the bright flower colors are seen by the visually impaired. Also fully double, the 'Inca' series has two- to three-inch flowers on fourteen- to sixteen-inch stems in orange and yellow; the yellow, gold, and orange 'Jubilee' series grow two feet or more tall and are best spaced fifteen to eighteen inches apart. At thirty-six inches tall the 'Climax' series and 'Cracker Jack' mixture may have flowers four inches or more across. Indeed, there are marigolds for gardens of all sizes. *T. lucida* is a fine addition to the dry-climate gardens. It blooms late in October and continues until frost. *T. lemonii* is another marigold for dry climates.

TALINUM PANICULATUM JEWELS OF OPAR *Portulacaceae*

Also known as the panicled fame flower, jewels of opar is native to the West Indies and South America. In some southern parts of the United States it has become naturalized and overwinters by means of tuberous roots. This curious plant is seldom grown outside of botanical institutions, but could find a place in many a home garden if better known. It should be grown for its attractive leaves rather than for its ten-inch-long airy panicles of tiny pink flowers on wiry stems. The variegated-leaved form is especially attractive for container

TALINUM (JEWELS OF OPAR, FAME FLOWER) Two-foot-tall plant with attractive elliptical or oval three-inch-long leaves and ten-inch long flowers in panicles. Needs full sun and dryish soil.

THUNBERGIA ALATA (CLOCK VINE) Three- to six-foot climbing vine with arrowhead-shaped medium green leaves. Cream to white to yellow to orange flowers with dark centers. Blooms in summer. Plant in partial shade to full sun in moist soil. Flowers best in cooler weather.

TITHONIA ROTUNDIFOLIA (MEXICAN SUNFLOWER) Four- to six-foot coarse-textured plant with large lobed leaves. Flower heads about three inches across. Orange-scarlet ray flowers and orange-yellow disk flowers. Blooms in summer. Plant in full sun. Tolerant of extreme heat and dry soil.

TORENIA FOURNIERI (WISHBONE FLOWER) Twelve-inch rounded plant with heart-shaped leaves on long petioles. Violetlike flowers of pale purple, yellow, and dark purple. Blooms summer to frost. Flowers have tiny wishbone-shaped stamens inside. Plant in shade or semishade and moist soil.

plantings; the flowers and stems with berries are wonderful in fresh and dried arrangements. Try underplanting with annual dianthus for a double display, or use it in front of white shrub roses for a see-through effect. A solid foliage background of artemisias or cannas might also be effective. Self-sown plants emerge late in spring or early summer; start seed indoors early in the season. Plant out about nine inches apart in well-drained, dryish soil in full sun. They are tolerant of drought conditions but not of wet feet. Lean soils are preferable to rich ones. Self-seeding and low maintenance.

THUNBERGIA ALATA CLOCK VINE *Acanthaceae (Acanthus family)*

Many of us may associate clock vine or black-eyed Susan vine with pleasant memories on Grandma's porch. Not as popular as it once was, this tropical African perennial can, if given support, lend a welcome vertical note to hanging baskets, mixed containers, and arbors, where it will climb five or six feet high. Take cuttings from overwintered plants or sow seed indoors six to eight weeks before the last frost. With a soil temperature of 70-75° F., germination takes two to three weeks. The seedlings grow slowly, but do not hurry to plant outside. It is wise to wait until the soil has warmed up and the night temperatures remain above 50° F. After hardening off, set out transplants six inches or so apart and about three inches from a support. Strings, twiggy brush, trelliswork, or even chain-link fences will be covered quickly after the plants become established. A moist soil, high in organic matter, is ideal. Select a position that is sunny during the morning but is protected from the noon-day and afternoon heat. In cool climates, afternoon shade may not be necessary–they do well in Chicago in full sun. Clock vine does not bloom well during high summer heat and humidity, but will make up for lost time once the heat abates and keep going strong until October. The best-known strain is 'Susie', sold mixed or as 'Susie White with Eye' or 'Susie Orange with Eye'. White-flowered *T. fragrans* 'Angel Wings' is sometimes offered.

TITHONIA ROTUNDIFOLIA MEXICAN SUNFLOWER *Asteraceae*

Mexican sunflower is one of the most striking annuals for strong summer color. Its brilliant orange-red daisy flowers may reach three inches across, borne on stems up to six or even eight feet tall. This is not a plant for the faint-hearted! Attractive to insects, butterflies, and hummingbirds (it is used in the butterfly garden at Brookside Gardens every year), Mexican sunflower is excellent as a summer screen or hedge, grouped at the back of sunny borders associating with sunflowers and rudbeckias or grouped among large shrubs. In cold climates sow seed indoors in small containers six to eight weeks before the last frost; stronger plants result from direct sowing after frost and when the night temperature remains above 50° F. Cover the seed lightly; germination may take up to three weeks. Nursery-grown transplants are offered, but growth checks of any sort may result in an unsightly dropping of the lower leaves. Plant out two to three feet apart into average, very well-

TRACHYMENE CAERULEA (BLUE LACE FLOWER) Eighteen- to thirty-six-inch-tall, open plant with finely dissected delicate foliage. Soft blue four-inch flowers. Blooms early to mid summer. Plant in full sun and well-drained organic soil.

TROPAEOLUM MAJUS (NASTURTIUM) One- to two-foot bushy plants or six- to eight-foot climbing vines with round lime-green leaves with slight whitish bloom. Scented flowers in orange, yellow, red, white, scarlet, or bicolored. Blooms summer to frost. Plant in full sun in poor soil.

VERBENA PERUVIANA (VERVAIN) Twelve- to twenty-four-inch creeping plant (roots at nodes) with deep green, finely toothed leaves. Flowers in bright red clusters. Plant in full sun in well-drained sandy soil.

VERBENA X HYBRIDA 'IMAGINATION' (VERVAIN) Eighteen-inch-tall trailing plant with dissected dark green leaves. Bright purple flowers in small heads. Blooms early summer to frost. Plant in full sun, well-drained soil. Heat can deter flowering; water heavily during hot spells.

drained soil; overly rich soil produces enormous plants with abundant foliage and rather weak stems, and overly wet soil is deadly to them. Mexican sunflowers take heat and humidity with ease and even tolerate drought. In windy sites, stake if necessary. If used as a cut flower, sear the stems and condition in warm water. Very susceptible to whitefly, especially when grown in containers. Scarlet orange 'Torch' and chrome yellow 'Yellow Torch' are popular; only three-foot-tall 'Goldfinger' and 'Sundance' are better suited to smaller gardens.

TORENIA FOURNIERI BLUEWINGS, WISHBONE FLOWER
Scrophulariaceae (Figwort family)

One of the few annuals adapted to shady gardens, wishbone flower deserves a wider audience. This tender annual from Vietnam makes a fine edging plant and is also attractive in shaded rock gardens, in containers, or in less-than-sunny beds, perhaps as a companion for hostas, ferns, or impatiens. For winter color in sun rooms and conservatories, they bloom freely through the winter in containers. Wishbone flower is slow growing at first, so seed indoors about ten weeks before the last frost date; in warm climates direct seeding out of doors is satisfactory. Torenia performs well through the beginning of the season even in humid climates, but tends to turn scraggly as the heat and humidity increase. The fine seeds are best covered only lightly; keep the soil temperature at 70-75° F. for germination in fifteen to twenty days. Nursery-grown transplants are readily available. When the soil has warmed up outside, plant about six to eight inches apart into well-drained, fertile soil amended with plenty of organic matter. Keep well watered. Be alert for slugs. Deadheading is not really necessary since the seedheads are quite attractive and the plants will rebloom by themselves. However, to avoid self-seeding, keep the spent blooms removed. For winter bloom, lift plants and pot them well before cold weather to allow time for them to become acclimated. The typical species has light blue and violet flowers on twelve-inch plants, but compact strains six to eight inches tall are available. Recently developed eight-inch-tall 'Clown Mix' has rose, white, blue, and violet flowers. 'Clown Rose' and 'Clown Violet' are also offered.

TRACHYMENE CAERULEA BLUE LACE FLOWER *Apiaceae*

Blue lace flower is an Australian wildflower, grown here as a tender annual. Formerly listed as *Didiscus caeruleus*, the flowers resemble a pale lavender blue Queen Anne's lace and are especially grown for cutting. In the mixed border they create an airy effect and assort well with summer-blooming bulbs and perennials. For early bloom, sow seeds indoors six to eight weeks ahead of the last frost date. Be sure to cover the weeds adequately since darkness enhances germination, which takes up to three weeks at about 70° F. To avoid disturbance of the strong taproots, sow seed in peat pots or prick off into individual pots early. Outdoor sowings made after the frost will

As much as we might like it to be spring, we must be careful not to sow seeds prematurely. Seeds planted too soon will produce oversized transplants–large, but so stunted by their small pots that they will fail to make good growth when planted in the garden.
ROGER SWAIN, *THE PRACTICAL GARDENER,* 1989

Many annual flowers are edible; nasturtium for example, has a peppery taste that adds tang–as well as its bright color–to salads. A word of caution, though: some flowers are poisonous or upsetting to the digestive system. Nigella, the blue flower in the picture on the right, was considered edible but is now questionable. Never eat any flower, or any part of any plant, unless you are absolutely sure it's safe.

result in an early fall crop. Plant out or thin blue lace flower to nine to twelve inches apart; close spacing encourages more flowers. Select a site in full sun where the soil is well drained. Deadhead to prolong flowering; stake if necessary or site where the plants will be supported by stronger neighbors.

TROPAEOLUM MAJUS NASTURTIUM, INDIAN CRESS *Tropaeolaceae*
What would the Grand Allee at Giverny be without the sprawling nasturtiums on the path? These showy, old-fashioned tender annuals have been grown by generations of gardeners in flower gardens, herb gardens, and cottage gardens. Several different types are available; some, such as 'Jewel Mix', remain bushy and about one foot tall, while others, such as the well-known 'Gleam' varieties, sprawl or climb by twining leaf stems. Both single and double flowers, mostly fragrant, in a full range of cream, yellows, and oranges to scarlet and crimson are on the market. The leaves of 'Alaska' appear to be splashed with white paint; 'Moonlight' has pale yellow flowers and is great mixed with salmon nasturtiums. The large seeds are best started outside two weeks or so after the last frost, sown six inches apart and one inch deep. In cold climates or for earlier bloom, sow indoors in peat pots several weeks before the last frost date. Germination takes eight to ten days. Plant out or thin to one foot apart; avoid injuring the brittle taproot when transplanting. Average to poor soil in full sun or with afternoon shade is best; overly rich soil results in an abundance of foliage at the expense of flowers. Drought tolerant,

but not at their best in humid climates except in the cool early spring; they are outstanding winter- and spring-blooming annuals at the Desert Botanical Garden. Excellent in hanging baskets and especially welcome in children's gardens. Black aphids and mealybugs are often a problem; avoid toxic sprays if the leaves, seeds, or flowers are to be consumed.

TROPAEOLUM PEREGRINUM CANARY VINE *Tropaeolaceae*
This beautiful, dainty vine from Peru has been neglected by the gardening public, but deserves to be grown more often. It can be started indoors in the same way as its relative the garden nasturtium. For best results use peat pots and sow two to three per pot and thin to the strongest. Once set out, the plants grow rapidly and produce their yellow, birdlike blooms from late June until cut down by frost. Slender stakes, wires, or netting should be provided for the plants to climb upon, or plant them so that they can hoist themselves into and about a conveniently near shrub, preferably an evergreen which would contrast attractively with the flowers. Both foliage and flowers are seen to good effect scrambling over evergreens, such as hemlocks, yews, or junipers. In late summer root cuttings from the lateral shoots to overwinter indoors. These plants will be the source of new material for next spring, enabling an earlier start and longer flowering season.

VERBENA BONARIENSIS VERVAIN *Verbenaceae (Vervain family)*
In recent years *V. bonariensis* has become a well-known feature of public and private gardens alike. It is a perennial in its native South America, but here it persists as a self-seeding annual; indeed, it has become naturalized in mild

Verbena bonariensis with Polyantha roses.

parts of the country. In fact, it sometimes reseeds to the point of weediness, though it is easy to pull out by the handfuls. From midsummer through fall its clusters of deep lilac flowers are held aloft on stiff but slender three- to four-foot stems, which though gawky when young develop a rare architectural grace. If young seedlings are pinched back hard they will grow into well-branched plants. Long-lasting as a cut flower, *V. bonariensis* is useful as a tall see-through plant to vary the height in flower borders and is especially attractive intermingled with grasses and Queen Anne's lace in the wild garden. Sometimes it is underplanted with lower annuals, such as 'Blue Horizon' ageratum or 'Green Envy' zinnias, for a double effect, and to keep weeds down. It also combines well with *Salvia greggii*, 'Cherry Rocket' snapdragons, and 'Strawberry Fields' gomphrena. It is always the last plant to finish blooming at Blithewold Gardens. Raise from seed as for *V.* x *hybrida* or take cuttings from overwintered plants; when plants have four sets of leaves, pinch them so that they branch lower and become larger and more branched. Mildew often attacks the foliage late in the season, especially if the plants are stressed from drought.

VERBENA X HYBRIDA   HYBRID VERBENA *Verbenaceae*

This short-lived perennial group, sometimes listed as *V.* x *hortensis*, is derived from several species, notably *V. peruviana* and *V. platensis*. (They are now correctly known as *Glandularia* x *hybrida*.) As a long-blooming annual it is indispensable as a low-growing groundcover, edging, or border plant, in rock gardens and even as cut flowers, as well as trailing out of tubs, windowboxes, and other containers. In hot, humid climates the hybrid verbenas are difficult to keep going for the whole season. Frequently they are attacked by thrips, whiteflies, and mites and often brown out in the center or succumb to mildew. However, on a small scale they are well worth growing and in more suitable climates are regarded as one of the staple annuals. For the front of the border, select mounding types, such as the white-eyed 'Novalis' mix in blue, scarlet, pink, and white and the striking All America winner 'Peaches & Cream', which has pastel salmon-apricot flowers on strong eight-inch plants. Among the trailing sorts rose pink 'Sissinghurst', said to cover four square feet and to be less mildew-susceptible than other cultivars, is popular and long-lasting if deadheaded; 'Silver Ann' fades from bright to pale pink and has attractive silvery leaves. 'Imagination' has dissected foliage and brilliant purple flowers, which hold their color best in light shade. The 'Amour', 'Romance', and 'Showtime' series are all available in mixed or solid colors. Sow seed indoors at about 65-75° F. ten weeks before the last frost. Germination takes ten to twenty days or longer but tends to be spotty. The 'Novalis', 'Romance', and 'Showtime' series reputedly have an eighty percent germination rate. Take special care not to overwater. Prick out and lower the temperature before hardening off prior to planting outside. Direct seeding is seldom successful due to poor germination. Widely grown as nursery transplants. Pinch for bushiness and plant out into average, well-drained soil about one foot apart, as soon as it has warmed up. A position in full sun is best; provide afternoon shade in the South. In the New York area, they do not do very well in the heat and humidity, but thrive near the shore. Unusual or special cultivars should be lifted at the end of the season and overwintered to produce cuttings for the following year. Regular water only during very hot times is recommended; fertilize routinely for a continuous supply of flowers. Keep deadheaded to prolong flowering; be alert for pests and diseases. Our native rose vervain (*Verbena canadensis*) is found from Pennsylvania to Colorado and south to Florida, Texas, and Mexico. Pink, red, and white forms are available in the nursery trade. One of the best recent introductions is fragrant 'Homestead Purple', which thrives however hot and humid the summer (it's highly recommended by Susan Nolde at Maryland's Brookside Gardens, and used to great effect with perennial *Calamintha nepetoides* at Botanica in Wichita); 'Abbeville' is a lavender form. These make colorful, long-blooming groundcovers or container plants and are useful in the rock garden. Persistent in mild winters; mildew resistant. Its prostrate habit makes *V. peruviana* one of the best for baskets. This Brazilian native has become naturalized in the South. Treat as *V.* x *hybrida*.

VIOLA TRICOLOR JOHNNY-JUMP-UP, HEARTSEASE *Violaceae*

A favorite during Elizabethan times, these charming European natives still spell spring to many gardeners today. Small of stature with perky, fragrant flowers Johnny-jump-ups make wonderful additions to rock gardens and other informal settings as companions for crocuses, small daffodils, or squills. They also do well in baskets and other containers, perhaps with primroses and minor bulbs. They flower over a longer period than do pansies and are somewhat more tolerant of hot summer conditions. Often they will rebloom in the fall when nights are cooler. Self-seeds in some areas; at Missouri Botanical Garden, only 'Helen Mount' and tricolor hybrids self-seed. The best-known cultivar is 'Helen Mount', which has a catlike face in purple, lavender, and yellow with black whiskers. 'Prince John' and 'Yellow Charm' are all yellow. 'King Henry' has especially fragrant violet and yellow flowers; in the trade it is being replaced by 'Baby Lucia'. Others include 'Cutie', 'Pretty', and the 'Princess' series in blue, cream, and bicolored. Culture is as for pansies.

VIOLA X WITTROCKIANA PANSY *Violaceae (Violet family)*

This large group, sometimes listed as *V. hortensis,* is derived primarily from *V. tricolor* and *V. lutea*. It sports flowers in all colors in solids and bicolors, the latter often with "masks" or "faces." This is a cool-season plant treated as an annual, or biennial in short-season climates. Start seeds indoors in January or early February; for optimum germination chill the seed overnight at 35-40° F. Germination only takes about ten days, with a soil temperature of 65-70° F. As soon as the seedlings are large enough, prick off individually and reduce the temperature to 50-55° F.; pansies do not like to be overheated and will develop into soft, leggy plants if grown too warm. Harden off thoroughly before planting out six to nine inches apart, after heavy frost. Nursery-grown

Poppies, pansies and parsley are combined in this bed; laying out the plants in curves rather than in straight rows adds to its effect.

VERBENA CANADENSIS 'CHERRY' (ROSE VERVAIN) Twelve- to eighteen-inch erect or sprawling stems with hairy lobed leaves. Clusters of salmon-pink flowers. Plant in full sun, well-drained soil.

VIOLA TRICOLOR (JOHNNY-JUMP-UP) Twelve-inch clump with small heart-shaped leaves with scalloped edges. Irregularly shaped flowers, one-half-inch wide, with deep purple, light blue, and yellow faces. Blooms in spring through fall. Plant in cool, partial shade in well-drained organic soil.

VIOLA TRICOLOR 'PRETTY' (JOHNNY-JUMP-UP) Four- to eight-inch clump with small heart-shaped leaves. Irregularly shaped tricolor flowers in white, yellow, and dark purple. Blooms spring to fall. Plant in cool, partial shade in well-drained organic soil.

VIOLA X WITTROCKIANA 'MELODY BEACONSFIELD' (PANSY) Six- to eight-inch clump with rich green heart-shaped foliage. Irregularly shaped flowers with sweet fragrance. Blooms in spring. Plant in cool area, partial shade, in well-drained organic soil.

There are good reasons that some annuals, like pansies, are so common: they are easy to grow, available in a vast range of shapes, sizes, and colors, and absolutely beautiful.

transplants are widely available. Rich, fertile soil in a partly shaded position is ideal. The young plants will not be harmed by light frosts and do best when transplanted while it is still cool. In cold climates plants from late summer or early fall seedings are generally transplanted into a cold frame or are protected with a straw or salt hay covering through the winter. This is not necessary in mild-winter climates; some of the newer cultivars are more cold hardy. Because of their maturity, overwintered plants often bloom more prolifically. Plants will start blooming about two-and-one-half months from spring seeding; most will peter out, especially in sunny positions, as the day temperatures approach 90° F. Keep deadheaded to prolong the display. Pansies are popular as underplantings for spring bulbs like tulips and hyacinths, as edging plants along shaded borders, in front of foundation plantings and shrubs, and in rock gardens and containers. Be alert for slugs and snails. Several cultivars are well adapted to flowering as winter pot plants indoors. Among the most popular are the F1 hybrid 'Majestic' or 'Majestic Giant' series in a full range of colors with blotches; these reach about seven inches tall with four-inch flowers. The 'Universal' mix is also an F1 hybrid strain bred for tolerance to both cold and hot weather. A so-called multiflora type, its flowers are two to three inches across, but it blooms more freely. Separate colors, such as 'Beaconsfield', which is deep blue and violet, and 'Deep Yellow', are available. The 'Maxim' series in separate colored or mixed is similar but even more floriferous; its uniform plants tolerate heat well. The 'Joker' cultivars are F2 hybrids; All American winner 'Jolly Joker' is a striking purple and orange bicolor, 'Joker Light Blue' is tricolored light and dark blue, with a white halo and yellow eye.

ZINNIA ANGUSTIFOLIA MEXICAN ZINNIA *Asteraceae (Daisy family)*

Mexican zinnia, sometimes listed as *Z. linearis*, is among the best low-maintenance annuals, especially in hot, humid climates. Its tolerance of difficult weather conditions, together with its lack of mildew and self-cleaning habit over a very long blooming period, rates it at the top of the list for many public gardens. 'Classic' has the typical single, eye-opening orange flowers about one and-one-half to two inches across; it looks great with 'Buddy' gomphrena. Newer sorts, such as 'Starbright Mix', in gold, yellow, and white, are more compact, about ten to fourteen inches tall but just as long blooming; 'White Star' in the same series is quite a good white but needs companion plants to show off at its best. In the garden Mexican zinnias are top rate for slightly informal mass bedding purposes, in rock gardens, and as edging or border plants. They are excellent as pressed flowers. Similar *Z. haageana* [*Z. mexicana*], also known as Mexican zinnia, may be listed by nurseries as semi-dwarf varieties. These include double-flowered 'Old Mexico', a mahogany and gold bicolor, and 'Chippendale', with single red flowers tipped with gold. Culture is as for common zinnias, though they are more sensitive to overwatering.

Zinnias provide a splash of color wherever it is needed in the garden; although full sun is best, they will flower in filtered shade as well.

VIOLA X WITTROCKIANA 'DELFT HYBRID' (PANSY) Six- to eight-inch clump with rich green heart-shaped foliage. Irregularly shaped white flowers with purple and yellow markings. Blooms in spring. Plant in cool, partial shade, in well-drained organic soil.

VIOLA X WITTROCKIANA 'MAXIM ROSE' (PANSY) Six- to eight-inch clump with rich green heart-shaped foliage. Irregularly shaped purple flowers, banded in white, with yellow centers. Blooms in spring. Plant in cool area, partial shade, in well-drained organic soil.

ZINNIA ANGUSTIFOLIA 'CLASSIC' (MEXICAN ZINNIA) Twelve- to eighteen-inch spreading to erect plant with straplike small leaves covered with hairs. Two-inch bright yellow flowers. Blooms midsummer to fall. Plant in full sun and dry soil.

ZINNIA ANGUSTIFOLIA 'WHITE STAR' (MEXICAN ZINNIA) Twelve- to eighteen-inch spreading to erect plant with straplike small leaves covered with hairs. Small flowerheads with white ray flowers with yellow centers. Blooms midsummer to fall. Plant in full sun and dry soil.

ZINNIA ELEGANS 'DREAMLAND IVORY' (ZINNIA) Two- to three-foot-tall erect to rounded plant with clasping medium green leaves. Creamy white ray flowers with disk flowers absent. Blooms early summer to frost. Plant in full sun and very dry soil.

ZINNIA ELEGANS 'CHERRY SUN' (ZINNIA) Two- to three-foot-tall erect to rounded plant with clasping medium green leaves. Cherry red ray flowers with disk flowers absent. Blooms early summer to frost. Plant in full sun and very dry soil.

ZINNIA 'SUNRISE RED' (ZINNIA) Two- to three-foot-tall, erect to rounded plant with clasping medium green leaves. Bright red ray flowers with disk flowers absent. Blooms early summer to frost. Plant in full sun and very dry soil.

ZINNIA 'FLAME PRINCE' (ZINNIA) Two-foot-tall, erect to rounded plant with clasping medium green leaves. Bright orange ray flowers with disk flowers absent. Blooms early summer to frost. Plant in full sun and very dry soil.

ZINNIA ELEGANS COMMON ZINNIA *Asteraceae (Daisy family)*

Modern garden varieties of the common zinnia abound. They range in height from a few inches up to three feet or so; flower size also varies from about two inches to as large as six inches across, singles and doubles, in all colors except blue. Zinnias are extremely popular as cut flowers, grouped in flower borders with other annuals or perennials, in rock gardens, as edging plants, and in containers—in fact, anywhere in the garden that needs a splashy burst of color. Nursery-grown transplants are readily available, but for those who prefer to start their own they are not difficult. Where the season is long, direct seeding as soon as the soil has begun to dry out and warm up is successful. In colder climates start seed indoors, barely covered, about two months prior to the last expected frost date. Germination takes five to ten days with a soil temperature of 65-70° F. Prick off and grow on at about 50° F. until planting time. Except when large flowers are required for show or cut flowers, pinch young plants to encourage bushiness. For best results plant out four to twelve inches apart according to variety into rich well-drained soil in an open position in full sun. Zinnias do not tolerate waterlogged soil but must be kept well watered during dry times. A summer mulch helps to cut down on soil evaporation, but may harbor mildew spores which splash and reinfect the plants when it rains. Stagnant air and wet foliage also encourage the spread of mildew, which may become severe. Leaf blight can be a nuisance, causing loss of the lower leaves. In hot, humid climates a midsummer replacement sowing may be useful in cutting gardens. Site taller sorts behind lower-growing plants; staking may be necessary. Select varieties according to their purpose. For cut flowers the 'Zenith' series comes in pinks, reds, orange, yellows, and white in a mix or solid colors; its five- to six-inch flowers top thirty-inch plants. The two-foot-tall 'Cut and Come Again' series has two-inch flowers in a full range of colors on two-foot plants, perhaps better for garden display. 'Border Beauty' is another good series. Chartreuse-flowered 'Envy' is a novelty sought after by flower arrangers. The foot-tall 'Pinwheel' series is important for its resistance to mildew; 'Rose Pinwheel' is the best of the series in the Missouri area, while the other colors do not stay true. It has single three-inch flowers in separate colors of rose, salmon, cherry, white, and orange or as a mix. Dwarf types, such as the six- to ten-inch 'Thumbelina' mix and the slightly taller 'Peter Pan' series, both come in a full range of mixed colors or separately.

Some zinnia varieties grow as low as impatiens, and can provide bright accents in groundcovers; others grow up to three feet tall.

Abutilon hybridum.

Acalypha hispida.

Baileya multiradiata.

OTHER ANNUALS

Although we have described several hundred annuals in the preceding chapter, we did not come close to covering every plant useful in annual gardening. Many tropical plants, edible plants, and plants normally used as houseplants can be used to great effect in annual beds and baskets. The following pages cover just a few more of the vast number of annuals available.

Abronia umbellata (sand verbena) Trailing, low-growing plant with verbenalike flowers, usually white, pink, or yellow. They need sunshine, cool temperatures, and light, sandy soil. Since they need a long growing season, they are best started indoors in a cold frame.

Abutilon hybridum (flowering maple) Graceful drooping branches with bell-shaped flowers in many colors and maplelike foliage; grows to three feet long. Moist, fertile soil, sun or light shade.

Acalypha hispida (chenille plant) Two-foot tall shrubby plant with bizarre racemes of furry pink or red flowers. Needs very rich soil, full sun.

Actinotus helianthi (flannelflower) Two-foot-tall plant has daisylike flowers with white petals and yellow centers. It does best in full sun and dry soil, and is somewhat difficult to grow; it is usually direct-seeded in furrows soon after the last frost.

Adonis (pheasant's eye) Bright red buttercuplike flowers, feathery foliage. Best in cool weather, light but rich soil.

Aeonium These rosette-forming succulent plants are perennial in Zones 9-10, but can be grown as annuals in cooler climates; some cultivars have very deep brown, almost black leaves that contrast well with other plants. They need full sun.

Agrostemma (corn cockle) Two- to three-inch lilac pink flowers on willowy stems. Full sun, any soil.

Anagallis arvensis (scarlet pimpernell) Prostrate plant to eighteen inches long, with one-quarter-inch-wide white or scarlet flowers. Prefers warm weather, full sun, and average soil. Blooms in summer.

Anchusa capensis (Cape forget-me-not, bugloss) Clusters of small blue flowers on wiry stems. Prefers cool weather, light shade, dry soil; deadheading after the first blooms will aid in repeat bloom.

Baileya multiradiata Gray-green foliage and yellow ray flowers; extremely drought- and heat tolerant. Do not overwater. A favorite at the Desert Botanical Garden in Phoenix. Perennial in Zones 7-10.

Beta vulgaris (Swiss chard) Besides its nutritive value, Swiss chard is a great addition to the annual garden, with handsome reddish leaves. Some cultivars have bright red veins. Grows best in full sun and rich soil. Will withstand frost.

Borago (Borage) Fuzzy gray foliage; star-shaped light blue flowers. Needs moist, rich soil, full sun.

Bupleurum rotundifolium Like a euphorbia in flower, but with leaves like a eucalyptus. Good for cutting.

Calandrina grandiflora (rock purslane) Shrubby plant with long, needlelike leaves and red or purple flowers. It needs lots of sun and dry soil, and tolerates extreme heat.

Calceolaria (pocketbook plant) Two- to five-foot-tall plant with small, oddly-shaped flowers, usually yellow. Needs full sun, rich soil.

Campanula (bellflower) Several forms of this popular plant are used as annuals, particularly *C. medium*, Canterbury bells, which is a biennial grown as a hardy annual. It grows to four feet tall, with violet bell-shaped flowers. Does best in average to moist soil and full sun to partial shade.

Cardiospernum halicacabum (balloon vine) Vine with almost-black balloon-shaped seedpods and white flowers; climbs up to ten feet. Needs full sun; very drought tolerant.

Cheiranthus cheiri (English wallflower) Spikes of one-inch-wide blossoms in many bright colors on plant that grows up to eighteen inches. They require neutral pH soil, sun, and moisture. They prefer cool weather. This plant is very popular in England but does not thrive in many areas of North America except for the Pacific Northwest.

Chlorphytum comosum (spider plant) This common houseplant which has cascading variegated foliage should be grown outdoors more often. It grows well in full sun or partial shade and any soil.

Cirscium japonicum (plumed thistle) Sometimes weedy, a biennial treated as an annual. Two- to three-foot tall plant with deeply lobed very dark green foliage and round thistlelike flowerhead, usually red. Does well in full sun or light shade, and light well-drained soil.

Cladanthus Gold, daisylike flower, with yellow center, about two inches across, with lacy foliage on plant two to three feet tall. Needs sun, any well-drained soil.

Clianthus formosus (desert pea, Sturt pea) Spreading plant to four feet across with unusual red flowers, to three inches long with shiny black blotch at base. Drought- and heat-tolerant. Summer annual.

Coix lacryma jobi (Job's tear) Annual grass, two to six feet tall, grown for its beadlike hard-shelled seeds that are usually black and can be used to make jewelry. Does best in full sun and average soil.

Cynara cardunculus (cardoon) Massive palmlike green leaves and interesting purple thistle flower in late summer and early fall. Needs full sun, very rich soil. It needs a long season, and is usually started indoors in very early spring.

Cyperus papyrus (papyrus) Usually grown indoors, papyrus has delicate leaves that work well with many annuals. It needs partial shade outdoors and a lot of moisture; it is often grown near water or in bogs. *C. alternifolia* (umbrella plant) should also be considered.

*Dimorphotheca (Cape marigold) Three- to four-inch daisylike flowers in very bright colors, usually with dark centers. Need lots of sun and well-drained soil. Thrive in hot, dry areas.

Dorotheanthus bellidiformis (Livingstone daisy) Tender winter annual with large

Borago.

Chlorphytum comosum.

Coix lacryma jobi.

Cynara cardunculus.

Echium lycopisis.

Lysimachia.

showy brightly-colored flowers with dark centers. Tolerates drought, heat, and poor soil, but does not survive cold.

Dracaena These common, shade-loving houseplants are great foliage accents. Some species, like *D. marginata* have narrow, sword-shaped leaves; others, like *D. deremensis* have broader leaves, often with attractive variegations.

Echium lycopsis (viper's bugloss) Rough, gray-green leaves on plant to three feet tall. Bell-shaped flowers in pastel shades of blue, pink, lavender. Needs dry, sunny location, poor soil; rich soil will produce much foliage but fewer flowers.

Emilia javonica (tassel flower) Wiry stems, two to three feet tall with tiny but brilliantly-colored flowers in orange and red. Needs full sun, dry to average soil.

Exacum affine (Persian violet) Often grown indoors as pot plants, Persian violets do well in moist, well-drained soil and full sun.

Felicia bergeriana (kingfisher daisy) One- to two-inch-wide daisylike plants with light blue petals and yellow centers. Needs full sun; tolerates drought.

Foeniculum vulgare (fennel) The feathery foliage of this plant lasts until frost; a bronze variety is also useful. It grows three to five feet tall and needs full sun.

Fuschia Many varieties of fuschia are available. Most are best in hanging baskets in sunny locations and they can be overwintered indoors.

Gypsophila (baby's breath) Many-branched plant, up to three feet tall with clouds of tiny flowers. Full sun, poor soil is best.

Humulus lupulus (hops) Fast-growing vine grows up to twenty-five feet per season, with bright green, deeply lobed leaves. Needs very rich soil for fastest growth, full sun.

Iberis (candytuft) Low-growing subshrub with clusters of white flowers. Needs full sun, cool weather, rich soil.

Iresine (bloodleaf) Brilliant burgundy foliage, striped in lighter red, can grow to six-foot shrub. Needs lots of light and water.

Layia (tidytips) Bright yellow daisylike flower, feathery foliage. Needs full sun and well-drained, moist soil.

Lagenaria (ornamental gourds) Growing on vines up to thirty feet long, these thick-shelled, interestingly-shaped gourds can be used as containers or in dried arrangements. They grow well on trellises in full sun, but are appropriate only for large gardens, as they tend to be invasive.

Lagurus ovatus (bunny tail grass) Grows to about fifteen inches tall, with two-inch heads of downy hairs.

Limnanthes douglasii (meadow foam) Low-growing white flowers with bright yellow centers do best in full sun and moist soil.

Lupinus Mostly annuals with purple or purple and white pealike flowers in whorls on erect racemes. *L. densiflorus aureus* has bright yellow flowers.

Lycoris radiata Slender dark green leaves, with a pale midstripe are produced in winter, but spidery red flowers are borne in umbels atop one- to two-foot stalks in fall.

Lysimachia Trailing plant with bright green leaves and small yellow flowers. Does best in full sun and average soil; it flags during the heat of midsummer but perks up again as the days cool off.

Mina lobata (love vine, dancing ladies) Twining vine with dark green fleur-de-lis-shaped leaves and sprays of tubular blossoms in graduated cream to red.

Myosotis (forget-me-not) Tiny blue flowers (pink and white varieties also available) on twelve- to eighteen-inch plant. Sun or shade, any soil, best in cool places. Reseeds prolifically.

Nicandra (shoo-fly plant) Three-foot-tall plant, somewhat coarse in appearance, but with interesting papery lanternlike seed cases.

Oenothera deltoides (sundrops) Yellow, cup-shaped flowers (white variety also available). Full sun or light shade, any well-drained soil.

Ophiopogon japonica (mondo grass) This grass is so dark it appears almost black; grows twelve to eighteen inches tall. Although it is perennial in Zones 7 and above, it is usually grown as an annual; full sun or part shade.

Ophiopogon japonica.

Origanum (oregano) There are many ornamental species of oregano; all need full sun and average soil. Some are grown for their foliage, others for their showy bracts.

Phacelia Winter annuals, usually blue or purple, sometimes white or pink flowers densely arranged on coiled fiddleheadlike inflorescences. Extremely drought and heat tolerant.

Reseda (mignonette) One- to two-foot tall plant with thick stems and spikes covered with green or yellow flowers. Fertile soil, partial shade, cool weather are best. Mignonette can be planted in spring and again in late summer to prolong bloom.

Phacelia.

Romneya coulteri (Matilija poppy) Tall plant, growing to six feet or more, with crepe-textured white flowers with a yellow ball of stamens in late spring or early summer. Zones 6-10.

Tibouchina urvilleana (glory bush, princess flower) This lanky subtropical shrub looks better when combined with plants that have profuse foliage, but its large purple flowers are stunning. It needs full sun and average soil, and is hardy only in Zones 7 and above.

Trachelium caeruleum (throatwort) Round, cloudlike clusters of tiny violet or blue star-shaped flowers on plant two to three feet tall. Full sun or partial shade, any soil.

Tulbaghia violacea has garlic-scented evergreen tufts of grassy foliage and clusters of lavender flowers much of the year.

Zauschneria californica (syn. *Epilobium canum;* California fuschia) Spreading, shrubby evergreen, perennial in Zones 9 and 10, with gray foliage and bright red tubular flowers.

Zea mays (ornamental corn) Tall stalks with multi-colored ears—sometimes deep red and navy blue—can provide strong vertical accents to the garden. Plant at least two kinds for pollination. Start indoors and plant out after all danger of frost is passed. Ornamental corn needs full sun and rich soil.

Trachelium caeruleum.

It is an established fact of horticulture that gardens bloom perfectly only in the imagination. This is especially true of annuals, whose brilliant colors and striking forms attract pollinators and gardeners alike but make designing with annuals an aesthetic challenge. Before leafing through a single catalogue, setting out a single start, or consigning a single seed to earth, consider your needs and desires: What is it that you want from your annuals—all-season color? fragrance? an abundance of cut flowers? Where do you plan to put them—in a formal bed? a mixed border? containers? among the vegetables? A little forethought and footwork can make the difference between an annual garden that delights the eye and a jumble of mismatched plants.

FUNCTION Versatile annuals can fulfill any number of functions in the garden; it's likely, in fact, that you'll be using them for more than one purpose. You may want to mass them, in a bed or border, for knock-your-socks-off drama. Or perhaps you'd like to plant them discreetly among shrubs and perennials to add spots of season-long color. Maybe your eye is to the harvest, and you plan to grow annuals for cutting or drying. Or, like many gardeners, you might want to add them to the vegetable garden, to attract bees and other beneficial insects. Annuals make wonderful short-term stand-ins: vining annuals like morning glory and cup and saucer vine can clothe a trellis or wall in a single season while you wait for slower-growing perennials like clematis and climbing hydrangea to fill in, and larger plants, including bishop's weed, helianthus, and cleome, make effective "instant" hedges; in a newly dug perennial garden, annuals can disguise bare patches, and seduce the eye away from first-season stragglers. They also serve a number of "secondary" functions: Many—like nicotiana and stock—are highly fragrant, while

In this border at The New York Botanical Garden, tall (castor bean, canna, fountaingrass), short (zinnias and marigolds), and medium-height (gomphrena, *Nicotiana sylvestris*) plants create a sweeping effect that draws the vertically as well as horizontally.

others–including the aptly named moonflower–are especially beautiful at night, and still others–tithonia, for instance–attract butterflies and humming-birds.

GARDEN TYPES Once you've decided *how* you want to use your annuals, you can begin to consider *where*. Annuals are most likely to be grown in one of three basic garden types: bed, border, and cutting garden. A bed is a free-standing garden, often surrounded by grass, whereas a border, as its name suggests, is a plot that runs along the margins of something else–a hedge, lawn, wall, walk, or building, for example. A cutting garden, strictly speaking, can be a bed or a border, but since its purpose is essentially plunder, it is often sited in a less conspicuous area of the landscape. If your main goal in growing annuals is to reap armloads of freshly cut flowers, you'll probably want a cutting garden. This doesn't mean that you have to forgo aesthetics altogether, just that they'll take a back seat to more practical considerations like abundance of bloom and easy accessibility for cutting.

If, however, you prefer to admire your flowers where they grow, you'll want to consider either a bed or a border (or perhaps one or more of both). As a rule, borders have a less artful look, as though nature, and not the garden-er's hand, had swept the plants into a harmonious drift. (Nothing, of course, could be farther from the truth, but more about that later.) Beds, on the other hand, are usually more formal; where borders are often serpentine or free-flowing, beds tend to be stylized or geometric: squares, rectangles, circles, semicircles, horseshoes, and so on. The size and shape of a border are more or less dictated by whatever it abuts, whereas the configurations of a bed are determined largely by the gardener's imagination. Nevertheless, a bed's shape

This less formal bed at Longwood Gardens uses foliage plants (fountain grass and alternanthera), accented by bright red celosia; a vertical accent is supplied by cannas in the background.

should reflect the surrounding landscape in some way, perhaps following the contour of the land or echoing the shape of a nearby element in the garden.

As a rule, borders offer the greatest diversity: They can include a wide variety of plants, from trees and shrubs to annual and perennial flowers. And because they often lie along buildings and other structures, they can go strikingly vertical with the use of twining and climbing vines. Beds, however, have an inherent drama; their essential purpose is to inject into the landscape a sense of the unexpected–a horseshoe of deep purple pansies and white alyssum set amid a green expanse of lawn, for example. Perhaps the most dramatic style of bed was the Victorian carpet bed, in which annuals were tightly interplanted to mimic works of art, family crests, and the intricate designs of Persian carpets. Luckily for those of us with more imagination than time, these beds–garish and contrived to many a modern eye–have long since fallen out of fashion.

GARDEN STYLES Though fashion continues to exert its influence, the most important factors to consider when choosing a garden style are your own personal aesthetic, the prevailing style of the house, and the overall condition of the landscape. A formal garden–usually consisting of a number of stylized beds (known as parterres) laid out in perfect symmetry and demarcated by walkways–would be appropriate for a more classic residence–a Federal-style urban townhouse, for instance. A cottage garden, on the other hand, in which

The garden below is used mainly for cutting, which does not detract from its loveliness.

In the garden above, over a dozen different plants (fuschias, snapdragons, marigolds, petunias, to name but a few) of differing heights, colors, and shapes are combined; it achieves an effect of lushness and abandon. In the garden at the left, at the Bronx's Wave Hill Garden, a more sophisticated, and no less sensational effect is achieved using a bed of golden coleus, two kinds of salvia (*S. farinacea* and *S. splendens*) and huge artichoke foliage under a morning glory vine.

a loose profusion of different plants blooms together in surprising harmony, is best suited to a smaller, less formal house–perhaps a California bungalow. Garden style is often dictated by the lay of the land. If your house is bordered by a sunny, rocky slope, a rock garden would probably be the most likely choice. If, on the other hand, you live in a heavily forested area, you might consider a woodland garden, where flowers, shrubs, and trees will be planted to achieve a deliberately natural look. Don't feel, however, that you're bound to some preordained landscape style; gardening is, in the end, a highly personal endeavor and, like any craft, is most successful when tradition and imagination converge.

PLANNING ON PAPER The best way to begin a garden from scratch, or even to revamp an established one, is to plan it out on paper. Scale is important: for larger gardens, or an entire yard, letting one-eighth inch equal a foot is useful;

Above: 'White Star' zinnias and 'Nicki Bright' nicotiana. Top: 'Nicki Pink' nicotiana with 'Celebrity Blue' petunias. Top right: An almost monochromatic yellow garden, using 'Yellow Rocket' snapdragons, 'California Girl' petunias and bright yellow marigolds.

for smaller gardens or individual beds, one-quarter inch to a foot may be more practical. Begin by marking in permanent structures like buildings, patios and decks, paths and driveways, pools, ponds, walls, and so on. Then pencil in semipermanent structures such as fences, arches, trellises, and benches, along with any existing shrubs, trees, beds, borders, and the like. When planning a new garden or making major renovations, consider your overall needs: Will you want paths that lead from one area of the garden to another? Are open spaces, for sports or play, important? What about quiet corners for rest and meditation? Will you want to dine among the flowers, or do your entertaining closer to the house? And unless you're in a very isolated area, you'll probably have to consider your neighbors as well: Do you need to screen out an unappealing view? Is privacy a priority? Taking all these factors into consideration, you can now begin to sketch in new trees, shrubs, and the beds and borders that will be home to most of your annuals.

Traditional mixed borders (comprising shrubs, flowering and foliage perennials, and sometimes trees) are usually at least twelve feet wide, but borders using only annuals can be considerably narrower–and must be, if garden space is limited. If you are planning a spacious border or bed, you'll need to incorporate room for routine maintenance–a path, for instance, or a series of

Top far left: Lime green coleus, bright pink zinnias, and white Yucca fila-mentosa. *Center:* Alternanthera and 'Big Daddy' petunia. *Above:* A mostly orange scheme of celosia, dahlia, and lantana on a standard.

stepping stones. Edging is another consideration. If you want a natural edge (say, between a border and a lawn), you can simply use an edger to dig deep into the turf (you'll probably have to re-edge several times during the season, as the grass makes its inevitable march into the border). For a more sculptural look, both borders and beds can be edged in brick, stone, wood, tile, masonry (if the bed is raised), even gravel—as long as the edging is harmonious with the rest of the garden.

PRINCIPLES OF DESIGN Once you've settled on the backbones, you can begin to consider the heart and soul of your annual garden—its flowers. The joy of gardening with annuals is that they lend themselves to experimentation, allowing you to start anew every spring in a way that would be impossible with trees, shrubs, and costly perennials. Annuals virtually beg the gardener to be daring, to try fanciful combinations of color and form. Some of the most impressive annual gardens feature unlikely but striking combinations, or unexpected plantings—a bed of lavender petunias and deep burgundy alternanthera, for example, or a drift of spider plants among the flowers. No matter how unorthodox, however, all successful gardens reflect certain basic principles of garden design.

Color Nature intended annuals to dazzle the eye, and so they do, primarily

Top: 'Newland' celosia picks up and highlights the red in 'Color Pride' coleus. *Above: Hibiscus sabdariffa* 'Coppertone' with dusty miller. *Right: Salvia farinacea, Salvia splendens,* sweet alyssum, petunias, and fountain grass at Kingwood Center in Ohio.

through the use of color. This makes color an essential element (perhaps *the* essential element) in annual garden design. Most of us respond viscerally to color; we get that "have to have it" feeling when we spot an intensely red canna, or a deep purple salvia, or a riot of orange and yellow nasturtiums. We tend to prefer specific color "temperatures"–either cool tones in the blue, green, and violet family or hot ones like reds, oranges, and yellows. By all means, follow your preferences, but don't be slavish; hot combinations can be

cooled down slightly by intermixing blues and grays, while cool hues like lavender, blue, and pink can be enlivened with a burst of fuchsia or hot pink. Many people who know nothing at all about the science of color manage to create striking color schemes in the garden simply by following instinct and personal preference. Alas, just as many are disappointed by colors that clash or fade into the background.

A rudimentary knowledge of color systems can help avert this kind of disappointment. There are four essential color schemes in garden design: monochromatic, polychromatic, complementary, and analogous. Monochromatic schemes use flowers of one basic color, though usually in a variety of tints and shades–an all-pink border, say, composed of geranium, candytuft, cosmos, snapdragon, and cleome, or a small but dramatic red-only bed of poppy, celosia, nasturtium, and geranium. The polychromatic garden, on the other hand, is a riotous profusion of colors, both complementary and contrasting. Even polychromatic gardens, however, reflect certain basic principles of color theory, separating colors that clash with other, more congenial hues or a gentle drift of white. (White, in fact, is quite useful as a color buffer, but make sure you use it in sufficient mass or it can look spotty.) Complementary schemes use colors that stand opposite one another on the color wheel: red and green, yellow and violet, or orange and blue. As in art, complementary-colored gardens tend to be highly dramatic, relying on contrast for their effect–imagine a planting of blue lobelia with orange calendula, for instance,

Above: Hibiscus acetosella with orange marigolds. *Top:* low-growing *Hakonechola* 'Aureola', *Pennisetum setaceum* 'Rubrum', *Impatients glandulifera. Top left: Cuphea ignea* and cannas.

Above: Cuphea ignea, coleus, nicotiana. *Far left:* Tansy, snapdragons, clary sage, and vinca. *Center:* A border of impatiens and petunias. *Above:* Annuals mixed with coniferous shrubs.

or an undulating river of red salvia against a deep green lawn. Where complementary schemes tend to grip the viewer by the throat, analogous schemes–using colors that abut one another on the wheel–rely on the horticultural equivalent of a stroke and a nudge to achieve their effect; subtler in their appeal, they tend to be easier to work with. If you're fond of the purples, for instance, you might choose annuals in shades of blue, blue-violet, purple, and pink–say, blue campanula, blue-violet lobelia, purple alyssum and stock, and pink dianthus, nicotiana, and annual phlox. For a touch of drama, you could then inject a single complementary note–a yellow nasturtium, for instance.

If you have more than one bed or border, of course, you can have a variety of color schemes throughout the garden. Whatever your scheme, keep in mind that colors are most dramatic when massed–that is, planted in groups of three or more, or in large drifts as they occur in the wild. And when considering color, don't forget foliage, which offers not just a vast array of greens from forest to chartreuse, but gray, silver, and purple as well. Annuals prized for their foliage–including coleus, dusty miller, and summer cypress–can be as striking as any flowering plant, and they make highly effective buffers between other, less congenial hues.

Size, shape, and texture Unless you'll be planting a single-variety bed or edging, consider a mix of sizes, shapes, and textures. Annuals come in a wonderful array of shapes and textures, from flat-headed daisies to trumpet-shaped datura to columnar delphinium; their overall effect can be lacy, feathery, or nebulous and ethereal; they can be round and flat as dinner plates or globular as marbles. They may rise in spikes like snapdragon, grow into fat mounds like impatiens and marigold, or hug the ground like sweet alyssum and lobelia. Both leaves and blossoms can be crinkly, velvety, or smooth as stretched rubber. Don't hesitate to make neighbors of plants with contrasting shapes and textures, but do try to tie them together in some way. You might, for example, group plants with very different shapes but in similar hues.

As a general rule, plants should be grouped according to size: In a border, site plants in descending order of size from back to front; in a freestanding bed, the tallest plants should be in the center. Don't be dogmatic about this, however; you can achieve a more natural look by planting just slightly on the bias, or by designing overlapping drifts of various sizes.

COMBINATIONS Annuals are wonderful mixers; as in nature, they blend harmoniously with trees, shrubs, perennials, even grasses and succulents. If it's drama you're after, don't be bound by the predictable. There's nothing wrong with a bed of marigolds, say, backed by yews and fronting a neatly clipped lawn, but why not take advantage of annuals' inherent diversity? For a tropical look, you could mix towering cannas with sculptural succulents like New Zealand flax and fountain grass. In a woodland garden, try a spectacular stand of green-and-white-striped zebra grass softened by white summer forget-me-nots. If space allows, take a cue from Monet's Giverny and interplant an allee of rambling roses, rows of brilliant perennials, and a rainbow of creeping nasturtiums to line the path below. And if you don't have room for a separate vegetable garden, imagine moonflowers lacing through the runner beans and sunflowers nodding over the eggplants. Annuals allow you—even encourage you—to experiment and, yes, make mistakes. Indeed, like many creative gardeners, you may find yourself most pleased, not with your well-planned successes, but with the felicitous errors that are at the very heart of annual gardening.

Dahlia with Glory Bush (*Tibouchina urvilleana*).

Key:
A: 'Cherry Red' zinnia
B: 'White Star' zinnia
C: 'Excel Primrose' marigold
D: 'Blue Horizon' ageratum
E: 'Polo Orchid' Petunia
F: *Miscanthus sinensis*

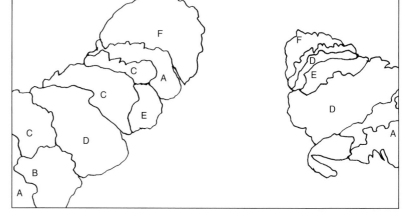

The path to this garden seat is paved with annuals; their colors repeat in patterns and all are kept to a low height. This arrangement includes low-growing 'White Star' and 'Cherry Red' zinnias, purple ageratum and petunias, yellow marigold. Anchoring the border are large clumps of ornamental grass. Later in the season, taller cannas will take over as the other plants begin to fade.

Key
A: Ageratum
B: Dusty miller
C: Red wax begonias
D: White wax begonias

With careful planning, you can draw pictures with your annuals. This flag design is a classic, often used in municipal plantings. It includes ageratum as the blue background, dusty miller as the white stars, and red and white wax begonias as the stripes. When choosing annuals for such designs, avoid those that reseed, producing colors and shapes where you don't want them.

The life of an annual is splashy, colorful, kinetic–and short. Because true annuals live out their life span in a single growing season, they often demand more in the way of time and attention than many of the longer-lived perennials. Watering, fertilizing, weeding, pinching back, and particularly deadheading–all take on a special significance when applied to the May-to-October romance that is annual gardening for most Americans. Of course, some annuals require less care than others; the ubiquitous impatiens, for example, often thrives under the most appalling neglect (which no doubt helps to explain its ever-increasing popularity)–but even impatiens require decent soil preparation and regular moisture. To get the most from your annuals–in terms of color, vigor, and extended bloom–you'll need an understanding of the basic techniques outlined in this chapter. Don't imagine, though, that maintaining an annual garden requires backbreaking labor: proper spacing will obviate the need for constant transplanting or pruning; mulching keeps watering and weeding to a minimum; and careful soil preparation will eliminate any number of tedious tasks.

CHOOSING A SITE With a few exceptions, annuals require a sunny location and fertile, moisture-retentive, well-drained soil. To find the most welcoming site, observe the landscape over the course of a sunny day; any area that receives at least five or six to eight hours of full sun offers the kind of exposure that most annuals prefer. Lightly filtered sun will work almost as well, but dense shade is hospitable only to a handful of annual plants. Because annuals like an ample supply of water and nutrients, it's best to site them well away from trees, like maples, with fibrous, spreading root systems.

Another element to consider when choosing a site is microclimate. A microclimate occurs when some alteration to the general landscape–a building, large tree, or change in the terrain, for example–exerts sufficient effect on a small space to render its climate different from that of the surrounding area. Plants at the bottom of a slope, for instance, often suffer frost damage earlier than those at the top, and the soil in front of a south-facing wall–especially one that's been painted white–tends to warm up faster, allowing earlier sowing of seeds and a longer growing season. It's worthwhile to observe the landscape carefully over a year's time for possible microclimates, noting which plants are earliest to bloom, which suffer the greatest damage from frost, where they are most likely to be buffeted by wind (especially if you live near the shore), which areas dry out most quickly, and so on. Growing annuals in a site can help identify these subtleties, which can help you plan for permanent plantings.

SOIL After sun, the most important consideration in the annual garden is soil. There are essentially three types of soil: clay, sand, and loam. Clay is generally rich in nutrients and organic matter but is so dense and heavy that roots have a hard time absorbing water–and anything else–from it. If the soil in your garden tends to be sticky when wet, it is probably clayey. Sand, on the other hand, drains well, but isn't capable of retaining much in the way of nutrients or water. Sandy soil is easy to recognize; it's grainy and won't hold together in your hand even when saturated. The most desirable soil for the vast majority of annuals is loam, a mixture of sand, silt, and clay. Add in a generous amount of the decayed organic matter known as humus (most easily available as compost from your own compost pile) and you have the perfect growing medium for annuals (and most other plants as well). Loam is easy to work and friable (that is, it crumbles readily in the hand); unlike sand, it has the capacity to retain water, and unlike clay, it is very well drained.

An easy way to determine how well your soil drains is to dig a hole about the same size and shape as a one-gallon pot, then fill the hole with water. If the soil drains in two to four hours, it is almost certainly loamy. Clay soil drains significantly more slowly, and sand in under two hours.

One way to correct poor drainage is to add sand to the soil, but make sure you mix in generous amounts of organic matter as well; sand and clay alone will yield cement—a less than hospitable environment for plants and the microorganisms they depend on to keep the soil fertile. However, this method is not as simple as it sounds; you will need to incorporate a great deal of sand before you begin to improve soil structure. Preferably, use raised beds; they not only promote drainage, but allow you almost complete control over the quality of the soil. A plastic drainage pipe, leading to a stone- or gravel-filled dry well, can also solve drainage problems; dig a trench about a foot deep and wide, install the pipe (available at hardware stores and some garden centers), cover it with a layer of geo-textile fabric or landscape fabric, then with gravel, then replace the dug-out soil. Drain tile can be installed in a similar fashion. More extensive drainage problems may necessitate the services of a professional landscaper, who can discuss with you the pros and cons of tile and gravel beds and more elaborate drainage ditches.

The best way to determine the all-around quality of the soil, especially when digging a new garden, is to have it professionally tested by a county extension service or agricultural university. The testing service will give you specific instructions for taking soil samples, but generally it's a good idea to remove small amounts of soil from five or six sites in the yard; dig down about six inches until you've got two cups of soil. Lab reports should include the percentage of nitrogen, phosphorus, potassium, and trace minerals present, as well as the soil's pH (the measure of its acidity or alkalinity). Most annuals like their soil slightly acidic to neutral. Should you need to alter pH, a reputable lab can suggest appropriate additions to the soil. Generally, if soil is too acidic, it can be corrected with lime or fast-acting calcium sprays or pellets; alkaline soils can be improved with elemental sulfur. Talk to the experts at your local nursery, botanic garden, or county extension service; they can probably give you information on the soil in your area and the best ways to fix it.

There are a number of ways to improve nutrient-poor soil. For a quick fix, you can add fertilizers, either chemical or organic, that supply the missing nutrients. But throwing down fertilizer willy-nilly is neither good for the environment nor particularly helpful to the soil in the long run. The best way to build up soil is to add generous amounts of well-composted organic matter, to

To determine whether your drainage is adequate, dig a hole large enough to hold a gallon pot. Fill the hole with water, and see how long it takes to drain.

COMPOST

In forests and prairies, swamps and backyards, an amazing process is continuously taking place. Plant parts and animal leavings rot or decompose with the help of fungi, bacteria, and other microorganisms. Earthworms and an assortment of insects do their part digesting and mixing the plant and animal matter together. The result is a marvelous, rich, and crumbly layer of organic matter we call compost.

BENEFITS OF COMPOST Compost encourages the growth of earthworms and other beneficial organisms whose activities help plants grow strong and healthy. It provides nutrients and improves the soil. Wet clay soils drain better and sandy soils hold more moisture if amended with compost.

HOW TO MAKE COMPOST A compost pile keeps organic matter handy for garden use and, as an added advantage, keeps the material from filling up overburdened landfills. To make your own compost, start with a layer of chopped leaves, grass clippings, and kitchen waste like banana peels, eggshells, old lettuce leaves, apple cores, coffee grounds, and whatever else is available. Keep adding materials until you have a six-inch layer, then cover it with a three- to six-inch layer of soil, manure, or finished compost.

Alternate six-inch layers of organic matter and two- to three-inch layers of soil or manure until the pile is about three feet tall. A pile that is three feet tall by three feet square will generate enough heat during decomposition to sterilize the compost. This makes it useful as potting soil, topdressing for lawns, or soil-improving additives.

COMPOST CARE Keep your compost pile in a semishaded area to keep it from drying out too much. But if your compost pile is near a tree, turn it frequently to make sure tree roots don't grow into it. Make an indentation in the top of the pile to hold water and sprinkle the pile with a garden hose when it looks dry. Keep the compost moist, but not wet. Beneficial organisms cannot survive in soggy conditions.

USING COMPOST When your compost is ready, it can be mixed into the soil before planting, or applied to the surface of the soil as a soil-enriching mulch.

QUICK COMPOST If you need compost in a hurry, speed up the process by turning the pile with a pitchfork once a week for a month. Mixing the compost allows oxygen into the center of the pile, where it encourages the growth of bacteria and fungi. A pile that is turned regularly will become finished compost in four to eight months.

MAKING A COMPOST BIN As illustrated below, many elaborate compost bins are sold. Some of these have devices for turning the compost and for removing it from the bin. Although these store-bought bins don't do the compost pile any harm, they are really not necessary. An enclosure made from chicken wire or from five wood pallets (one on the bottom, and four wired together for the sides) does the job just as well.

WHAT TO COMPOST
- kitchen waste
- lawn clippings (in thin layers so they do not mat down)
- chopped leaves (large leaves take a long time to break down)
- shredded branches
- garden plants
- shredded paper
- weeds (but be sure to use before they go to seed or weeds may sprout in the garden)
- straw or hay

WHAT NOT TO COMPOST
- orange and other citrus peels
- meat scraps, fatty trash (to avoid rodents and animals)
- excessive wood ashes

use organic mulches, and to garden wisely. That means retaining as much of the topsoil as possible when weeding or clearing the site, rotating crops so that no one plant will tip the balance of nutrients in the garden, sowing cover crops like clover, winter rye, and mustard that can be plowed under to become "green manure," and making sure that the plants you do grow are well matched to the soil type.

However, richly fertile soil is not right for all types of flowers; marigolds, for example, will produce abundant foliage and few flowers in overrich soil. Mary Irish of the Desert Botanical Garden in Phoenix advises against overfertilization of soil for annual beds in that area; in general, beds there are not turned more than a few inches. If they have been worked before, they are often only scrunched with a rake. Mulch and/or compost are added, seed put in or broadcast, then very lightly raked the other way to cover.

PREPARING THE BED If you're beginning an annual garden from scratch, the first order of business is to mark off its boundaries, preferably with string or garden hose (both of which can be easily moved about until you determine the garden's size and form). Clear the area of debris and vegetation; grass should be removed, roots and all, with a shovel, spade, or pitch fork, but make sure you knock off as much of the precious topsoil as possible before disposing of the grass (preferably in a compost pile). If you clear the site just after a rainfall (or a good soaking with a hose or sprinkler), your job will be infinitely less difficult. Remove weeds and other vegetation or grass and weeds will haunt you for years.

There are two ways of digging a bed: single or double after turf and other vegetation is removed. Double digging–a kind of super-aeration and -enrichment that entails lifting and loosening the soil to two spades' depth–is an arduous chore and unnecessary to the preparation of an annual garden (unless, of course, you plan to mix annuals and perennials). Single digging will work the soil to a depth adequate to the relatively short roots of most annuals.

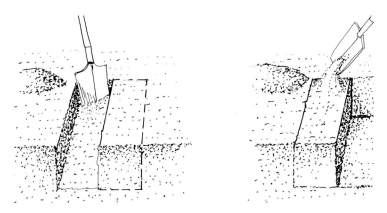

Double digging is a method of creating a loose, well-tilled bed; it requires digging two shovels deep, breaking up clods as you dig. Soil from the first digging is used to fill the adjacent rows.

Plants are not happy in the trunk of your car. Keep them there for as short a time as possible, and water them well and give them time to recover from the trip before planting them in a spot where they will be stressed.

Begin by loosening the soil to a depth of four to six inches; remove any tender vegetation still growing on the site and turn the soil, then wait at least two weeks and once again turn the soil under to a four- to six-inch depth. After this initial re-loosening, add compost (two inches spread over the entire bed, or eight to sixteen cubic feet per hundred square feet) and any other necessary soil amendments, then re-till to a depth of eight to twelve inches using a spade, fork, or rotary power tiller.

Galen Gates of the Chicago Botanic Garden recommends using glyphosate or Roundup to destroy weeds before planting a new bed. Although he does not usually promote chemical fertilizers, he feels that in this instance it is a safe, worthwhile practice.

When adding fertilizer to a newly dug annual bed, use one to two pounds of either 5-10-5 or 4-12-4 over each hundred square feet (or a ratio in line with your soil test results); one pound per hundred feet is sufficient for established gardens. The numbers on a fertilizer signify its percentages of the essential plant nutrients nitrogen, phosphorus, and potassium, of which phosphorus is, by far, the most important to the vast majority of annuals. If you're adding chemical fertilizers, do it close to planting time, since they break down fairly quickly. In some soils, phosphorus and potassium are naturally high, and a 10-0-0 fertilizer may be sufficient.

CHOOSING PLANTS

Transplants There are two basic ways to start an annual garden: from seed and with transplants. Though starting from seed has certain advantages (including economy, a greater degree of quality control, and wider selection), nothing is easier than setting out transplants from a nursery or garden center–provided, of course, that the plants have been well started and carefully nurtured. Look for young, healthy, pest- and disease-free plants, with turgid, evenly green, upright foliage; try to avoid anything leggy or root-bound no matter how desperately it calls out to you, since even the most fervent TLC can prove useless if initial neglect was severe enough. Roots should be white, sturdy, and relatively abundant but not matted. Great streams of roots flowing out of a pot's drainage holes are a sure sign that the plant has outgrown its pot; another tip-off is a yellowing of the leaves at the base of the plant (which can also signify over- or under-watering, but in any case it is a sign that the plant has been stressed). Another warning signal of problems to come is early bloom; it is not a sign of a healthy plant and can stunt its later growth. Look instead for good vegetative growth

Insect damage can provoke even greater troubles, since you run the risk of infesting the entire garden. Avoid plants with mottled, striped, or distorted leaves, and make sure that nothing swarms when you give the plant a good shake (whiteflies and aphids are the major insects to look for). You may be able to salvage a particularly desirable specimen by washing it in a strong stream of water, but keep it segregated from other plants until you're sure the pests haven't resurfaced (and try to wangle a discount from the supplier).

Seeds If you prefer a more hands-on approach, by all means start your annual garden from seeds. You'll save money, if not time, and your choice of annuals will be virtually unlimited–everything from heirloom varieties that have fallen out of favor to the very latest hybrids too new to appear on nursery pallets. And nothing is more comforting, in the dark of midwinter, than curling up with a great pile of seed catalogues and letting your imagination fast-forward to spring.

Catalogues, in fact, are your best source for anything but run-of-the-mill seeds, but order early–the more enticing the flower, the sooner inventories will be depleted–and don't be seduced by the hyperbole and glossy portraits (which, come the depths of February, are seductive indeed). For flowers that need to be started indoors, give yourself sufficient lead time, and when they arrive, check the packets for expiration dates (this goes for store-bought seeds as well).

PROPAGATION

Starting from seed The seeds of certain annuals, including sunflower, cosmos, zinnia, and nasturtium, can be sown directly in the garden as soon as the danger of frost has passed. (Indeed, some others–like morning glory, moonflower, and sweet pea–resent transplanting so much that you're best off letting them grow where they germinate.) Simply plant the seeds and thin seedlings according to the directions on the seed packet, making sure to keep the soil evenly moist until germination. (Water gently, though, to keep from washing seeds out of their beds.) It's best to plant seeds in a straight line, a practice that makes it easier to distinguish desirable seedlings from the generation of weeds that will inevitably spring up around them. Certain seeds can be broadcast over lightly raked soil in fall, preferably after the first frost to discourage early germination; try this with alyssum, bachelor's button, cleome, cosmos, portulaca, and nicotiana, among others, to get a head start on the following season. This is not a foolproof method, and you will find that results are uneven–nicotiana, for example, hardly ever comes up after winter in the Midwest–but you will also learn, after time, which plants can be grown successfully from broadcast seed.

Annuals with longer germination periods or growing seasons like begonias, geranium, impatiens, pansy, petunia, salvia, and vinca will need to be started indoors. Make sure they germinate early enough to be planted out after the last frost date in your area, but don't start them too soon or you risk growing a crop of leggy, weakened seedlings. It's best to start seeds in flats, in a sterile, soilless growing medium prepared specifically for germination (for example, equal portions of peat moss and sand, perlite, or vermiculite). All flats–shallow, topless boxes between two-and-one-half and four inches deep–should have drainage holes in the bottom, but otherwise the possibilities are endless. You can recycle plastic crates and aluminum foil roasting pans, or purchase any number of pre-designed flats, including those already filled with a growing medium and seeds. If you choose to re-use a container, wash it in a 1:9 solution of water and bleach to kill off any lurking microorganisms and to deter the seedling rot known as damping off (see Pests and Diseases). Julie

VIEWPOINT
MIXTURES FOR SEED STARTING

We use Metro Seed Mix 350. We use small seed trays to germinate seeds. When plants are large enough to prick out, they get planted in plastic cell-packs. We usually plant out annuals before complete full growth growth, usually in a four-inch-square pot.
KIM JOHNSON, OLD WESTBURY GARDENS

I prefer Redi-Earth with a top dressing of vermiculite. I have also used milled sphagnum as a seed starter or top dressing as it is supposed to be a natural fungus inhibitor. However, you have to be very careful that it doesn't dry out. Also the soil mixes usually have a starter fertilizer in them them that gives the seedlings a boost once they've germinated. Sphagnum has no real nutrients and seedlings need to be transplanted when ready. I generally use fibre packs (six to a flat) to start the seeds, with a clear plastic top that fits over the flat holding the paks. I bottom water the seed paks until transplanting. Bottom watering helps keep the leaves from getting wet and helps cut down on damping off.
JULIE MORRIS, BLITHEWOLD MANSION AND GARDENS

We use Metro Mix and two-and-one-quarter-inch peat pots, thirty-two to a flat. They are planted into the ground from these.
JUNE HUTSON
MISSOURI BOTANICAL GARDEN

For starting seeds of annuals, I prefer to purchase one of the many soilless seed starting mixes. I find that these mixes are fine in texture, which allows them to stay free from compaction and hold some moisture, yet are not too wet for most varieties of annuals. When sowing seeds of some annuals that have a tendency to damp off, I much prefer wooden flats or clay pots to plastic, for they allow excess water to pass more easily.
MIKE RUGGIERO, THE NEW YORK BOTANICAL GARDEN

STARTING SEEDS

1. Fill the container almost full with the potting mixture.

2. Space seeds the correct distance apart and cover with the recommended depth of soil.

3. Water well. The soil must be kept moist, but care should be taken not to batter the tender seedlings. Overwatering promotes disease problems.

4. When the first two leaves appear, thin or transplant the seedlings to the correct distance. Seedlings grown too close together can develop damping off (a soil-borne fungal disease that attacks the seedling stems at soil level). When the next set of leaves appear, transplant

into individual pots and a slightly heavier soil mixture. **5.** When transplanting, hold the plant by the leaves rather than the stem. (New leaves will grow back, but if the stem is damaged, the entire plant suffers.)

6. Gently and thoroughly water the transplants to settle soil around roots.

Morris at Blithewold Gardens finds that a sprinkling of milled sphagnum on top sometimes helps prevent damping off.

To begin, moisten the sowing medium in a large bowl or plastic bag (the proportion of medium to water should be about 8:3), or fill the flats to the top and let them stand in a larger pan of water overnight. When the flats are ready for planting, there should be about one-and-one-quarter inch of space at the top. Small seeds can simply be pressed into the top of the medium, while medium-sized seeds will need to be covered to a depth of one-eighth to one-quarter inch; large seeds should be planted at a depth equal to three or four times their diameter. Check the seed package to see which need light to germinate, and how to cover with soil. After seeding, water with a mister or fine overhead spray from a watering can; you can also immerse the flats in a shallow pan of water–a process that may help deter damping off. Whatever your method, keep the soil evenly moist, but never allow it to become water-logged.

Most seeds need high humidity and a temperature of about 70° F. to germinate (though certain annuals, including forget-me-not, sweet pea, and annual phlox, germinate at about 55-60° F., and should be started in an unheated room for best results). To maintain sufficient humidity, place the flat beneath a thin pane of glass or inside a plastic bag or greenhouse enclosure, removing the enclosure as soon as germination occurs. For only a small investment, you can also purchase a specially waterproofed heating cable to ensure proper soil temperature, which is important because seeds germinate in response to soil temperature, not air temperature.

Some seeds need strong light to germinate; others, in fact, require darkness (see individual entries). If you have insufficient sunlight, you'll need to augment it with artificial, fluorescent light. Keep the lights on around the clock until germination; then turn them off at night, allowing the plants about ten hours of darkness per day. Lights should be about six inches above seedlings.

The earliest green evidence of your labor will be the food storage cells (or "false" leaves) known as cotyledons; when the first true leaves appear, you can begin to add a water-soluble fertilizer at about one-quarter the recommended strength. (As the plants mature, you can gradually increase the strength.) When seedlings have developed two or three sets of true leaves, transplant them to individual pots filled with potting soil, adding one-quarter cup of 5-10-5 fertilizer to each gallon of soil. Just before transplanting, water the seedlings, then lift them delicately out of the flat with a small spoon or use the technique known as "pricking out"–gingerly unearthing the seedling with a pencil point or similarly sharp stick. Use your fingers (holding the leaves, not the stem) to place each seedling into its pot, and carefully firm the soil around the roots. Water gently but well, and allow the seedlings to acclimate to transplanting by keeping them out of direct sunlight for a few days.

Although seed starting is done routinely and successfully in most botanic gardens, some beginning home growers find it difficult and give up after a few tries. This is usually due to the fact that they've tried to grow too many

TAKING CUTTINGS

1. Select a strong, healthy shoot and with a sharp knife, make a diagonal cutting two to three inches long.

2. Dip cut end into water, and then into a rooting hormone if possible. Insert cutting into prepared hole.

3. Rooting seedlings or seeds need humidity. Wrapping the pot or flat in a plastic bag with a few holes cut in it raises the humidity level.

PREPARING A NEW BED FOR ANNUALS

1. Add soil amendments as necessary–compost, leaf mold, peat moss, etc. Shovel necessary amendments on top of bed to be prepared.

2. Turn over soil, one shovel deep, incorporating amendments and breaking up any clods of soil. If you can, do this two or even three times. Soil should become loose and friable.

3. Using a steel rake, smooth and level surface of bed. Remove any stones, debris, or clods of earth.

seedlings and could not supply enough light for them. In most home situations, it is difficult to find a windowsill that gets enough sunlight for young seedlings; lights are very helpful. Another problem is starting seeds too early, which leads to overgrown plants that don't do well once they get into the garden. If you fail the first few times, keep trying. Once you get the hang of it, seed starting is easy and economical and allows you to grow a vast assortment of plants not available through other methods.

Cuttings Many annuals, including coleus, dianthus, and pelargonium, can be propagated with relative ease from cuttings. (Indeed, begonia, impatiens, marigold, and nasturtium are so easily propagated that they will root almost instantaneously in nothing more than a glass of tap water.) If possible, cuttings should be taken from young plants in the middle of their growing season. Simply remove several established three- to five-inch shoots–preferably those that haven't flowered–at their base, making sure that the cut is clean and sharp. Place the cuttings in a well-watered, preferably sterile rooting medium (sand, perlite, or equal parts sand and vermiculite work well), taking care to keep the medium evenly moist. Cuttings will need bright, indirect light, high humidity, and a room temperature of about 70° F.; to maintain humidity you may want to place them in a plastic bag or greenhouse enclosure. Watering and misting frequently is a must. After a few weeks, give each cutting a light tug; if it pulls back, it has most likely rooted. When the roots are one to two inches long, start acclimating the plant to normal humidity by removing the plastic bag or taking the plant out of the greenhouse for a few hours each day. After about a week, the plants can be transplanted to the garden or potted up for the winter in regular potting soil.

Self-seeding Though all annuals set seeds, some are more determined about the process than others. So-called "self-seeders" like alyssum, cleome, lobelia, nicotiana, nasturtium, and salvia prodigiously reproduce themselves without a lick of work on the part of the gardener. This is either a nuisance or a boon, depending on your gardening philosophy. You'll soon learn to recognize these seedlings (known as "volunteers") when they appear in early spring, or later, when the ground has warmed up, and you can uproot them, move them, or leave them alone as you see fit.

PLANTING Whether you're transplanting bedding plants from the garden center or seedlings you've nurtured along yourself, setting out young annuals requires care and a modicum of finesse. Home-grown transplants will need to be hardened off: A week before planting, set them outdoors in a protected, shady spot, bringing them in at night for the first three or four days. Each day keep them out for a slightly longer period, beginning with about three hours; after four or five days they should be sufficiently acclimated to wind and temperature to stay outdoors until planting. You can also harden off plants in a cold frame, a four-sided box set outside on the ground and topped with glass or heavyweight plastic: Keep the top off, closing it only during severe cold or high winds. If possible, set out young annuals on a cool, overcast day, avoiding at all costs the midday scorch. Late afternoon, when air and soil are nicely

VIEWPOINT
BROADCASTING SEED

Most of our annuals are planted from seed that is broadcast. Planting is done in October for all annuals, but summer blooming plants may be reseeded again in April
MARY IRISH, DESERT BOTANICAL GARDEN

I've broadcast a variety of poppy seeds in late October/early November so that they germinate the following spring and bloom in June. Zinnia seeds at Blithewold are broadcast the first of June and bloom at the end of July. A second sowing is broadcast the end of July and start blooming in September. They look especially fresh, are great for butterflies, and usually just miss Japanese beetles.
GAIL READE, BLITHEWOLD MANSION AND GARDENS

We don't broadcast seed for several reasons. When seed it broadcast, it must be monitored very closely so that the seedlings can be watered when they come up. Then, in our public garden–and the same would hold true for most home gardeners–there's a great chance that the seedlings would be trampled by foot traffic. Finally, the percentage of seeds that germinate is much lower than those that do so in a controlled environment that it's just not worth doing.
JUNE HUTSON
MISSOURI BOTANICAL GARDEN

I normally don't broadcast seed, but rather grow plants in flats or pots but in the past I have grown larger beds of *Portulaca grandiflora* using this technique. When broadcasting portulaca, I have always mixed the rather small seeds with fine sand, which helps evenly distribute the seed. Since portulaca is a warm weather annual, I wait until the ground has sufficiently warmed up and in the New York area, this means late May to early June.
MIKE RUGGIERO, THE NEW YORK BOTANICAL GARDEN

IRRIGATION METHODS

Many of our beds are under automatic watering systems; others are watered by hand.
JUNE HUTSON,
MISSOURI BOTANICAL GARDEN

Unfortunately, we use overhead sprinkling systems; we also handwater with a wand at transplanting time.
SUSAN NOLDE,
BROOKSIDE GARDENS

I have used soaker hoses and hand watered if absolutely necessary. I usually water for just the first month and then hope mulch will hold in enough moisture. But if it doesn't rain we'll use soaker hoses, etc., once a week. We don't use overhead irrigation.
JULIE MORRIS, BLITHEWOLD MANSION AND GARDENS

Most of our beds are on a drip irrigation system, and there are special emitters that send water out in a fine spray. These are used throughout the life of a bed with annuals. In some areas, where the system is not in place, hand watering with a fine wand is used. We have two very large annual beds, and there we have a popup sprinkler system with fine mist heads. In all cases, beds are watered daily until germination. Once the plants have about five true leaves, watering is done twice a week, until the plants get two inches tall. At that time, we water about once a week, unless the weather is unseasonably warm.
MARY IRISH, DESERT BOTANICAL GARDEN

In larger beds, we use sprinklers as early in the day as possible, but for plants that don't appreciate moisture, we water by hand using a water breaker attached to a hose. We use drip irrigation for container plants when possible; when not feasible we water by hand.
MIKE RUGGIERO, THE NEW YORK BOTANICAL GARDEN

We use oscillators or Rainbirds, or water by hand with a watering wand.
KIM JOHNSON, OLD WESTBURY GARDENS

warmed, is an ideal time for transplanting.

SPACING Each plant requires a specific amount of space in which to spread out and grow; crowding too many plants into a small area will result not only in smaller plants but weaker ones as well, as each plant competes in vain for water and nutrients. For individual requirements, check plant descriptions, and space accordingly. This is especially important because so many annuals are deceivingly small in spring–and then take over the garden, overwhelming small varieties. It is a common error on the part of many beginners to crowd as many plants as will fit into the ground.

TRANSPLANTING Before digging your planting hole, make sure the soil, both in the garden and in the original container, is well watered. Remove plants from the container, using a knife or your hands to pull the roots away from the sides; this will encourage stronger root growth. To make a proper hole, use a trowel and pull the soil toward you till you've pulled away enough to accommodate all of the roots without crowding. Place the transplant in the hole, making sure the roots are well covered, then firm (but don't compact) the soil around the plant, leaving a slight depression around the base of the plant where water can pool.

INITIAL CARE The most important thing you can do for your transplants (after you've provided a well-prepared area and soil) is water them well, immediately after planting and then once a day for about a week until roots begin to establish themselves. A watering can or hand-held hose is best at this stage, since overhead sprinkling can pelt immature plants. Always water the soil around new transplants, rather than the delicate foliage. For the first two weeks, monitor plants and soil carefully for signs of dryness; never allow the soil to dry out completely.

ROUTINE CARE

Watering After about two weeks, your annuals should be sufficiently well established to get by with about an inch of water a week. During dry spells or especially hot weather, you'll have to provide the water yourself, which you can do with a garden hose (preferably a soaker hose, laced strategically through the garden), a drip system, or an overhead sprinkler. (A caveat about sprinklers, however: Watering in the evening encourages the growth of fungal diseases in some annuals, among them calendula and zinnia, and overhead watering in general can damage tender blooms.) Whatever your chosen method, it's better to water deeply, once a week, than to provide a meager daily sprinkle, since deep watering encourages equally deep root growth; make sure that the soil is wet to a depth of about six inches.

Check the garden periodically for signs of dryness. These include yellowing or browning of the leaves, usually along the bottom third of the plant; wilted stem tops; flagging–a folding, drooping, or turning of the foliage; an inability to set blossoms or the dropping of buds; and dry, crumbly dirt around the root zone. Note, however, that all but the last are also signs of overwatering; if you spot any of the above-mentioned symptoms along with waterlogged soil and a dark stem incapable of supporting the plant, you've probably gone

PLANTING

1. Hole should be at least as deep as the original pot; measure the pot against the shovel of your trowel to be sure.

2. Dig the hole. If you haven't already prepared the bed, see page 190.

3. Place the plant in the hole, spreading its roots as much as possible.

4. If you're planting a peat pot, make sure to rip off the top part so that a lip does not appear above ground. This lip would act as a wick, stealing water from the plant.

5. Fill the hole with loose soil.

6. Firm the soil around the newly planted transplant, but don't compact it.

VIEWPOINT

MULCHING

I feel mulches should always be organic so that they carry on the normal functions of a mulch and improve the soil. Black plastic is not only unattractive, it also draws the root systems to the surface where they are exposed to the stresses of heat.
GALEN GATES, CHICAGO BOTANIC GARDEN

We don't use inorganic mulches
DON BUMA, BOTANICA, WICHITA

We use shredded, composted leaves.
KIM JOHNSON, OLD WESTBURY

We use leaf mold and oak mold; we never use inorganic mulch.
JUNE HUTSON, MISSOURI BOTANICAL GARDEN

We use buckwheat mold more than anything, and chopped up leaves from previous seasons if available.. I put down some fertilizer first–5-10-10 or Electra–if I'm using leaves and work mulch into the soil in the autumn at the end of the season.
JULIE MORRIS, BLITHEWOLD

We don't use inorganic mulches. We usually use shredded hardwood bark for mulch.
SUSAN NOLDE, BROOKSIDE GARDENS

We use organic mulch, finely shredded, for some of the large beds–as a top covering and as an amendment. Home gardeners find that an inorganic mulch of fine gravel is one of the best materials to use to encourage good annual wildflower germination. It is never advisable to use black plastic here–it brings soil to lethal levels.
MARY IRISH, DESERT BOTANICAL GARDEN

We mulch some smaller beds with pine needles during the summer, but the only mulching done on large beds is a shallow cultivation (dust mulch) that keeps weeds down and slows evaporation of water from the soil.
MIKE RUGGIERO, NEW YORK

overboard and will need to let the garden dry out for a while. Cut off any damaged areas, pull away mulch, and cultivate the soil lightly, to a depth of one or two inches. However, if the stem is truly damaged, the plant probably can't be saved; consider discarding it.

Mulching The benefits of mulching are many, some more apparent than others. A good mulch not only retains moisture, it helps keep roots warm in spring and cool in summer, discourages the growth of weeds, prevents soil compaction, and–if the mulch is organic–adds nutrients to the soil as it decomposes. In addition, mulch can have an aesthetic benefit, especially when the annual garden is young and just beginning to fill in.

Inorganic mulches–clear or black plastic, or paper-backed aluminum foil–suppress weed growth and warm the soil in early spring. Make sure, however, that the mulch you use is porous, or punch holes in it yourself, so that water can penetrate to the soil below. If you don't like the look of plastic or foil, you may want to cover it with a more decorative, organic mulch. Inorganic mulches have several drawbacks; they are not recommended by many of our experts. Most are very unattractive and will need to be discarded at the end of the season. They also get very hot in hot climates and impede the flow of water into the soil; they are never used at the Desert Botanical Garden for these reasons. Organic mulches, on the other hand, can overwinter in the garden and then be tilled into the soil the following spring, or a year later depending on the type of mulch. Among the most popular organic mulches are pine bark, shredded leaves, compost, grass clippings, straw, sterile hay, sawdust, and cocoa or peanut hulls. The leaves, clippings, and straw take nitrogen from the soil; add extra nitrogen before applying those mulches. Add the mulch when plants are about four to eight inches tall, spreading it at a depth of at least two inches–preferably four–to keep down weeds. At Blithewold Gardens, mulch is applied after the soil has warmed up, which is well into June. Susan Nolde at Brookside Gardens recommends decreasing the depth of the mulch around the base of the plant to not more than one-half inch to avoid stem rot.

WEEDING Even with mulch, you'll probably have to weed occasionally. Not only are weeds unsightly, but they also compete with annuals for the scarce resources of water, nutrients, light, and air. By far the best approach is to get to the weeds while they're small, before they've had a chance to set the seeds that will usher in a new, and more abundant, weed crop. This usually means hand-pulling, which isn't as tedious as it sounds if the garden is well mulched. You can also cultivate the soil around plants with a small hoe (difficult if the garden is well-mulched), but this can damage not just the weeds but the fine roots of nearby annuals as well, so proceed with caution.

FERTILIZING Many annuals respond well to periodic applications of fertilizer, especially if growth seems to be lagging, but some simply hate the stuff. If you fertilize amaranthus, cleome, cosmos, gazania, nasturtium, or portulaca, they will produce foliage at the expense of bloom. Depending on the individual needs of the plant, use a balanced fertilizer such as 20-20-20 or a low-

Controlled watering with a watering wand get the water just where you need it; it is often better than overhead systems.

Weeding is a time-consuming but necessary task. Weeds are not only unsightly, but also compete with your plants for nutrients and water.

Often seeds or transplants will come up too thickly. Remove extra seedlings until they are the proper distance apart. The thinned seedlings can be planted elsewhere.

Deadheading is one of the chief tasks of the annual gardener. It keeps the garden looking neat and encourages new blooms.

Seeds can be collected from most annuals. Store in envelopes marked with the plant's name in a cool dry place.

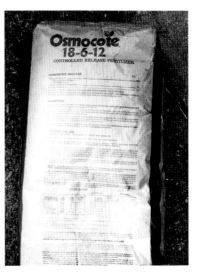

Fertilize only when necessary; osmacote is a popular fertilizer. Too much fertilizer can produce an abundance of leaves with few flowers.

nitrogen blend like 5-10-10, either in liquid form or slow-release granules. With fertilizer, however, the concept of too much of a good thing can become strikingly apparent: A surfeit will stress annuals, making them leggy and unattractive; it can also reduce the amount of oil in the leaves, rendering foliage dry and burned around the edges. A safer method of boosting the soil's nutrient content is to apply a top dressing of compost or well-rotted manure, which will break down slowly to enrich the soil over the growing season. Well-conditioned soil needs less or no fertilizer; proper preparation of a bed will save time and cost later on.

PINCHING BACK/PRUNING Nearly all annuals benefit from pinching back–the process of removing the plant's growing tip to encourage side branching and bushiness. Begin pinching when young plants are between two and four inch-es tall and have developed several sets of leaves, or when seedlings are ready to be transplanted into the garden. Pinching back can also help to revive leggy plants that have languished too long at the garden center. Pruning–the removal of one or more branches just above a node (the site at which leaf meets stem)–is simply another, more dramatic way to induce branching. Annuals grown for cutting are, by their very nature, routinely pruned and tend to develop into husky, freely blooming plants.

DEADHEADING Like pinching back and pruning, deadheading–the act of remov-ing spent flowers before they go to seed–is an efficient means of producing more plentiful blooms. Since the essential goal of an annual is to reproduce itself through seed, it will go on madly pushing out blossoms until sufficient seeds are set or the season changes; by deadheading, you are, in effect, frus-trating the plant into abundance. Note, however, that some annuals–impa-tiens and fuchsia among them–effectively deadhead themselves by dropping most of their blossoms before they can go to seed. Some plants, like cosmos, zinnias, and scabiosas, need to be deadheaded more frequently than others.

STAKING Many of the taller annuals, unless planted in a very sheltered location, will require staking to remain upright, usually when they've attained a third of their projected height. It is usually easier to stake plants before they need it than when they are already flopping. These include cosmos (excepting dwarf varieties), larkspur, castor bean, tithonia, sunflower, and delphinium, as well as some of the weaker-stemmed annuals such as clarkia. Plants with heavy stems can be tied to individual stakes of reed or bamboo, which should be four to six inches shorter than the plant's ultimate height; insert the stake close to the plant (but be careful of damaging surrounding roots), and sink it deeply (about eight inches) into the ground. Loosely tie the plant at intervals as it grows, using heavyweight twine, twist ties, or plastic clips. Cosmos and other delicate-stemmed annuals can be supported as a group between two rows of stakes that have been criss-crossed with string (preferably green); if the string is low enough, foliage will ultimately disguise it. This is also true of the process known as "pea staking," which involves the use of needleless ever-green or other leafless branches as supports; these multibranched "stakes" should be about six inches shorter than the plant's mature height. Garden centers and catalogues also offer an abundance of ready-made supports, including hoops and interlocking stakes. More natural-looking equipment–string as opposed to plastic ties, bamboo stakes rather than bright green plastic ones–blend in more easily. The ultimate goal is for plants to look like they have not been staked; supports should be hidden by foliage or blend in, and plants should not look stiff or tortured.

PESTS AND DISEASES

In an era of increasing concern over the use of chemical pesticides, the first line of defense against insects and disease is good planning. That means proper soil preparation, even moisture, moderate, not excessive, fertilizer, good air circulation, and the choice of disease-resistant plants. Even carefully planted and cultivated annuals, however, are subject to their share of blights, rots, and infestations, so it's wise to keep a watchful eye on the garden to catch problems before they become disasters. If you can recognize pests and their damage, as well as the early symptoms of disease, you can take rapid action to keep problems–and the chemical solutions they sometimes necessitate–to a minimum. Not all these pests and diseases occur in all parts of the country; the upper Midwest is usually free of significant pest and disease problems. See page 214 for more information on organic gardening and biological controls.

APHIDS These small, soft-bodied pests come in a rainbow of colors–black, brown, yellow, green, and red–and plague a wide variety of annuals, sucking the juices from young stems, leaves, and flower buds. They usually seek out soft new growth. The safest treatment is a strong jet of water from a mister or garden hose, or you can apply insecticidal soap. A homemade solution of equal parts water and dishwashing liquid is also effective, but as this can burn some susceptible annuals, use it sparingly at first to make certain of its safety. For limited infestations, you can also hand-pick aphids and, if you aren't squeamish by nature, simply squash them between thumb and forefinger.

BEETLES Annuals attract a number of beetles, which feast happily on their tender blossoms; you may find the beetles in mid-munch right on the flower, or notice leaf holes and tiny, chewed-looking flower particles dotting the foliage. They are rare in the Midwest. If there are only a few beetles about, they can be hand-picked and disposed of. Asters and zinnias are often host to the black blister beetle, which can wreak havoc not only on petals but on human skin, in the form of poison ivy-type blisters. Remove this pest with tweezers, or knock it off with a stick into a coffee can of soapy water. Larger beetle infestations may require the use of chemical pesticides, although a long-range solution would be the application of an organic grub-proofer like milky spore. Commercial or homemade traps are virtually useless, since they attract more beetles to the garden than they snare.

CATERPILLARS Though caterpillars tend to leave flowers alone, they can make quite a meal of your foliage. The best solution is to hand-pick them as soon as they appear. In addition, the caterpillars known as corn and stalk borers can make their way inside the stems of a variety of annuals. As a preventative,

Japanese beetle.

make sure you do a thorough cleanup of the annual garden in late fall, destroying all plant stalks. Once again, individual pests can be removed by hand if you find them inside a damaged stem. Remember that crushing a caterpillar can end the life of a beautiful butterfly; if you learn to recognize butterfly larvae, you can selectively remove the caterpillars. Chemical pesticides can be effective, as can a good spraying with *Bacillus thuringiensis*, a microbial insecticide harmless to humans, wildlife, and beneficial insects.

CUTWORMS Novice gardeners are often mystified to find young plants sawed off at the base and left dying on the soil, but old hands recognize this as the work of the cutworm. If you've had a problem with cutworms before, you can protect your seedlings with a plastic or cardboard collar placed around the base of the plant. Once plants mature, cutworms are usually not a problem.

LEAFHOPPERS These small, light-green, tent-shaped insects suck plant juices and stunt growth. Serious infestations often respond to an application of pyrethrin.

LEAFMINERS Leafminers literally tunnel through plants, producing wavy, ivory-colored lines on the surface of the foliage. Remove and destroy affected leaves promptly.

NEMATODES These microscopic insects affect roots and can cause susceptible annuals to wilt and lose their color. Many gardeners swear that nematodes are repelled, or even destroyed, by marigolds and vincas. If you find this doesn't work (or can't bear the thought of planting marigolds), try rotating plant varieties every three to four years. Incidentally, the theory about nematodes and marigolds is the subject of much dispute; tests have shown that nematodes are actually attracted to marigolds, and that marigolds can act as bait for them.

PILLBUGS, known as roly polys, are a real pest in Kansas, stripping off foliage at night. Snail bait is a control.

SLUGS It's a wonder that something that moves so slowly can do so much damage in so little time: slugs can mow down seedlings and inflict serious injury on established plants. If great portions of your plants are disappearing, but you see no other evidence of pests, you might try taking a midnight stroll through the garden, since slugs do most of their work after sundown. Look carefully, too, for shiny snail tracks across the soil or on surrounding surfaces. They thrive in moist, shady locations. For small gardens, slugs can be hand-picked and destroyed, or you can make your own slug traps: Sink a tuna or small cat food can into the soil so that its rim is at ground level, then fill the can with beer (malt beer works best). The aroma of fermentation is irresistible to slugs, and they almost inevitably plunge to their death. Grapefruit rinds have also been found to attract slugs. (Commercial snail bait is also available, but can harm birds as well.) If you'd prefer deterrence to destruction, try scattering wood ash or some other gritty substance, such as builder's grade sand, around the base of plants.

SPIDER MITES AND THRIPS The bane of many an indoor gardener, spider mites can also damage outdoor garden plants. They thrive on dry, stressed plants. Well before their delicate webs are evident, you may notice discoloration or fading of foliage. Hosing with water can usually prevent or reverse an infestation. Both spider mites and thrips do their damage by rasping–stripping the foliage of its chlorophyll. As with mites, regular hosing can prevent or ameliorate a thrip infestation.

WHITEFLIES If your plants are ailing and you raise a dustlike cloud of tiny white insects every time you brush against them, whiteflies are almost certainly your problem. They usually attack soft, new growth. After removal of all affected areas, give the plants a high-pressure jolt with the garden hose, which is generally quite effective at controlling infestation. They can also be treated with insecticidal soap or pyrethrin. Many garden supply centers also sell a sticky paper that attracts the whiteflies.

BOTRYTIS BLIGHT This grayish powder, appearing on buds and flowers, is a fungal disease common on geraniums and pansies in cool, cloudy weather; it can also attack petunias during times of high humidity. Remove and destroy all affected flowers; don't use them in the compost pile. Spraying with a fungicide may be necessary to keep the problem from reappearing.

DAMPING OFF Primarily affecting seedlings grown in flats, this fungal disease is almost certainly the culprit if young plants germinate and then fall over and die without warning. Starting seeds in a sterile mix is the best way to avoid the problem. Other precautionary measures include bottom watering (immersing the flat in a pan of shallow water) and resisting the urge to overseed and overwater; you can also improve air circulation by installing a small fan in a corner of the room, far enough away so that it doesn't blow directly on the seedlings.

POWDERY MILDEW As its name implies, this fungal disease, afflicting a number of annuals including snapdragons and zinnias, is evident as a whitish powder on foliage. Since it flourishes when days are warm and humid and nights are cool, it is often most apparent in late summer or early fall. You can reduce the likelihood of infection by planting resistant varieties, watering only in the morning, and avoiding overcrowding in the garden–poor air circulation is one cause of powdery mildew. If your plants are still affected, cut off any diseased foliage, thin the remaining leaves and stems to boost air circulation, and keep the plants well watered to reduce stress. A home remedy that has worked for many gardeners is the application, once a week or so, of water, vegetable oil, baking soda, and dishwashing liquid (use one tablespoon of each of the last three ingredients to every gallon of water, and shake well). This won't work unless it's done on a regular basis. Horticultural oils now on the market can also help; be careful using them with zinnias as they can burn the foliage.

RUST Rust appears as rust-colored or orange spots on foliage, especially the undersides of leaves, and commonly afflicts a number of annuals including dianthus and snapdragon. As a preventive measure, water only in the morning. If plants become infected, remove and destroy all affected foliage. Some gardeners have achieved success with applications of fungicide, especially sulfur, but if infection is severe, your only recourse–since the fungus spores remain in the soil–may be to remove the plants and replant the area with resistant annuals.

Powdery mildew.

WINTER

All climates • Plan and finish garden projects like compost enclosures, fences, benches. Request and study catalogs for new plants; order seeds early to avoid the rush.

• Check stored corms and tubers (like gladioli and dahlias) and trim away dead material.

• Clean and repair garden tools.

Warm climates • In late winter, plant snapdragons in trenches. Plant out early annuals like pansies and petunias; be prepared to protect them in case of a late frost

Moderate climates • In late winter, start seeds for spring annuals.

Cold climates • Start seeds for slow-growing annuals like impatiens and coleus in late winter.

EARLY SPRING

All climates • Turn over the compost heap.

• Prepare garden soil as soon as it is warm enough to work. Have the soil tested early, and add amendments as necessary.

Warm climates • Plant seeds outdoors for spring and summer annuals.

• Plant out all annuals except those that need hot weather, like vinca and lantana.

Moderate climates • Check plants you've stored over the winter, like geraniums and lantana, trim them and start hardening them off for outdoor planting.

Cold climates • Plant out frost-hardy species.

• Start tuberous begonias.

MID TO LATE SPRING

All climates • Start checking for pest problems; the least harmful methods of control are most effective when started early.

Warm climates • There is still time to transplant seedlings.

• Consider planting marginally hardy plants at this time; if they have a chance to establish themselves well, they might survive the winter.

Moderate climates • Start pinching early blooming annuals.

• Sow seeds of fast-growing annuals in vegetable beds and around spring bulbs.

Cold climates • Most bedding plants can be planted out by late spring; check all transplants you've not planted and if you don't think it's time to plant them out, at least repot into more spacious containers.

LATE SPRING TO EARLY SUMMER

All climates • Continue to monitor for pests and diseases.

• Trim back spent flowers to promote a new flush of growth.

• Weed as necessary.

• Replace some early bloomers that can't tolerate the heat of summer.

Warm climates • Direct-seed warm-weather annuals.

Moderate climates • Most bedding plants can be put out in the garden by early summer.

• Pay attention to the compost heap. Turn and water is occasionally.

Cold climates • All but the most heat-loving plants can be planted out by early summer.

MIDSUMMER

All climates • Continue pest control, weeding, pinching.

Warm climates • Water as necessary.

• Deadhead and replace plants that have wilted in the summer heat (unless you expect them to revive in fall).

• Start seeds for fall flowers.

Moderate climates • Plan the fall garden; start seeds or buy transplants for fall-flowering species.

• Keep cutting back spent flowers to promote a second bloom.

Cold climates • All plants can be planted out by this time. Check container plants to see if they need extra fertilizer or water.

LATE SUMMER TO EARLY FALL

All climates • Continue deadheading to maintain garden appearance and for cut flowers.

• Plant cool-weather annuals to replace those that have not lasted through the summer.

• Continue pest control.

Warm climates • Check continuously for watering needs.

• Plant out fall-flowering annuals.

Moderate climates • Take cuttings of flowers that you wish to grow next year; note which can be grown as houseplants.

Cold climates • Prepare mums for fall gardens; many can be planted in bare areas of the garden.

• Keep the garden well watered

FALL

All climates • Dig up and take in bulbs.

• Remove spent flowers from garden; replace with mums or other fall-flowering varieties. Some berries or pods can be used in dried arrangements.

• This is a good time to test soil and amend it as necessary.

• Sow seeds for early spring annuals.

FLOWER CRAFTING

There are almost as many ways to use flowers as there are ways to plant them. In addition to fresh arrangements (an art in itself) many types of flower crafts have been developed. A few of them:

Flower pressing involves placing fresh flowers between heavy weights for a long period of time. Using single flowers is better, because the final result is one-dimensional. Pressed flowers can be used in pictures and greeting cards.

Dried flowers can be made simply by bundling the flowers and hanging them in a cool, dry place for several weeks. Once the flowers are completely dry, they can be used in all sorts of dried arrangements. Just about any type of flower can be dried. Consider using foliage, fruits, and berries in dried flower arrangements. Wreaths are a particularly attractive form on dried arrangement, using a base made of straw, wood, or any other material.

Preserved flowers can be made using silica gel or other specialty ingredients, as shown on this page. Preserved flowers look almost real, and can last for many years if kept in the proper environment.

To preserve flowers with silica gel, first insert a wire which will act as a stem. Place the flower in a bowl with a tight lid, and cover with silica gel, making sure it gets between the petals. After a few days, inspect to see if the flower is totally dry. Preserved flowers (as seen if the photo at left) must be stored carefully, away from heat and humidity.

SPECIAL CONDITIONS 5

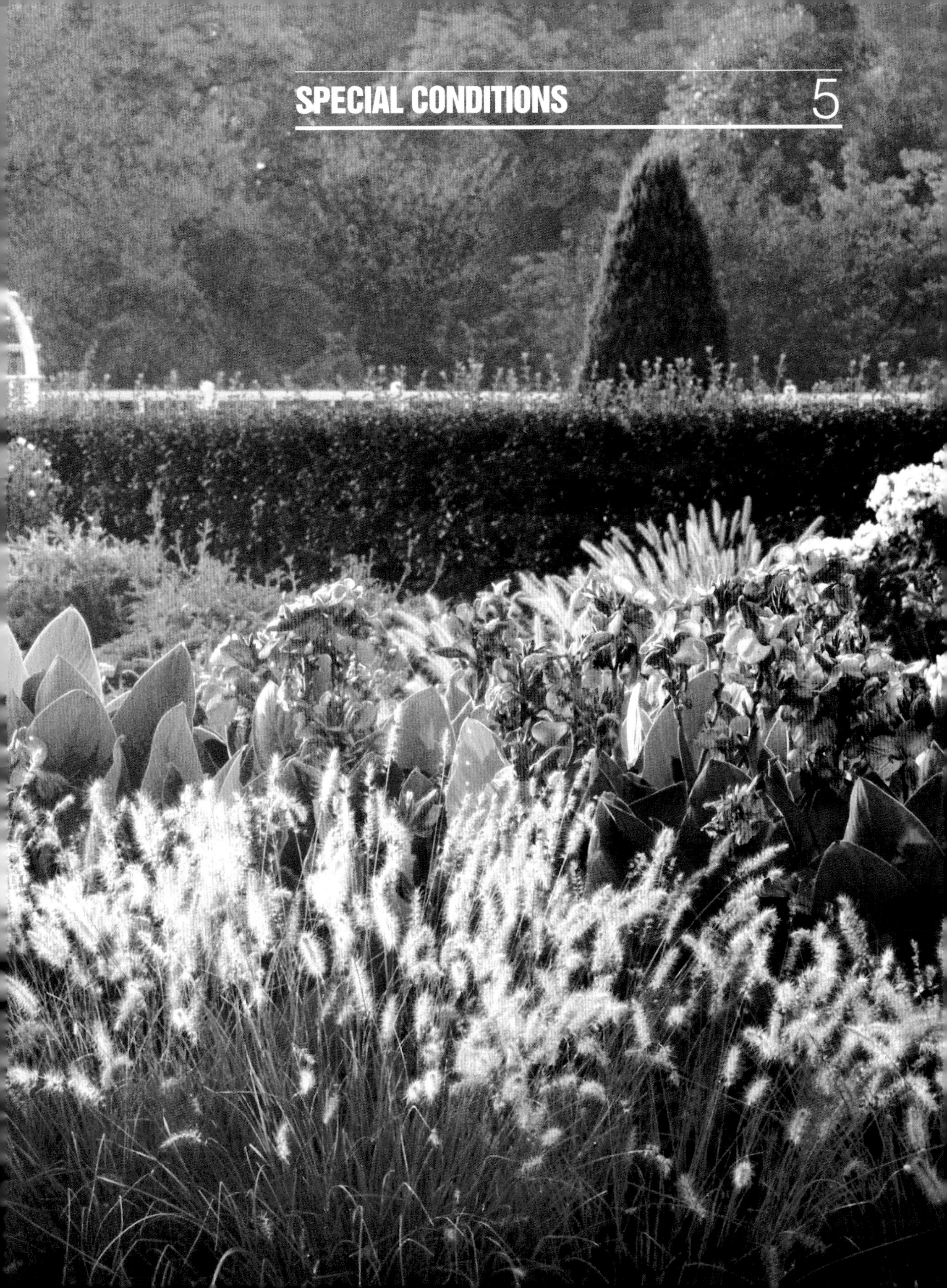

HANGING BASKETS AND CONTAINERS

Many a full-blown passion for gardening has begun innocently enough with a few colorful annuals troweled into a white plastic hanging basket. Basket gardens mature quickly, require a minimum of upkeep, make a glorious display even in hard-to-brighten spots, and—when they begin to show wear and tear—can be moved or tossed away with only a twinge of guilt. To create a successful hanging garden you need neither a degree in horticulture nor a grand estate (in fact, you don't even need a backyard); the only requirements are access to the outdoors, some basic knowledge, and a love of annuals.

Siting the basket Inventive gardeners have found innumerable spots for hanging baskets, from porches, pergolas, and arbors to ivy-covered walls and horizontal tree branches. If you have good air circulation, shelter from strong winds, and any exposure with the exception of extremely deep shade, you can grow annuals in baskets—provided you choose your plants carefully. If the area receives little or no direct sun, you'll need to pick shade-loving plants like browallia, caladium, coleus, or impatiens; if it bakes all day, choose plants that hold up well in bright light like geranium, heliotrope, vinca, lantana, verbena, and nasturtium. Consider factors other than sun as well; nasturtiums, for example, don't like humidity any better in a basket than they do in the ground, but they're great for Chicago. A mixed exposure—a partially shaded porch, for example—gives you the greatest choice of annuals, since you can pick from both sun- and shade-tolerant plants. In addition, you'll need to site your baskets where they can be easily tended, or install a pulley system for watering and general upkeep.

Containers Choosing a container will probably represent your most important aesthetic decision—after your choice of plants, of course. Don't forget that you'll be looking at the container as well as the plant. The most common containers are plastic pots with hangers and saucers attached; if you buy your baskets pre-planted, this is, indeed, the container you're likely to get. There's nothing wrong with these basic baskets, but they're by no means your only choice. Terracotta, pottery, wood, heavyweight wicker, and wire are all popular materials, and many have been designed specifically to function as hanging baskets. One of the most pleasing alternatives is a rounded wire basket lined with sphagnum or carpet moss, which combines a natural look with a nostalgic material and form; this type of container allows you to plant all around the it for a fuller look and can be watered by sinking the whole basket in a tub or sink. Or consider hanging your flowers flush to the wall in a recycled hayrack or one of the many decorative half-baskets now on the market. Many baskets are self-hanging, but if not, you can choose among a great variety of hangers, from elaborate macrame to nearly invisible lucite and wire. In addition to personal preference, take into account the surrounding decor: Is it rough-hewn and rustic? Laden with Victorian gingerbread? Sleekly postmodern? Pick a pot that either blends with or highlights its surroundings. And finally, consider the basket's intended occupants: Heavy trailers like fuchsia will virtually cover the entire basket, so there's little point in planting them in something

Above: A basket with a single plant, 'Pampas Fire' petunias. *Top:* White petunias with sweet potato vine (*Ipomoea batatas* 'Blackie').

Previous page: Missouri Botanical Garden at dusk. See "The Night Garden", p. 212.

expensive and ornate. For more upright plants, or those that trail less profusely, the look of the pot is more important.

Choosing plants Whether grown at home from seed or bought well-started at
the garden center, basket annuals should be planted when they're young and
vigorous. The two most important considerations are habit and mature size.
If the plant is upright, it shouldn't grow much taller than roughly one-and-
one-half times the height of the basket, or the effect will be ungainly and top-
heavy. If bloom is profuse–as with impatiens–or the form is dramatic–as with
ivy-leaf geranium–you may want to restrict your basket to a single specimen.
Otherwise, consider mixing both color and form. Some of the most impressive
hanging baskets combine trailing plants like petunia and lobelia with bushy
or upright annuals like ageratum and vinca. Galen Gates suggests mixing
dark-foliaged plants with light: ornamental peppers with dusty millers. Don't
always stick to the usual; try plants like nemophila, *Zinnia angustifolia,* mimu-
lus, diascia, sanvitalia. All-foliage plants, including ivy, vinca vine, and dusty
miller, add a pleasing counterpoint to vivid color combinations. Consider
herbs and vegetables as well: basil, thyme, parsley, and cherry tomatoes are
decorative as well as delicious and fragrant. Combine colors, shapes, and
styles, bringing in elements from all parts of the garden; Galen Gates has
combined pink impatiens, pink hypoestes, green parsley, and cherry tomatoes,
for a basket with interesting flowers, fruit, and foliage.

Planting Before planting, place the plants on top of the soil until you've
achieved a felicitous arrangement, and, once again, consider mature size and
habit. Don't, for example, surround a trailing petunia with a bunch of
upright salvia; taller plants should be placed in the center of the basket (or, if
you're using a half-basket, at the back). You can crowd your plants a bit more
than you would if planting them in the garden–after all, you're going for
maximum drama in minimum space–but make sure the roots have sufficient
room to spread out and grow.

With wire planters, you can grow plants from the base as well as the top;
simply insert them from the bottom up in two or three layers directly through
the moss liner, adding soil as you begin each ring.

Many professional gardeners advocate the use of moss or commercial pot
liners in *all* hanging baskets. This certainly helps to conserve moisture, maintain an even soil temperature, and reduce watering, but it isn't necessary.
Some of the most impressive hanging displays have been grown in ordinary,
unlined plastic pots.

Containers should have proper drainage in the form of drainage holes. You
can make your own soil mix from equal parts topsoil, peat moss, and vermiculite, or buy one of the excellent potting mixes available commercially; these
should feel light in the hand when you lift the bag–an indication of well-
draining soil. Fill the basket to within two inches of the top, then dig holes
equal to or slightly larger than the rootballs. Cover the roots firmly but gently, then fill the pot with additional soil to within three-quarters of an inch of
the top. Slowly water the newly planted baskets until the water runs out of

V I E W P O I N T

HANGING BASKETS
I use sixteen-inch wire baskets lined
with a two- to three-inch layer of
sphagnum moss, then filled with lightweight soil-less potting soil with two
tablespoons slow-release fertilizer
pellets incorporated into the soil. The
potting mix is usually a combination of
peat, perlite, and sand, such as Pro
Mix, Jiffy Mix, or Metro Mix. For containers that aren't hung, and so can
be heavier, I use a mix of three parts
soil-less mix and one part garden soil
to slow water drainage. Our heavy
clay soil retains water, so this mix cuts
down on frequency of watering.
LUCINDA MAYS,
CALLAWAY GARDENS

We use plastic containers with a
saucer for hanging baskets that contain annuals. Plastic holds water
longer here, and that small gain in
water retention is important in this
warm, dry area.
MARY IRISH, DESERT BOTANICAL
GARDEN

We use wire baskets lined with sheet
moss. I use the long-fiber sphagnum
as the planting medium and fertilize
regularly. Using warm water to soak
the sphagnum seems to make it
absorb water more easily; wring it out
well before using.
JULIE MORRIS, BLITHEWOLD

The most attractive baskets are made
of wire mesh lined with sheet moss
and filled with a soil-less potting medium. The effectiveness of a basket's
display can be significantly improved
if small sections are removed from the
basket and plants are placed in the
"side" of the container. The basket
looks much fuller this way, as
opposed to when plants are placed
only on top.
GALEN GATES, CHICAGO BOTANIC

We use a soil that is made up of a
sandy loam to which we add peat
moss. The sandy loam gives us
drainage while the compost adds
micronutrients and increases water
holding.
MIKE RUGGIERO, NEW YORK

Why stop at one basket? The photos above show arrangements of several baskets, above at the United States Botanical Garden in Washington, on top at a home in the Bronx. Among the plants included in these displays are verbena, petunias, zinnias, impatiens, clock vine, setecreasa, and *Cuphea hyssopifolia*.

the drainage holes. Baskets will need less maintenance if you add a slow-release fertilizer at planting time.

Hanging Whether your container is suspended from a hook or bracket or mounted against a wall, the device for hanging should be well anchored; hanging baskets look deceptively light and airy, but soil and water make for a weighty combination. Brackets as well as hooks should be installed with screws and molly bolts. Make sure, too, that the basket is low enough for the flower display to be appreciated; too often, baskets are hung so high that only their drainage holes are clearly visible. A good rule of thumb is to hang baskets at or just above eye level, from at least one perspective–for example, if your basket is suspended from a doorway overhang, it should more or less meet your eye when you stand on the top step; that way, it can be appreciated by visitors and residents as they come and go, as well as by passersby on the street below. If the hanger on your basket isn't long enough, simply extend it with a length of medium-weight chain (available at hardware stores).

Upkeep Because their roots heat up so quickly, all containerized plants should be watered frequently–once daily, and even twice a day in extremely hot weather, especially if the containers are overplanted, until the water runs freely through the drainage holes. Hard-to-reach baskets can be watered with a compression unit, a device that moves water from a hand-held bottle into a long, narrow tube. Hanging annuals also need more frequent fertilizing than garden plants. Every two weeks, water them with a soluble fertilizer designed specifically for potted plants. (Some gardeners prefer to water weekly with the same formula diluted to half-strength.) Pinching, disbudding, and deadheading are as important to hanging annuals as to their garden-bound cousins; to avoid that neglected-and-gone-to-seed look, remove spent blossoms each time you water. If you'd like to try to overwinter your baskets indoors, inspect them well for insects, knocking off any that are visible with a strong spurt of the garden hose. Though the arid winter environment that prevails in most houses is more conducive to growing succulents than tender annuals, some may survive quite nicely in a sunny window, serving as a constant reminder of the bounties of summer.

Other container plants Containers, large and small, are an integral part of the displays at most botanic gardens. As for hanging baskets, containers require excellent drainage and must be monitored a bit more carefully than in-ground plants to make sure their water and nutrient needs are being met. After all, their roots cannot spread through the garden looking for what they need. Using containers brings an architectural element into the garden, especially if the container is well chosen; stone urns filled with ivy geraniums atop pillars at Old Westbury Gardens, for example, add immeasurably to the magnificence of its mansion. Standing containers can be considerably heavier than hanging ones, so they can be any size at all, particularly if you don't plan on moving them. This allows the possibility of elaborate arrangements using dozens of different annuals in containers, and taking advantage of the excellent soil and drainage that you can provide in the "raised bed" environment of a container.

Above: An all-foliage windowbox, with purple alternanthera and ivy. *Below left:* Zinnias, New Guinea impatiens, and trailing browallia. *Below right:* Marigolds, dusty miller, *Celosia spicata.*

Above: Green and bronze fennel with pansies. *Right:* Kale and parsley with sweet alyssum.

LATE SEASON ANNUALS

Annuals are usually considered for their long bloom through the summer. There are numerous flowers that keep our gardens alive with color during the season of warm temperatures and long days. Unfortunately, as the season progresses, we see a decline not only in temperature and day length but also in the performance of these plants. It seems that as the plants wind down so do we gardeners. There is, however, an underutilized group of annuals that actually come into their own in late summer and fall. The following plants provide fragrance, bold foliage, bright stem color, verticality, and winter effects–and some are even edible.

BETA VULGARIS Swiss chard's ornamental effects reach a crescendo in fall. With increased sophistication in gardeneing, people are becoming more creative in extending the growing season. Swiss chard works well with this mentality because its iridescent red stalks are evident into November and December. Though color alone is reason enough to grow this jewel, there is another–its nutritious aspect. To harvest, pull the outer stalks off first so new ones form inside–harvesting continues with temperatures into the mid twenties. Although drought tolerant, it flourishes in soil enriched with compost.

DATURA Angel's trumpet is a dramatic, bold-foliaged plant that is well established in August, at which time it produce large, fragrant, trumpet-shaped flowers late each afternoon. Datura can be used as a large mass in a perennial bed with its ten-inch leaves, or as a lone accent. The species *D. metel* is five feet tall and is effective in the back of a border. Datura's spreading habit (two to three feet) and its drought tolerance make it a candidate for large containers which too often sport small-scale, wimpy annuals that

look out-of-place. Discretion is required in placement since both its leaves and fruit are poisonour if eaten (it has been used since ancient times for its narcotic properties). Datura is well-suited to full sun and is tolerant of a half day of shade.

CYNARA CARDUNCULUS (cardoon). Late in the day, silver- and gray-foliaged plants like cardoon are the last to fade out of sight. I include these at the far reach of the garden to give greater depth for a longer period of daylight. Though often considered too large for today's vegetable gardens, cynara is well suited for combination in a perennial or mixed border. It resembles its relative the artichoke with large, dramatic, prickly. almost dagger-shaped leaves. Vase-shaped, three feet tall and wide, it is imposing near the back of the border. It is definitely not a plant for small, delicate beds or the faint of heart. One plant in full sun can make an imposing statement in any bed. The large silver to white leaf stalks are edible and with the steel-colored flowers combine nicely late in the season with the clear blue flowers of fall asters.

BRASSICA OLERACEAE (ornamental cabbage) Many people turn to mums for fall color, and in some cases asters and pansies. These plants do offer color at this slower time of year, but their effectiveness is diminished with temperatures in mid to low twenties. Ornamental cabbages retain their form and foliage color in -10° in Chicago—a truly remarkable feat for any annual when you think about it. This is an excellent item to use in highlighting beds void of sturdy perennials. and for accenting and noting the locations of steps and walks in winter. Colors range from deep pink to white, plus every shade of green from bright lime to almost black; some cultivars have standard cabbage leaves, others have very frilly ones. Ornamental cabbages are best used in the fall; in the spring they bolt, sending up flower stalks. You will be most impressed with these when they are placed where you can see them from a kitchen window or as a warm greeting on your porch when you return home on fall or even winter days.

TROPAEOLUM PEREGRINUM (canary creeper) is a relative of nasturtium and like its more famous cousin has leaves that can be used in salads. This unique plant has attractive two- to three-inch gray-green leaves that are deeply divided like the palm of a hand. This beauty is also prized for its bright yellow flowers (three-quarter to one-inch long) that appear in late summer and last well into the cooler temperatures of fall. Upon close inspection, one notes that the erect upper petals resemble yellow wings with fringed or feathered tips. Carary creeper climbs ten to fifteen feet and has a somewhat open and airy habit. It is effective when coiling up through other plants or small trees but is most strking when allowed to festoon an evergreen hedge. It is best placed within close view or along a path so one can appreciate the delicate flowers that resemble birds in flight.

Some gardeners equate autumn with garden cleanup. Using the plants described on these pages, gardening with annuals need not end in September! GALEN GATES, CHICAGO BOTANIC GARDEN

Other late season annuals for cold climates (Zone 7 and colder)

Asters (used as annuals)
Canna x *generalis*
Chrysanthemums (mums)
Cleome hasslerana
Datura inoxia ssp. *inoxia*
Euphorbia marginata
Foeniculum vulgare 'Rubrum'
Kochia scoparia
Nicotiana sylvestris
Ruta graveolens
Gourds
Kale
Lettuce
Peppers (ornamental and edible)

SOME SOURCES
American Horticultural Therapy
Association
 362A Christopher Avenue,
Gaithersburg, Maryland 20879
800-634-1603

Canadian Horticultural Therapy
Association
c/o Royal Botanical Garden
PO Box 399, Hamilton, Ontario,
Canada, L8N 3H8
416-529-7618

ENABLING GARDENS

Being forced to stop gardening is one of the worst fates that can befall a gardener, but the inability to get down on one's hands and knees owing to arthritis, a bad back, a heart problem, the need to use a wheelchair–or the normal aches, pains, and fatigues of advancing age–is no reason to stop gardening. By using a few different gardening techniques, modifying tools, following new criteria in the selection of plants, and tapping into the many resources available for information and help, no one should ever have to stop gardening.

Begin by thoroughly and frankly assessing your situation.
•How much time can you devote to gardening?
•Do you need crutches, a cane, or wheelchair to get around?
•Can you get up and down from the ground without assistance?
•How much sun or heat is wise for you?
•Can you bend at the waist easily?
•Is your coordination impaired? balance? vision? ability to hold tools?

Consult your doctor, occupational or physical therapist, and most importantly speak to a horticultural therapist.

Horticultural therapists are specially trained in applying horticulture in therapeutic programs for people with disabilities and older adults. They have developed specialized gardening tools and techniques that make gardening easier for every situation.

Once you've decided how much you can and want to do, the garden can be planned. For example, people with relatively severe mobility impairments should have firm, level surfaces an easy distance from the house and should use containers or raised beds to bring soil up to a comfortable working height–usually somewhere around two feet high with a maximum width of thirty inches if worked from one side and sixty inches if both sides of the container or bed are accessible. People with more mobility can work with easily worked, light soils mounded to eight to ten inches above grade and should use lightweight, long-handled tools. Smaller containers can be hung within easy reach on poles or fences, and an overhead structure can be used to support hanging baskets on ropes and pulleys so the baskets can be lowered for care and then replaced to an out-of-reach position.

Important considerations when planning the garden layout include:
•Start small: keep it manageable
•Use or create light, easily worked soils so less force is required to work them either by hand or with tools
 •Keep all equipment and tools in accessible places
 •Arrange for a nearby water source–soaker hose or drip irrigation, perhaps–to minimize the difficulties in watering
 •Use mulches to cut down on weeding

Annuals can be the backbone of the enabling garden. Their very nature allows the gardener to avoid the overwintering problems of trees, shrubs, and some perennials, in containers. Annuals offer a never-ending pallet of texture, scent, and hue from which to choose.

DRY CLIMATE GARDENING

A gardener new to the desert will find that many of his tried-and-true practices and plants no longer work. Some of the most common annuals, like begonias and impatiens, fail almost reliably. After a while, though, he or she will realize that gardening in dry, hot climates opens a whole new set of opportunities.

There are two basic seasons for annuals in the desert: cool season annuals are planted in the winter and bloom in early spring, which is usually around February. There are many treasures to choose from: Arizona poppies (also called Mexican poppies), desert bluebells, lupines, tidy tips, several species of nemophila, *Clarkia amoena, linum grandiflorum* are just a few. By combining these with winter-flowering shrubs, the desert gardener can enjoy color right all through the year–and rarely contend with pests and diseases.

Summer annuals are planted in spring and bloom through the hottest part of the year. There are relatively fewer plants that are able to tolerate the extreme heat of desert summers, but that has not stopped gardeners from finding plants that enliven their gardens at that time. Three old standbys are sunflowers, gaillardias, and golden fleece. A less-known but beautiful and heat-tolerant plant is *Kallstroemia grandiflora* (also known as Arizona poppy).

Among the best choices are native plants that not only offer fantastic color and strongly regional flavor but also perform quite well with minimal care and almost no pest problems. Desert gardeners should look for plants that are native to their own regions as well as to neighboring desert areas.

All of these annuals combine with a vast array of incredible desert shrubs, succulents and perennials that the desert gardener is able to grow. Many plants that can only be grown as annuals in the North are perennials here; *Baileya multiradiata,* California poppies, *Penstemon parryi,* and *Hibiscus rosa-sinensis* (which becomes woody), for examples. These perennials have the brilliant colors that annuals are known for and the added attraction of overwintering. Desert shrubs, including *Encelia farinosa* (brittlebush), *Calliandra californica* (red fairyduster), *Leucophyllum species* (Texas ranger) have interesting foliage and long-lasting fascinating flowers. Another element in desert gardening is cacti and other succulents; the solid masses of cacti and succulents like aloes and agaves are beautifully complemented by small, bright annuals.

Although many of these flowers survive in the wild, it is overly optimistic to expect them to flower abundantly without additional water. Most annuals are watered generously until germination, then about twice a week until the plants are two inches, then about once a week unless it becomes unseasonably warm. Organic mulches or fine gravel help keep roots cool and conserve water. Little or no additional fertilizer is needed for annuals; overfertilization usually results in too much foliage and too few flowers.

MARY IRISH, DESERT BOTANICAL GARDEN

In very dry and hot regions, many plants fare better if provided some shade, even those normally considered as full-sun annuals.

Lighting at Missouri Botanical Garden is accented by hanging baskets of verbena. Vertical plantings–standards, tall plants, vines growing on trees, hanging baskets on posts, poles, and trellises–are an imporant feature of the night garden. When low-growing plants get lost in the shadows, those at eye level are still visible.

THE NIGHT GARDEN

A garden at its best in the evening is a wonderfully romantic notion, and one that can be easily fulfilled by following a few basic guidelines. You can plan a garden that is primarily to be enjoyed at night or incorporate a few evening beauties into your existing garden. Plan your evening garden along a winding path through the trees just made for a moonlit stroll or beside a pergola with a bench that is perfect for enjoying coffee at sunset

Without the light of the sun, most colors in the garden are reduced to shades of gray. However, white and silver do not fade with the light, but begin to shine brighter and brighter as dusk falls. White and silver blossoms and foliage become luminescent with the rising of the moon, reflecting available light. A garden filled with white snapdragons, baby's breath, white garden balsam, sweet alyssum, white poppies, lupines, and white zinnias amidst white roses and clematis is a beauty to behold under a velvet night sky.

Although any scented plants make the garden delightful, there is something particularly appealing about plants that scatter their scent at night. There are plants that are pollinated by night creatures such as moths, that don't waste their scent during the day. As dusk falls, their perfume begins to waft through the soft evening air. Some, such as the old-fashioned favorite evening-scented stock, are not particularly striking as garden accents, but are worth planting for the clove fragrance alone. Their flowers are purple to white and arranged loosely on stalks, and most gardeners suggest planting them behind or among something else that is showy. A long-time favorite, flowering tobacco, comes in a range of colors from yellow to white to red to rosy-pink. It releases its heady scent beginning at dusk, a perfect plant for window boxes right at nose height. Woodland tobacco stands four to six feet with abundant clear white flowers that are scented at night like freesias.

There is an unusual group of plants that open only in evening, another drawing card for the night garden. The plants, such as the evening primrose and four o'clocks, are fairly nondescript during the day, but as the cool of evening approaches they come into their glory by opening wide, often shedding sweet perfume at the same time. Putting them into a garden that is meant to be enjoyed in the evening lets them draw the same sort of raves as other plants that are in their prime in the bright morning sun. Moonflower vine has pure white fragrant flowers that open at dusk, giving all three traits that are special for the evening garden. Not only does the white sparkle at night, but the flowers also perfume the evening air. Moonflowers on a trellis are like stars suspended in the evening sky.

Lighting for the night garden should be subtle. It is not efficient or even attractive to flood the garden with bright lights; their brilliance will detract from the flowers and look artificial anyway. But a few soft lights will allow the viewer to pick through the shadows and observe shapes of flowers as well as night pollinators like the sphinx moth. Lighting can be placed overhead or be recessed into the beds, which is sometimes more difficult because it requires electricity to be woven into the ground. In winter, twiggy plants like Siberian dogwood and Harry Lauder's walking stick add interest when lit from below.

ANNUALS FOR THE VEGETABLE GARDEN, VEGETABLES FOR THE ANNUAL GARDEN

Annual beds and vegetable and herb gardens can use many of the same plants. Some of our favorite food crops are also extremely ornamental; varieties of cabbage, kale, basils, peppers, and other vegetables have been bred specifically for their ornamental value and are less tasty (or in the case of peppers, so hot that you wouldn't want to use them) than normal varieties. But many other vegetables and herbs, such as lettuces, fennel, kale, and perilla can do double duty, going from the annual bed to the dining room table. A row of small green and red lettuces or large blue and purple cabbages enhance any annual bed; even corn can add a vertical accent (and indian corn adds interesting color and shape as well). Some vegetables bear remarkable flowers; squash or okra blossoms rival the beauty and brilliance of hibiscus, and the tiny blossoms on bean plants, such as scarlet runner beans are beautiful as well. Fruit and fruitpods, such as those of the hyacinth bean have long been used in annual gardens and are often used in dried arrangements.

Inedible annuals have their place in the vegetable garden as well. Although the theory that some annuals, such as marigolds and nasturtiums repel insect pests has never been proven (see page 142 for our expert's opinions on the subject), they serve other purposes. Bright flowers attract pollinating insects and birds to the garden, increasing the rate of pollination and the production of fruit. Borders of fast-growing flowers mark the ends of vegetable beds, allowing the gardener to identify what is planted and how it is to be maintained. And, of course, flowers dress up the garden, making it an even more enjoyable place to work!

Pansies dress up the raised vegetable beds at The New York Botanical Garden.

ORGANIC GARDENING

Few gardeners today are unaware of the devastating effect pesticides and other chemicals used in the past have had on our environment. Rachel Carson's searing exploration of the subject, *Silent Spring* (1962), exposed the "needless havoc" wrought by products designed to promote healthy plants. Not only were the chemicals poisoning our environment, they were also killing the natural predators of the pests we were seeking to destroy, making it impossible for nature to come to its own defense.

In the past few decades a vast and successful effort has been made to find new ways to garden without using harmful chemicals. The approach is directed at the soil and at the measures taken to control pests.

The soil is built up through the addition of organic materials, especially compost. The addition of compost, homemade or store-bought, and other organic material such as peat moss, green cover crops, and bone meal makes the soil so fertile and productive that petrochemicals are not needed.

Pest problems are handled through a practice called Integrated Pest Management (IPM), developed by the Council on Environmental Quality. IPM is defined as "maximum use of naturally occurring pest controls, including weather, disease agents, predators, and parasitoids. In addition, IPM utilizes various biological, physical, chemical controls and habitat modification techniques. Artificial controls are imposed only as required to keep a pest from surpassing tolerable population as determined from accurate assessments of the pest damage potential and the ecological, sociological, and economic costs of the control measures." In other words, gardeners must make reasonable assessments of how much damage a particular pest will do. If the pest is just munching on foliage, let it be. If controls must be taken, nonharmful ones should be tried first. Only in extreme cases is chemical warfare waged—and then in the most nonharmful ways possible.

The weapons in the IPM arsenal include:

• Careful monitoring to identify problems before they become widespread.

• Beneficial insects, such as ladybugs, praying mantises, and some nematodes, which feed on garden pests. Some of these reside naturally in your garden; others can be bought and placed there.

• Bacteria such as Bt (*Bacillus thuringiensis*) that attack garden pests. These bacteria can be bought by the pound and dusted on the plants; strains have been discovered that breed and attack many common pests.

• Insecticides such as rotenone, pyrethrum, and sabadilla and insecticidal soaps.

• Pest-repellent plants such as marigolds, which may repel bean beetles and nematodes, and garlic, which repels whitefly (see page 142).

• Hand-picking pests off foliage wherever seen in small numbers.

See pages 197-199 for more information about pest control.

ANNUALS IN THE ROCK GARDEN

Making a rock garden is not simply mounding soil and spreading rocks on top. A good rock garden is created much as a painter paints a picture or a flower arranger combines a bouquet—with creativity and at least a little technical knowledge. The purpose of most rock gardens is to emulate the dramatic beauty of natural rock outcroppings, splashed with the textures and flowers of nature's alpines. Few gardeners restrict their choice of annuals for the rock garden to true alpines; any plant that fits the proportions of the garden and is not invasive can be used. Small, low growing plants are most often used to fill the numerous nooks and crannies in the rocks.

Placement of a rock garden requires some planning. Site selection should be governed by topography, incorporating any existing rock. It is best to work with an existing or created slope, which brings the rock into better view. If the slope is steep, take special care to make sure the rocks are anchored and stable. Choose a site that receives full sun or partial shade; a southeast exposure is best. The soil must be graded and amended so that water will percolate through it rather than wash over it. Ideal pH is 6.2-6.8; add lime if pH is too low, and add leaf mold if it too high. If subsoil comes to the surface while you are regrading, you will need more soil additives or topsoil. Sculpt the soil into the desired shape. If you move a lot of the soil in the process, it is likely to settle. Wait for several days for the settling to occur, then work in your soil amendments with a digging fork or rototiller.

Native rock is not only less expensive than imported, it also looks more natural. Limestone is a superb rock because it porous and retains moisture that encourages plant growth. (If you have limestone in your rock garden, you should check the soil periodically for high pH.) Granite is so hard that few plants can grow on it. Study natural rock outcroppings for inspiration on placing additional rock. Place the rock so that it is visible from the main viewing area. Select focal points or areas by deciding where a person will stand when looking at the garden, then arrange the rock sot that it is visually balanced within each focal point, between focal points, and with the garden as a whole. Bury the rocks enough to make them look as though they belong there; if they are shallow, they will appear to have been set on top of the soil A good rule of thumb is to cover one-half to two-thirds of each rock with both soil and plants. Begin placing the rock at the highest point and work downward, making sure the rocks won't wobble or give way when you step on them. You will need access to the rocks for weeding and harvesting, so consider natural stepping stones or meandering paths throughout the garden.

Plan your rock garden to contain some fairly large spaces where you can plant a low ground cover such as cheddar pinks. Fill in the spaces between the rocks with slow-growing small annuals, usually one to three plants for each space. You do not need the large number of plants you would use in an annual border. As you gain expertise in rock gardening, you will find that this specialty is a challenging and rewarding way to garden.

ANNUALS FOR THE ROCK GARDEN
For spring
Brachycome iberidiflora
Centaurea cyanus
Diascia barbareae
Nigella damascena
Agrostis nebulosa
Eschscholzia californica
Silene oculata
Linaria maroccana
Viola tricolor 'Pretty', 'Cuty', 'Baby Lucia', 'Yellow Charm', Helen Mount'
Nemophila menziesii
For summer
Ageratum 'Blue Horizon'
Antirrhinum majus 'Rocket', 'Floral Carpet', 'Silks'
Catharanthus rosea
Cuphea hyssopifolia
Cosmos sulphureus 'Lady' series
Dianthes chinensis cultivars
Gazania rigens 'Garden Sun', 'Mini Star'
Heliotropum arborescens 'Mini Marine'
Gaillardia pulchella 'Red Plume', 'Yellow Sun'
Lobularia maritima
Nierembergia violacea 'Purple Robe', 'Mount Blanc'
Verbena canadensis cultivars
Verbena bonariensis
Verbena 'Imagination'
Zinnia angustifolia 'Classic', 'White Star'

acidic soil: Soil with a pH below 7.0.

alkaline soil: Soil with a pH above 7.0.

annual: A plant that lives for only one year or one growing season.

anther: Part of a plant's stamen that bears pollen grains.

aphid: Insect that sucks the juices from a plant's tissue.

biennial: A plant that lives for two years or growing seasons, producing leaves the first season and flowers and seeds the second.

blackspot: Fungus disease that produces black spots on leaves, which then yellow and fall off.

blanch: Whiten a plant's leaves, stems, or shoots by excluding light: e.g., by covering with soil.

bolt: Go to seed, especially prematurely.

botrytis: Tiny fungus that causes many destructive blights.

bract: A small, modified leaf, with or without a stem.

broadcast: Scatter seed, fertilizer, or other materials over a large area instead of placing in specific rows or planting holes.

Bt: *Bacillus thuringiensis,* a bacteria that attacks and kills many common garden pests; can be bought by the pound.

bud: Unexpanded leaf, stem, or flower that will develop at a later time.

bulb: Encased leaf or flower bud, as an onion or tulip.

calyx: All the sepals, the outer parts of a flower.

chlorophyll: Green coloring matter in plants, essential to photosynthesis.

clay soil: Soil composed of many very fine particles, sticky when wet but hard when dry; water and air have a hard time moving through clay soil.

cold frame: A low box or frame on the ground with a light-transmitting cover that protects young plants from frost and helps transplants to harden off.

companion planting: Practice of planting different plants near each other for their helpful effects, such as repelling insects or shading.

compost: Decomposed plant material that adds nutrients to the soil and improves soil composition.

corm: Bulblike underground stem.

corolla: The inner set of a flower's petals; the petals as a whole.

crown: The section of a plant where stem and root meet; the topmost part of a root system, from which the leaves and shoots emerge.

cultivar: A variety of a plant that has been created by human intervention rather than naturally.

cultivate: Stir the soil surface to eliminate the weeds, aerate the soil, and promote water absorption.

cutting: Part of a plant (stem, leaf, root) cut off and then rooted to form a new plant.

cyme: A fairly flat-topped, often branched cluster of flowers.

damping off: Fungous disease that causes seeds and seedlings to rot and die.

deadhead: Remove old flowers to prevent seedpods from forming and improve the plant's appearance.

deciduous: Shedding leaves or other plant parts each year.

die back: Process by which a plant appears to die back to the ground during its dormant period; the plant begins growing again in the spring.

diploid: Having two sets of chromosomes.

direct seeding: Sowing seeds directly into the garden rather than starting seeds indoors.

disbud: Remove buds to encourage production of larger or more flowers.

disk flower: Small flowers in the center of a flowerhead, found in most members of the daisy family.

division: Method of propagating by separating parts from a plant to produce new plants.

drainage: The ability of the soil to move water so the roots of the plant don't become waterlogged, and so nutrients move through the soil.

fertilizer: Any material that supplies nutrients to plants.

filament: Structure that supports the anther; filament and anther together make up the stamen.

friable: Term for soil that easily breaks apart or crumbles when handled.

germination: The beginning of plant growth from a seed.

harden off: The process of gradually accustoming a young, indoor-started plant to the outdoors.

herbaceous: Dying to the ground; not woody.

humus: Decayed organic matter, black and crumbly, that improves soil texture and moisture retention.

hybrid: A plant created by crossbreeding two or more different plants.

inflorescence: The arrangement of flowers on a plant, as spikes or umbels.

insecticide: A product that kills insects.

knot garden: Herb garden formally planted in tight patterns.

lace bug: Insect with broad, lacy wings that sucks sap from plants.

layering: Method of propagating by putting stems of a plant in contact with soil so that roots will form, and then separating the rooted stem from its parent plant.

loam: The best garden soil, a balanced mix of silt, sand, and clay.

manure: Livestock dung used as an organic fertilizer, rich in nitrogen.

mealybug: White, cottony-looking insect that attacks plants.

mildew: Fungal disease that produces white dust or downy tufts on leaves.

mosaic: Virus disease that causes mottled, yellow, curled leaves and discolored fruit.

mulch: Any material spread on the soil surface to conserve moisture, check weed growth, and protect the plant from excessive heat or cold.

nematode: Microscopic wormlike animal that may be beneficial or harmful to plants.

neutral soil: Soil with a pH of 7.0.

nitrogen: One of the three most important plant nutrients, needed for production of leaves and stems.

node: Place where the leaf is attached to the stem of a plant.

nutrients: Elements in the soil absorbed by plants for growth.

open-pollinated: Pollinated by the wind or animals, not by human manipulation.

organic gardening: Practice of gardening without the use of synthetic chemicals.

organic matter: Part of the soil that consists of decayed or decaying plant and animal matter (humus).

panicle: Grouped flowers.

peat or **peat moss:** Decayed remains of ancient plants, added to soil to increase the soil's ability to absorb and hold moisture.

perennial: A plant that lives for more than two years.

perlite: Volcanic glass used in seed-starting and growing mediums.

pesticide: A product that kills garden pests.

petal: Part of the flower's corolla, next layer after the sepals, often colorful.

petiole: Leaf stem or stalk.

pH: A measure of the acidity or alkalinity of the soil, on a scale of 1 (extremely acid) to 14 (extremely alkaline), with 7.0 being neutral.

phosphorus: One of the three important plant nutrients; good organic sources are bonemeal and powdered rock phosphate.

photosynthesis: Process by which plants capture energy from the sun and convert it into compounds that fuel growth and life.

pinch: Snip back new growth, to keep plants compact and encourage bushiness.

pistil: Innermost part of a flower, the female reproductive organ consisting of sigma, style, and ovary.

pollination: The movement of pollen from one flower to another, necessary for fertilization and therefore fruit production.

potassium: One of the three most important plant nutrients; good organic sources are greensand and small amounts of wood ashes.

potbound: Condition of a pot-grown seedling or plant whose rootball is thickly matted and contains little soil.

prune: Remove dead or living plant parts, to improve the plant's form or increase fruit or flower production.

pyrethrum: Insecticide made from chrysanthemums.

raceme: Long flower cluster, with flowers opening from the bottom first.

ray flower: One of the marginal flowers of the head in a composite plant.

receptacle: The end of the flower stalk which bears the flowers of a head.

rhizome: Underground stem, thick and fleshy and usually creeping.

rosette: Dense cluster of leaves on a very short stem.

rotenone: Biological insecticide.

runner: Stem that grows along the ground and takes root at its nodes or tips.

rust: Fungal disease that produces rust-colored blotches on leaves.

sabadilla: Insecticide made from a Mexican plant of the lily family.

sandy soil: Soil with a high percentage of sand, or large soil particles; water travels through sandy soil very easily, so nutrients leach out quickly.

scale: Insect that forms a brown dome around itself on a plant.

scape: Leafless flowering stem that arises from the ground.

seedling: A young plant, especially one grown from seed.

set (fruit): Develop fruit or seeds after pollination.

set out: Plant a seedling in the garden.

sidedress: Apply fertilizer along a seed row or around a plant or hill.

slug: Slimy, short, worm-shaped creature that eats leaves.

soil test: Analysis of the soil to determine its pH and available nutrients.

species: Related strains of a plant that occur naturally.

spider mites: Insects that rasp chlorophyll off of broadleafed plants.

spike: Elongated flower cluster.

spittlebug: Sucking insect that deposits a small bit of spittle (a bunch of bubbles) on a plant's stem.

stamen: The pollen-bearing, or male organ, of a flower; consists of filament and anther.

steep: Soak in a liquid under the boiling point.

stem: Plant tissue that supports leaves and connects leaves with roots.

stigma: Tip of the pistil; it receives the pollen.

succession planting: Process of planting a new crop as soon as the earlier one is harvested.

succulent: Plant with juicy, water-storing stems or leaves.

sucker: Leafy shoot at a stem junction.

taproot: Main root that grows downward.

thin: Pull up or pinch out young plants so remaining plants have room to grow and mature.

thrips: Insect that rasps chlorophyll off of broadleafed plants.

till: Cultivate the soil, especially with a mechanical tiller.

trace elements: Soil compounds essential to plant growth and development but present and needed in only very small amounts.

transplant: Move a plant to another location; also, the plant so moved.

tetraploid: Having four sets of chromosomes.

tuber: A short, naturally swollen underground stem, as a potato.

umbel: Flat-topped, umbrellalike flower cluster.

vermiculite: Lightweight, highly water-absorbent mineral used in seed-starting and growing mediums.

virus: An ultramicroscopic disease-causing organism.

whiteflies: Tiny flies that suck a plant's juices; often look like a cloud of smoke.

wilt: Disease that causes leaves to turn brown; often causes sudden death of plant.

SEED COMPANIES AND NURSERIES
NOTE: INCLUSION IN THIS LIST DOES NOT
IMPLY RECOMMENDATION AND THIS LIST
DOES NOT INCLUDE MANY FINE NURS-
ERIES

Abundant Life Seed Foundation
PO Box 772
Port Townsend, WA 98368
206-385-5660

Appalachian Wildflower Nursery
Route 1, Box 275A
Reedsville, PA 17084
717-667-6998

Burpee Seeds
Caprilands Nursery
Silver Street
Coventry, CT 06238
203-742-7244

Companion Plants
PO Box 88
Athens, OH 47501
614-592-4643

Edgewood Farm and Nursery
Route 2, Box 303
Standardville, VA 22973
804-985-3782

Fox Hill Farm
440 W. Michigan Avenue
Parma, MI
517-531-3179

Fox Hollow Herb & Heirloom Seeds
PO Box 148
McGrann, PA 16236
Horticultural Enterprises
PO Box 810082
Dallas, TX 75381

Gurney's Seed & Nursery Co.
110 Capital
Yankton, SD 57078

Harris Moran Seed Co.
60-A Saginaw Drive
Rochester, New York 14623
716-442-6910

Harris Moran Seed Co.
1155 Harkins Road
Salinas, CA 93901

H.G. Hastings Company
1036 White Street SW
PO Box 115535
Atlanta, Georgia 30310
404-755-6580

Henry Field's Seed and Nursery Co.
415 N. Burnett Street
Shenandoah, IA 51602

605-665-9391
J.L. Hudson, Seedsman
PO Box 1058
Redwood, CA 94064

Jackson & Perkins
1 Rose Lane
Medford, OR 97501
503-776-2000

Johnny's Selected Seed
305 Foss Hill Road
Albion, Maine 04910
207-437-4301

Jung Seeds and Nursery
335 S. High Street
Randolph, WI 53957
414-326-3121

Logee's Greenhouses
141 North Street
Danielson, CT 06239
203-774-8038

Mellinger's
2310 W. South Range Street
North Lima, OH 44452
216-549-9861

Merry Gardens
PO Box 595
Camden, ME 04843
207-236-9064

Native Seeds/SEARCH
2509 N. Campbell, #325
Tucson, AZ 95719

Nichols Garden Nursery
1190 North Pacific Highway
Albany, OR 97321
503-928-9280
800-432-5858 (Iowa)
800-831-4193

Park Seed Company
Cokesbury Road
Greenwood, SC 29467
803-223-7333

Plants of the Southwest
Agua Fria Road
Route 6
PO Box 11A
Santa Fe, NM 87501

Seeds Blum
Idaho City Stage
Boise, Idaho 83706

Siskiyou Rare Plant Nursery
2825 Cummings Road
Medford, OR 97501
503-772-6846

Stallings Nursery
910 Encinitas Blvd.
Encinitas, CA 92024
619-753-3079

Stokes Seed Company
PO Box 548
Buffalo, NY 14240

Territorial Seed Co.
PO Box 157
Cottage Grove, OR 97424
503-942-9547

Thompson & Morgan
PO Box 1308
Jackson, NY 08527
201-363-2225

Twombley Nursery
163 Barn Hill Road
Monroe, CT 06468
203-261-2133

Wildseed Farms
1101 Campo Rosa Road
Eagle Lake, TX 77454
1-800-848-0078

Wrenwood of Berkeley Springs
Route 4, Box 361
Berkeley Springs, West Virginia 25411
304-258-3071

Publications

The Avant Gardener
PO Box 489
New York, NY 10028

Flower and Garden Magazine
4251 Pennsylvania Avenue
Kansas City, MO 64111

Horticulture
300 Mass Avenue
Boston, MA 02115

Organic Gardening and Farming
Organic Park
Emmaus, PA 18049

CONTRIBUTORS

Main Garden:
June Hutson
Missouri Botanical Garden
4344 Shaw Boulevard
St. Louis, MO 63110
314-577-5100

Julie Morris and Gail Reade
Blithewold Mansion and Gardens
Ferry Road
Bristol, Rhode Island 02809

Donald Buma
Botanica, Wichita
701 North Amidon
Wichita, Kansas 67203

Susan Nolde
Brookside Gardens
1500 Glenallen Avenue
Wheaton, Maryland 20902

Lucinda Mays
Callaway Gardens
US Route 27
Pine Mountain, GA 31822

Galen Gates
Chicago Botanic Garden
PO Box 400
Glencoe, IL 60022

Mary Irish
Desert Botanical Garden
1201 North Galvin Parkway
Phoenix, AZ 85008

Michael Ruggiero
The New York Botanical Garden
Bronx, New York 10458

Kim Johnson
Old Westbury Gardens
PO Box 430
Old Westbury, NY 11568

PHOTO CREDITS

All photographs ©James Cuidon with the following exceptions:

©Ian Adams: 18, 60, 97BL, 123B, 146R, 147, 148TL, 166-67, 174R.

©Galen Gates 29TR, 35BR, 38, 39TR, 44BR, 57BR, 72TL, 77TL, 78BL, 82TR, 92TR, 104BR, 124BR, 128BR, 140BR, 150BL, 155, 174BR, 175R, 208.

©John Glover: 15, 52, 73, 123T, 132, 153, 157, 171

©Dency Kane: 45B, 92BL, 98, 121BL, 152R

©Sylvia Martin: 41, 74, 113T, 183, 184

©Elvin McDonald: 58

©Jerry Pavia: 54, 59TR, 82BR, 89TL, 94TR, 116L, 128Tl, 133BL

©Photo/NATS: ©Anne Reilly: 29Tl, 83, David Stone: 150BL

©Sylvia Martin: 94TL, 130BR

©Steve and Sylvia Sharnoff: 162 bottom

©Albert Squillace: 6, 28, 29BL, 31, 34, 40B, 43, 43, 46, 47, 51TL, BR, 53, 55, 62BR, 66, 67BR, 68, 69, 70TL, 77TR, 86, 88, 90, 99BR, 102, 104, 105, 106TL, 109, 110TL, 111, 116BL, 116BR, 122, 124RT, BL, 126, 128TL, BR, 134, 137TR, 139, 145TR, 146L, 152L, 158, 161, 168, 170, 172, 176, 177, 178, 179, 180-81, 186, 189, 197, 201, 206T, 213.

©John Trager: 56, 57T, 59BR, 62TL, 64TR, 65, 72BR, 75, 78TR, 80

©Chani Yammer: 74, 113B, 117, 141

©Cliff Zenor: 40T, 81, 89TR, 163center.

llustrations on endpapers and on pages 16-17 by Delores Bego; all other illustrations by Eric Marshall

T=Top; B=Bottom; R=Right; L=Left

LEAF SHAPES

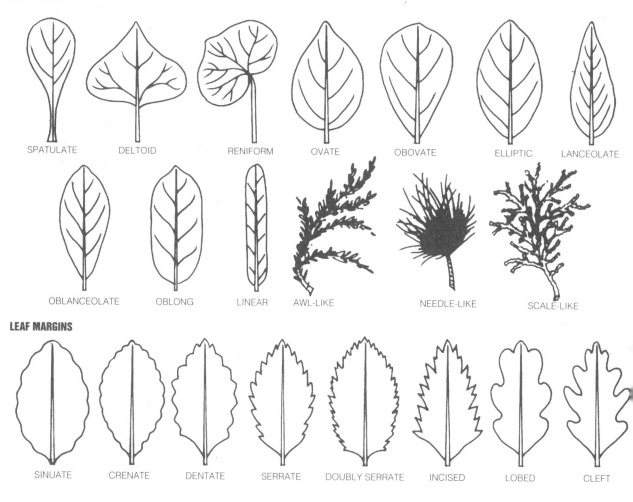

SPATULATE DELTOID RENIFORM OVATE OBOVATE ELLIPTIC LANCEOLATE

OBLANCEOLATE OBLONG LINEAR AWL-LIKE NEEDLE-LIKE SCALE-LIKE

LEAF MARGINS

SINUATE CRENATE DENTATE SERRATE DOUBLY SERRATE INCISED LOBED CLEFT

LEAF ARRANGEMENTS AND STRUCTURES

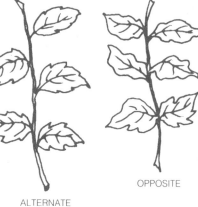

SIMPLE PALMATE COMPOUND BIPINNATE

ALTERNATE OPPOSITE WHORLED